# Windows Registry Forensics

## Advanced Digital Forensic Analysis of the Windows Registry

# Windows Registry Forensics

## Advanced Digital Forensic Analysis of the Windows Registry

Harlan Carvey

*Dave Hull, Technical Editor*

AMSTERDAM • BOSTON • HEIDELBERG • LONDON
NEW YORK • OXFORD • PARIS • SAN DIEGO • SAN FRANCISCO
SINGAPORE • SYDNEY • TOKYO

Syngress is an imprint of Elsevier

ELSEVIER

SYNGRESS

Acquiring Editor: Angelina Ward
Development Editor: Heather Scherer
Project Manager: Danielle S. Miller
Designer: Kristen Davis

*Syngress* is an imprint of Elsevier
30 Corporate Drive, Suite 400, Burlington, MA 01803, USA

**Notices**
Knowledge and best practice in this field are constantly changing. As new research and experience broaden our understanding, changes in research methods or professional practices, may become necessary. Practitioners and researchers must always rely on their own experience and knowledge in evaluating and using any information or methods described herein. In using such information or methods they should be mindful of their own safety and the safety of others, including parties for whom they have a professional responsibility.

To the fullest extent of the law, neither the Publisher nor the authors, contributors, or editors, assume any liability for any injury and/or damage to persons or property as a matter of products liability, negligence or otherwise, or from any use or operation of any methods, products, instructions, or ideas contained in the material herein.

**Library of Congress Cataloging-in-Publication Data**
Carvey, Harlan A.
 Windows Registry Forensics: Advanced Digital Forensic Analysis of the Windows Registry / Harlan Carvey.
    p. cm.
 Includes bibliographical references.
 ISBN 978-1-59749-580-6 (pbk.)
 1. Microsoft Windows (Computer file) 2. Operating systems (Computers) 3. Computer crimes—Investigation—Methodology. 4. Computer networks—Security measures. 5. Computer security. 6. Component software. I. Title.
 HV8079.C65C373 2011
 363.25'62—dc22

                                                                          2010043198

**British Library Cataloguing-in-Publication Data**
A catalogue record for this book is available from the British Library.

ISBN: 978-1-59749-580-6

Printed in the United States of America
10  11  12  13  14    10 9 8 7 6 5 4 3 2 1

*Typeset by*: diacriTech, Chennai, India

For information on all Syngress publications visit our website at *www.syngress.com*

# Dedication

To Terri and Kylie; you are my light and my foundation.

# CONTENTS

# Preface

I am not an expert. I have never claimed to be an expert at anything (at least not seriously done so), least of all an expert in forensic analysis. I am not an expert in Windows Registry analysis. I am simply, by profession, a responder and analyst with some work and research experience in this area. I have also performed a number of analysis engagements, in which information found as part of Registry analysis has played a rather significant role. In one such engagement, Registry analysis allowed me to provide a compelling argument to demonstrate that files known to contain credit card data had been neither found nor accessed by an intruder, thereby reducing the subsequent costs (with respect to notification and fines) to the customer. I have assisted with providing information to demonstrate that certain user accounts had been used to access certain files. More importantly, I have worked through the process of sharing what I have seen with others, by writing this book and sharing what I've observed from a practitioner's perspective. I am not an expert.

When I sat down to write this book, I did so because even in the year 2010, I am amazed at the number of analysts with whom I speak that have no apparent idea of the forensic value of the Windows Registry. Sometimes, when I talk to someone about demonstrating that a user account was used to view files, I get a blank stare. Or after talking about tracking USB devices across systems and no one asks any questions, I get approached by a dozen of the folks from the presentation, between the podium and my exit. It seems that, in many instances, the "abandon hope, all ye who enter here" warning that Microsoft displays on its knowledge base articles regarding the Registry really do a good job . . . of keeping the good guys out, as well as from "digging" or investigating. Sadly, there's nothing in that admonition that states, "oh, yeah . . . the bad guys are all up in yer Registry!" As a result, many analysts are consistently behind the power curve, learning from the bad guys the new uses for the Registry (persistence, data and executable storage, and so on), often months after they have been established and used.

Windows systems make use of a number of different file types that provide a great deal of value to incident responders and forensic analysts alike, and the Registry is only one of them. Quite a few file types include embedded time stamps that can be used to add significant detail to time lines and may include other valuable information. I chose to focus on the Registry because of the shear wealth of information available, if you know where to look and you're willing to do so. To make it easier for me to do this, in November 2008, I released an open-source tool I called "the Registry Ripper," or just RegRipper, and this tool seems to have, in some senses, taken off. RegRipper isn't a viewer application, as much as it is an extraction tool. Once you find something of interest in the Registry through research or some sort of analysis, you can develop a plug-in (the design behind RegRipper is based, in part, on a plug-in structure similar to what's used by the Nessus vulnerability scanner) to extract (and if necessary, parse) the information you're interested in. From that point on, it's no longer a matter of keeping lists, repetitively clicking your way through a Registry viewer, or simply forgetting what you were looking for . . . RegRipper will run the plug-in and extract the information for you, if it's available. This means that one person can write a plug-in, and a dozen or a hundred other people can run it and get the same results.

I've used RegRipper on just about every examination I've conducted, even before I released it. Once malware artifacts or persistence mechanisms have been identified, I can write a plug-in, and from that point on, run the plug-in against the appropriate Registry file. The same holds true for other artifacts, which are discussed in detail in Chapters 3 and 4. Most plug-ins take a second or less to run (there are a few that will take longer, and I've tried to point those out), and that's more than worth it to know if I'm dealing with another instance of Zeus or Conficker, or something else. Others have used RegRipper; RegRipper has not only been downloaded and run by a number of analysts, but also it's been included in a number of open-source forensic distributions, as described in Chapter 2. Many have spoken highly of RegRipper. Chris Pogue of Trustwave is but one of a number of analysts who has included references to RegRipper in his presentations at computer security and forensics conferences.

Throughout this book, the focus is on the Registry found on the Windows NT family of operating systems, from Windows XP (also including Windows 2000), through Windows 2003, Vista, Windows 2008, and Windows 7.

## Intended Audience

This book is intended for anyone interested in the forensic analysis of Windows systems, including analysts, incident responders, students, law enforcement officers, and researchers. Even system administrators and hobbyists will get something useful from this book. I've tried to point out how the information in this book can be used, by both forensic analysts and incident responders, alike. Whether you're either examining an image acquired from a system or connecting to remote systems through Matt Shannon's magnificent F-Response Enterprise Edition, you can use tools like RegRipper to look for indicators of malware infections, intrusions, as well as of misuse.

While reading this book, you'll notice that there are several tools, described throughout, that were written in the Perl scripting language. Fear not, true believer (see how I worked in that Stan Lee reference right there?), as this does not mean that you have to be a Perl programming guru, in order to use or understand the output of these tools. In most cases, Perl is simply the method I've used to solve a problem . . . and in most cases, solving problems is what it's all about. Although some programming capability would be beneficial if you want to develop your own RegRipper plug-ins, several folks with little to no Perl programming skill have written working plug-ins. Others have rewritten tools like RegRipper in other languages, because again, it's not about the tool you use to solve the problem, it's about solving the problem.

# Organization of This Book

This book consists of four chapters following this preface. Those chapters are as follows:

## Chapter 1 Registry Analysis

This chapter addresses the topic of analysis overall and what goes into it. Analysis is much more than simply pressing a button in a commercial forensic analysis tool and accepting the results that appear. Analysis may consist of finding one Registry value among what could be thousands, but more often it will consist of collecting and correlating a number of keys (including LastWrite times) and values, and even correlating that information with other data collected from other sources, such as the file system and event logs.

All analysis should begin with your goals; what are you looking for, what are you hoping to show, demonstrate, or reveal? For consultants such as myself, goals are paramount to an engagement, as someone is paying for my efforts, and spending time pursuing things not consistent with those goals will have a detrimental impact on the timely delivery of my final report. What I've found over the years is that customers often want timely, accurate information that they can act upon and use to make important business decisions, and the goals of the engagement will get me there. In many respects, the same thing applies to law enforcement examinations; there's something that the analyst is trying to show or determine often to support someone else's case.

Although goals direct the efforts of an analyst, documentation is a key component of analysis. Not only does our documentation allow approach analysis in a concise, consistent manner, but also it allows us to go back to something we did weeks or months after the fact, and answer the questions that arise.

Another aspect of computer forensic analysis that I think is very often overlooked is having an understanding of what is "normal" or "expected" on a system, and knowing that what's not there can be as important (or more so) as what is there. There are many aspects of Windows systems that are "normal" and consistent as a result of how the operating system works and how the user interacts with the system. The existence of these artifacts can tell you as much about the system as their absence. For example, if a user interacts with the system on a regular basis but does not have a RecentDocs key (this key is discussed in detail in Chapter 4 of this book), then this can tell you much more about what happened on the system than the user having that key populated with a number of values (in one case, a tool had been used to remove potential "evidence" including the key itself).

By discussing these topics, as well as others in this chapter, my hope is to put the reader in the right mindset for the rest of the book. Actually, what I'd really hope for is that at some point after this book is published, someone tells me that this chapter had an impact on how they approach all examinations, regardless of whether they involve Windows systems or not. Something like this would be very validating.

## Chapter 2 Tools

In this chapter, we discuss a number of tools that are used in Registry analysis, from two basic perspectives. One perspective involves determining Registry keys and values that are affected by various actions on a system; in short, either monitoring a live system's access to the Registry or determining changes made to the Registry following a specific action, such as running an application or installing malware.

The other perspective involves using the information we've discovered during forensic analysis of systems, specifically of Registry files from acquired systems. In both cases, we discuss some of the tools that can be used.

One thing you should not expect to find in this chapter is a great deal of detailed discussion of the use of commercial forensic analysis applications. As I was preparing to write this book, I had submitted my proposal to the publisher, who then had that proposal reviewed. Of the 11 anonymous reviews of the proposal that I had received, one of the comments consistent across all of the reviews was that I should include detailed commentary of the use of commercial forensic analysis applications. Well, I have to tell you . . . I simply do not have access to all of those tools. And yes, I did try to get access to one of them, and was told that no, I could not get even a temporary license for the use of the tool. Although I do have access to ProDiscover from Technology Pathways, that is the only commercial product that I could utilize while writing this book. The rest of the tools discussed in this chapter are freely available, and in the case of RegRipper, the tool is also opensource, allowing the analysts to modify the tool to meet their needs, rather than adapting their analysis to the confines of the tool.

## Chapter 3 Case Studies: The System

Throughout the process of writing my previous books, something that I've come to understand is that providing a lengthy list of Registry keys and values is of little overall value to most analysts. Yes, there may be a number of keys or values in that list that some analysts hadn't considered or heard of, but for the most part, providing just a list doesn't do much to demonstrate how that information can be used, particularly during the wide variety of possible examinations. So rather than providing a box of building blocks and expecting the analyst to assemble them into different structures, the approach I've taken in this chapter (as well as in Chapter 4) is to attempt to show how various keys and values have had a significant impact on various examinations, and how they can be used in conjunction with other data to further your analysis, and allow you to succinctly achieve your goals. My hope is that providing the information in this manner is engaging and educational, and leads the reader, regardless of background or job duties, to use the described tools, and if necessary, dig a bit deeper.

That being said, in this chapter, I attempt to answer a lot of the questions that I encountered while working on engagements, as well as address some of the questions that I've seen others pose in forums, on list servs, and at conferences. I think that this chapter contains a lot of really good information (well, of course *I* think that, right?), and I hope that everyone who reads it finds something new.

### Chapter 4 Case Studies: Tracking User Activity

In many ways, this chapter may be the most significant one in the book for some analysts. There are a number of examinations that center on activity associated with a user account (that is "user activity"), particularly when law enforcement encounters the "Trojan defense," or during investigations involving corporate espionage or the theft of intellectual property by a departing employee. I've also found a great deal of valuable data associated with particular user accounts during examinations involving the exposure or theft of credit card data.

Information described in this chapter can be used to address a number of issues. For example, in addition to demonstrating a user's interaction with the Windows Explorer shell, time stamps associated with the data can illustrate when the user account was logged onto the system. This can assist an analyst in demonstrating the use of a particular user account when auditing on the system has not been configured to record when users log in (determining the audit configuration is covered in Chapter 3).

## CD Contents

The CD that accompanies this book contains several of the tools I've written (in Perl) and described in this book, although other tools that are freely available on the Internet are not provided on the CD. The tools I've provided are open-source, so feel free to examine the code, and if necessary, modify it to meet your needs.

I've also provided executable versions of the tools, "compiled" with Perl2Exe, so that you do not have to install Perl to run the tools.

If you do decide to run the Perl versions of the tools (as opposed to the binary executables), you only need to install Perl on your system. One of the assumptions I see quite often is that to run the tools provided on the accompanying CD (as well as with respect to Perl scripts, in general) is that Perl needs to be installed on every system, and that simply isn't the case.

# Acknowledgments

I'd like to begin by thanking God for the many blessings He's given me in my life, the first of which has been my family. I count having the interest, ability, and heart for writing this book, as well as the others, as one of those blessings. I thank Him daily, but I find myself thinking that it's not nearly enough. A man's achievements are often not his alone, and I think in my heart that being able to write a book like this is a gift and a blessing in so many ways.

I'd like to thank my true love and the light of my life, Terri, and my stepdaughter, Kylie. Both of these wonderful ladies have put up with my antics yet again (intently staring off into space, scribbling in the air, and of course, there are my excellent imitations taken from some of the movies we've seen), and I thank you both as much for your patience as for being there for me when I turned away from the keyboard. It can't be easy to have a nerd like me in your life, but I do thank you both for the opportunity to "put pen to paper" and get all of this stuff out of my head. Yes, that was a John Byrne reference.

I'd like to thank Jennifer Kolde, a computer scientist with the federal law enforcement, yet again. Going through the process of working on my very first book with you has left an indelible mark on how I have approached and written books since then. Over the years we have had a number of opportunities to engage and exchange thoughts and ideas, and that has really been very beneficial for me.

Maggi Grace Holbrook, a law enforcement officer in Washington state, deserves a big "thank you," but not just from me. Maggi Grace is a dedicated officer with a grueling and often thankless job. With the people she encounters and the images she has to look at as part of her job, I don't know how she does it. But I do know that when I took some time to help her and answer some questions for her, she went out of her way to thank me. Exchanging e-mails with her, since then, have really validated my own avenues of interest and have led to a lot of my thoughts, and what I've included in this book regarding the "Trojan defense." God bless you! Maggi Grace.

I also want to thank Chris Pogue and Don Weber. Chris and I spent about 18 months working together on the IBM ISS team, and during that time, we had a couple of opportunities to work together. Working on engagements with Chris had been a great opportunity for me to really look at and question (or have questioned) some of my base assumptions; Chris came from a field of penetration testing and Linux, so sometimes his questions regarding forensic analysis of Windows systems, and in particular, of the

Windows Registry really made me take a step back and think about things. I know that this can be frustrating for some, but for me, it was and has been a good exercise. Chris is currently (as of this writing) doing good things with TrustWave and has been heavily focused on payment card industry (PCI) forensic assessments. Engaging with him regarding what he's seen has given me a view into a world I'd left. I also worked with Don while on the IBM ISS team, albeit not for as long. Don played a similar, but different (we are both former Marines … 'nuff said!) role, and now he's off doing good things for InGuardians.

I miss working with Cory Altheide. Cory and I exchanged e-mails several years ago and published some research articles with respect to tracking USB removable storage devices across Windows systems. At one point, Cory and I had an opportunity to work together, and while employment at that organization ultimately didn't work out for either of us, I'm going to be entirely selfish and say simply that when we did have an opportunity to work together, it was a blast!

I want to be sure to thank everyone who's inspired me by writing their own RegRipper plug-ins. Michael Hale Ligh comes to mind as I was reviewing a chapter of an upcoming book, of which he is a coauthor, and saw several custom plug-ins. Don Weber, a former IBM ISS teammate and former Marine, wrote some of his own plug-ins a while ago, as well (not bad for a Python guy). To the two of you and to the others who've done so, I thank you for what you've done in validating my efforts in creating RegRipper.

As far as RegRipper goes, I have to thank Brett Shavers yet again for his efforts in setting up and maintaining the RegRipper.net Web site. I thank you for your efforts and support, Brett.

# About the Author

**Harlan Carvey** (CISSP) is a vice president of Advanced Security Projects with Terremark Worldwide, Inc. Terremark is a leading global provider of IT infrastructure and "cloud computing" services, based in Miami, FL. Harlan is a key contributor to the Engagement Services practice, providing disk forensics analysis, consulting, and training services to both internal and external customers. Harlan has provided forensic analysis services for the hospitality industry, financial institutions, as well as federal government and law enforcement agencies. Harlan's primary areas of interest include research and development of novel analysis solutions, with a focus on Windows platforms.

Harlan holds a bachelor's degree in electrical engineering from the Virginia Military Institute and a master's degree in the same discipline from the Naval Postgraduate School. Harlan resides in Northern Virginia with his family.

# 1

# REGISTRY ANALYSIS

## Introduction

The Windows Registry is a core component of the Windows operating systems, and it maintains a considerable amount of configuration information about the system. In addition, the Registry maintains historical information about user activity; in order to provide the user with a "better", more personalized experience, the Registry maintains details about applications installed and opened, as well as window positions and sizes. This information is maintained within the Registry in a manner similar to a log file. By this, I mean that there's a great deal of time-stamped information maintained in the Registry, including, but not limited to:

- When a user opened an application or accessed a Control Panel applet
- The last time the system connected to a particular wireless access point
- When a graphic image viewing application was used to access a particular file

All of this information can be extremely valuable to a forensic analyst, particularly when attempting to establish a timeline of activity on a system. A wide range of cases would benefit greatly from information derived or extracted from the Registry if the analyst was aware of the information and how to best exploit or make use of it.

Information in the Registry can have a much greater effect on an examination than I think most analysts really realize. There are many Registry values that can have a significant impact on how the system behaves; for example, there is a Registry value that, on Windows XP and 2003 systems, tells the operating system to stop updating file's last access time so that whenever a file is opened (albeit nothing changed) for viewing or searching, the time stamp is not updated accordingly. And oh, yeah … this is enabled by default on Vista, as well as Windows 2008 and Windows 7 systems. A few other examples of Registry values that can impact an examination include (but are not limited to) the following:

- Alter or disable File System Tunneling [1]
- Modify System Crash Dump, Prefetcher, and System Restore Point behavior
- Clear the page file when the system is shut down
- Enable or disable Event log auditing
- Enable or disable the Windows firewall

## FILE SYSTEM TUNNELING

"File system tunneling" refers to an operating system's ability to "hold onto" file system metadata for a short period of time. How this can affect an analyst's examination is that if a file is deleted and then another file created in relatively short order that reuses the directory entry for the deleted file, the second file will actually take on the metadata (time stamps) for the previous file. It turns out that this also works for file renaming operations, as well, according to Microsoft. In short, when a file is removed from a directory, either by deleting or by renaming the file, the metadata for that file is temporarily cached. If, within a predefined amount of time (15 s by default), another file is added to that directory with the same name, the cached information is reused. This capability is meant for compatibility with earlier DOS programs that require the functionality and would affect an examination by providing false information about the creation date of a file in an analyst's timeline. The file system tunneling functionality can be controlled or simply disabled through specific Registry values [1].

There are a number of other values that can have a significant impact (possibly detrimental) on what an analyst sees during disk and file system analysis. Some of these values do not actually exist within the Registry by default and therefore must be added, usually in accordance with a Microsoft Knowledge Base (KB) article. At the very least, understanding these values and how they affect the overall system can add context to what the analyst observes in other areas of their examination.

## REGISTRY VALUES AND SYSTEM BEHAVIOR

The Windows Registry contains a number of values that significantly impact system behavior. For example, an analyst may receive an image for analysis and determine that the Prefetch directory contains no Prefetch (*.pf) files. Registry values of interest, in such a case, would include those that identify the operating system and version; by default, Windows XP, Vista, and Windows 7 will perform application prefetching (and generate *.pf files). However, Windows 2003 does not perform application prefetching (although it can be configured to do so) by default. The Prefetcher itself can also be disabled, per MS KB article 307498 [2]. This same value can be used to enable or disable application prefetching on Windows XP, Vista, and Windows 7 systems.

The purposes of this book are to draw back the veil of mystery that has been laid over the Registry, and to illustrate just how valuable a forensic resource, the Registry, can really be during malware, intrusion, or data breach examinations, to name just a few. The Windows Registry contains a great deal of extremely valuable information that can provide significant context to a wide range of investigations.

## What Is "Registry Analysis"?

When examining an acquired image, an analyst will many times include "Registry analysis" as one of their analysis steps. You'll see this mentioned during initial calls, listed in reports, mentioned during final close-out of a project or analysis engagement, and discussed online. Most times, this will amount to opening a Registry hive file in a viewer application and looking at the contents of a couple of the more well-known Registry keys or locating a couple of values. Sometimes, the keys examined are pulled from the analyst's previous experience, and in other cases, they may be part of an analysis plan or standard operating procedure for the organization. This list may expand to a significant number of Registry keys, and be included in a checklist or spreadsheet.

However, does this really constitute "Registry analysis"? I mean … really? When someone says "disk analysis," it usually constitutes much more than just looking at the disk itself, or just accessing the disk via the appropriate write-blocking hardware. Usually, the word *analysis* refers to (or infers) examining something from various angles and degrees, in an attempt to determine the context of the object of our attention in relation to other information or data from the same or other sources. The same holds true for the Windows Registry. There's much more to "Registry analysis" than simply looking at a couple of keys or values.

How does this approach differ from more "traditional" Registry analysis? The approach to Registry analysis has traditionally been one of looking at a specific key or at several specific values, and this approach has long been reflected in commercial tools. Commercial forensic analysis applications tend or attempt to represent the

Registry in much the same manner as one would expect to see it on a live system (with obvious limitations, of course, all of which we will discuss later in this chapter and throughout the book), providing a layer of abstraction to the analyst through that representation. Looking at a specific key or value may answer a specific question for the analyst, but how often is that all we're really looking for? Registry keys and/or values may be pertinent in and of themselves, but more and more, they are simply part of the story, rather than being the entire story themselves. Don't misunderstand; there will be times when one Registry key or value is all you need. However, what I'm trying to convey here is that there is much more information and context available, so don't stop at just that key or value because you may think that's all you need, or that's all that you have available to you.

In short, "Registry analysis" can run across a spectrum of activities, from extracting specific key and/or value information to searching within the Registry and correlating data retrieved from different areas of the Registry. All of these activities can constitute the scope of "analysis," although both analysis and the examination itself may often benefit from something more. For example, what do certain Registry keys or values *mean* within the context of others? As we mentioned earlier in this chapter, a specific Registry value [3] controls whether or not the operating system updates a file's last access times; so, how does this affect an analyst attempting to determine when a particular image file was viewed? If an analyst understands what information is maintained in the Registry, he/she will then be able to determine not only *which* user on the system viewed the image but also which application and when. Or, consider a flag value within a Registry value that determines whether or not a password is required for a user account? Is that flag value sufficient, or should the analyst check to see if the user account actually has a password (this is covered in detail in Chapter 3, "Case Studies: The System")?

Also, there may be far more information within the Windows Registry than meets the eye, particularly when the Registry is presented to the analyst via the abstraction layer of a viewing application. Much like files within a file system, Registry keys and values that are deleted do not simply disappear; as we'll see, the Registry files can contain significant information within the unallocated space of the files themselves.

Throughout the rest of this book, we're not going to be looking so much at this Registry key or that Registry value; rather, in most (albeit not all) instances, we'll be interested in examining the Registry as part of a postmortem analysis and as such, we'll use Registry analysis to help us determine not only the context of what we're looking at but also how that object of our attention plays into the overall context of our analysis. That context may be determined based on the analysis of other Registry keys and values, or it may be dependent upon other objects, such as file system metadata, Windows Event log records, entries in other logs, and so on.

## Analysis Concepts

Before we talk about Registry analysis specifically, there are a few analysis concepts that we need to discuss that are pertinent to examinations as a whole. Keeping these concepts in mind can be extremely beneficial when performing digital analysis in general.

### Locard's Exchange Principle

Dr. Edmund Locard was a French scientist, who formulated the basic forensic principle that *every contact leaves a trace*. This means that in the physical world, when two objects come into contact, some material is transferred from one to the other and vice versa. We can see this demonstrated all around us, every day … let's say you get a little too close to a concrete stanchion while trying to parallel park your car. As the car scrapes along the stanchion, paint from the car body is left on the stanchion and concrete, and paint from the stanchion becomes embedded in the scrapes on the car.

Interestingly enough, the same holds true in the digital world. When malware infects a system, there is usually some means by which it arrives on the system, such as a browser "drive-by" infection via a network share, USB thumb drive, or an e-mail attachment. When an intruder accesses a system, there is some artifact such as a network connection or activity on the target system, and the target system will contain some information about the system from which the intruder originated. Some of this information may be extremely volatile, meaning that it only remains visible to the operating system (and hence, an analyst) for a short period of time. However, remnants of that artifact may persist for a considerable amount of time.

## EVERYTHING LEAVES A TRACE

Almost any interaction with a Windows system, particularly through the *Windows Explorer* graphical interface, will leave a trace. These indications are not always in the Registry, and they may not persist for very long, but there will be something, somewhere. It's simply a matter of knowing what to look for and where, and having the right tools to gain access to, and understanding of how to correctly interpret the information.

The quote, "absence of evidence is not evidence of absence," is attributed to the astrophysicist Dr. Carl Sagan and can be applied to digital forensics, as well. Essentially, if an analyst understands the nature of a user's interaction with a Windows system, then the lack or absence of an artifact where one is expected to be is itself an artifact. During a recent examination, I was trying to determine a user's access to files on the system and could not find the RecentDocs (this key will be discussed in greater detail in Chapter 4, "Case Studies: Tracking User Activity") key within the user's NTUSER.dat hive file; RegRipper did not find it, and I could not locate the key manually. As it turns out, the user had run the "Window Washer" application, which reportedly clears the list of recently accessed documents. The time associated with the user launching the application (derived from the user's UserAssist key) corresponded to the LastWrite time on the RecentDocs parent key.

While examining a system that was part of a larger incident, our team had determined that there was a malware file on the system (a dynamic linked library, or DLL) but could not determine the method used to load and launch the malware. A timeline consisting of file system and Event Log events clearly showed the user logging in, the process being launched, the DLL file being accessed, and then the known file system artifacts being created. Our first thought was that there was some autostart location or trigger within the user's NTUSER.dat hive file, but we could not find anything. It turned out that the DLL in question was loaded as a result of some Windows shell extensions not having explicit paths listed in the Registry, and the operating system following its designated search order to locate a DLL by that name. In both instances, the absence or lack of an expected artifact was itself an artifact and spurred additional in-depth analysis.

So how does this apply to Registry analysis? When a user, even an intruder who has gained access to the system, interacts with the system and particularly with the *Windows Explorer* user interface (a.k.a., shell), some rather persistent artifacts are created. If a malicious user logs into the system and plugs in a USB thumb drive, there is an exchange of information that occurs, and some of those artifacts persist in the Registry. If the malicious user then launches applications (such as, U3, Moka5, MojoPac, and so on), there will be additional artifacts created. When a user connects his/her system to a wireless access point (WAP), information about the WAP persists on the system, again, in the Registry.

Analysts need to keep Locard's Exchange Principle in mind during an examination because it can not only tell them that there *are* artifacts but also point them to where those artifacts may be located.

### Least Frequency of Occurrence

I first heard the term "least frequency of occurrence" mentioned in the context of digital forensics at the SANS Forensic Summit during the summer of 2009. Peter Silberman (an analyst with the consulting firm Mandiant) used the term to describe malware infections on systems. His point was that in the old days, malware (and in particular worms) would spread rapidly, infecting and reinfecting systems. In short, a system would be so heavily infected that it would become completely unusable by anyone, let alone the attacker. The result was that not only the infected systems were unusable to the attacker, but the failing systems also provided a clear indication to the "victim" organization that they were infected. In order to address this, malware authors began using a unique "mutex," a software programming object that allows for mutual exclusion, within their malware in order to prevent the system from becoming reinfected. Once the system was infected, the mutex would be present in memory; on reinfection, the malware would check for the mutex and, if found, not proceed with the infection.

The offshoot of this is that the mutex is very often random (although, sometimes not so random) and always unique. This became an excellent indicator of a malware infection; in fact, Kris Harms (also an analyst with Mandiant) discussed (during a presentation) using the Microsoft SysInternals tool handle.exe to list all the mutexes available in memory for all of the running processes on the system and then sorting the output by the unique mutexes. Kris demonstrated that a quick look at those mutexes that only occurred once very often resulted in rapid and accurate detection of malware, even if the mutex name itself had been changed. Demonstrating Kris's use of handle.exe is outside the scope of this book, but it does serve as an example of how the concept of *least frequency of occurrence* (LFO) can be used, not only for malware but also for intrusions, and therefore can also be very important to our analysis.

The point of LFO is that during the lifetime of a system, malware infections and intrusions are often what occurs least frequently on that system. Operating system and application updates are extremely "noisy," generating a great deal of file system (file creations, modifications, and deletions) and Registry (keys being created, values updated, and so on) activity, and occurring fairly frequently. Windows XP, by default, will create a System Restore Point every 24 hours (as well as under other conditions) and will also launch its Disk Defragmenter utility every three calendar days to perform a limited defrag. Windows XP also generates or updates Prefetch files whenever an application is launched. Beginning with Windows Vista, the operating systems began maintaining Volume Shadow Copies (as opposed to the traditional Windows XP System Restore Points) in order to provide a recovery mechanism. When a user installs software from

Apple (such as QuickTime, iTunes, and so on), a Scheduled Task is created on the system to look for updates to those applications once a week, and the user can choose to install those updates by creating and modifying files within the file system. Microsoft releases operating system and application updates monthly, and sometimes does so "out of band," or out of the regular update release schedule. What this means is that there is a *lot* of normal file system and Registry activity that occurs on a system, but in contrast, when malware infects a system, a few files (and maybe Registry keys or values) are created, and there may also be some network connections as the malware communicates off the system. When an intruder accesses a system via Remote Desktop using an easily-guessed password, there may be several Event log records generated (we will discuss how to determine the audit configuration on a system in detail in Chapter 3, "Case Studies: The System") and some Registry keys may be created or modified, and depending upon the actions they take, there may be some files created, modified, or deleted on that system. Again, with the exception of turning the compromised system into a repository for pirated movies or music files, a malware infection or intrusion will very often constitute the least frequent activity on the system. In fact, many intrusions go undetected for long periods of time, as the intruder will use very simple techniques to minimize as much as possible the artifacts left on a system. This can also be true for other types of issues, such as viewing illegal images. A file (or a few files) are added to the system, the files are viewed (as we'll see in Chapter 4, "Case Studies: Tracking User Activity," some Registry keys will be updated), and then the files may be shared or deleted. Overall, adding, viewing, and deleting these files really do not constitute a considerable amount of activity, particularly when compared with operating system and application updates.

What this often means to our analysis is that during intrusions or malware infections, we wouldn't usually be looking for large numbers of files being added to the system, or for massive numbers of Registry keys or values being created, or regular or significant spikes in activity of any kind. Most often, spikes in file system and Registry activity will indicate an operating system or application software update (or much to the chagrin of the analyst, a system administrator running antivirus application scans), not a malware infection or system intrusion.

### Goals

Before starting any analysis, every analyst should carefully consider and document their goals. What are you looking for? What questions are you trying to answer? What do you hope to ultimately achieve through your analysis? We do this because this helps us understand what it is we should be doing, what data we should extract, where we should go to look for clues, and what data can be correlated to address the issue. Too often, analysts get caught up in the "find all bad stuff" mind-set (or allow customers to hem them into it) and in doing so spend hours upon hours "doing analysis," yet never actually answer the questions before them. Believe me, I understand how you'll be looking for one thing but find something else that, while interesting, may not have anything to do with your immediate analysis. Pursuing these kinds of things is called having "shiny object syndrome"; like a fish or a kitten, you're easily distracted by shiny objects. An example of this is locating all of the malware and spyware on a system, when the customer just wanted to know if a user on the system had accessed or copied a file (as in a fraud or exposure of intellectual property issue).

Your goals may vary depending upon your employer and the type of work you generally do. If you're a consultant, your goals may vary from case to case; during one examination, you may have to determine if a system was infected with malware and, if so, the capabilities of that malware (that is, what data did it extract, where was the data sent, was the malware specifically targeted at the organization, and so on). In another examination, you may have to determine if there was sensitive information (that is, personally identifiable information, credit card data, classified data, and so forth) stored on the system, whereas another examination may pertain to violations of corporate acceptable use policies. If you're a law enforcement officer, you may be faced with a possible issue of fraud, or you may need to demonstrate that a computer owner had knowledge of and viewed contraband images.

Regardless of the type of examination, your goals are where everything starts and ends. For consultants, who are not answering a customer's questions can lead to serious issues, such as spending far more time on your "analysis" than your contract allows, or attempting to bill a customer when you haven't answered their questions. Our analysis goals give us direction and focus, and allow us to provide those answers in a timely and efficient manner.

### Documentation

Perhaps the most important aspect of any analysis, after the goals, is documentation. Forensic analysts and incident responders should document all aspects of what they do, from the acquisition of hard drives and the transfer and management of acquired images to their analysis plan and actual case notes. Many organizations have their own acquisition methodology and chain of custody documentation, usually in some sort of form or checklist. This is a good start, but documenting case work should not stop there.

What can sometimes be missed is documentation of the overall analysis process. Before conducting analysis, do you sit down and ensure that you understand the goals of the analysis, or the questions that you're trying to answer? Whether you're a consultant working for a customer or an examiner performing work in support of law enforcement, there's usually some reason why you're sitting there with a hard drive or an acquired image. What is that reason? Most likely, it's that someone has questions that need to be answered. So start your analysis plan by documenting the goals that you're trying to achieve. From there, you can begin framing out your steps going forward and noting where you need to look and those tasks that you need to achieve. For example, if the goal is to determine the existence of specific e-mails, you'll likely want to check for .pst or .ost files, or may want to check the Registry and determine which e-mail client was used and determine if Web-based e-mail was used, and so on.

The analysis plan can lead the analyst directly into documenting the analysis process itself. So why would we do this? What happens if at some point during the analysis process, you get sick or become injured? What happens if the analysis needs to be handed off to someone else? Another very real possibility is what happens if 6 months or a year after you complete your analysis, you have to answer questions about it? I know several analysts to whom this has happened recently. For myself, I've worked with customers who've come back with questions 6 or more months after accepting the final report and paying their bill … had I not had clear, concise documentation, I would have had trouble answering their questions in an intelligible manner.

# Note

Many times when beginning an examination involving the Web browser on a system, I'll see analysts start off by saying, "I'd check the contents of the user's TypedURLs key." That key, located in the NTUSER.dat file within the User Profile, contains a list of the URLs typed into the Internet Explorer address bar. But is that really a good place to start? What if there are no entries? What does that tell you? Perhaps a better place to start would be to determine which Web browser the user was using, or at least which Web browsers were installed in the system before targeting browser-specific artifacts.

We've all been busy to the point where we can't remember what we had for breakfast, let alone the specifics of an examination from 6 months ago. Your case notes and documentation can be extremely important at that point, and it's best not to have to figure that out after the fact.

Another important aspect of documenting your analysis is that it allows you to go back and look at what you did and improve the process. Documentation is the basis for improvement, and you can't improve a process if you don't have one. Your documentation provides that process. If you didn't document what you did, it didn't happen. By listing out the steps you followed in your analysis, you can see which ones were perhaps less fruitful, which ones can be skipped or improved upon the next time, and which ones provided greater value. This also allows for other, less-experienced analysts to learn from what you have done, what worked, and what didn't so that more analysts are able to achieve a similar, greater level of analysis.

## Challenges of Registry Analysis

Although often fruitful, Registry analysis isn't always easy, and there are two primary challenges when it comes to Registry analysis. Depending on your particular experiences, there may be other challenges, but these are the two big ones as I see them.

The first challenge to Registry analysis is that the Registry itself isn't all that well understood by responders and analysts. To be honest, I'm not even sure that there's really *anyone* who completely understands the Windows Registry. The Registry is a critical, core component of the Windows operating systems, and it records a considerable amount of information about the system configuration and usage, as well as user activity, particularly when the user is interacting with the system through the Windows Explorer shell. With just the operating system itself, I don't think that there's really anyone who completely understands why some keys and values have the paths and contain the structures that they do, or what activities lead to the keys or values being created or modified, let alone the structure of various binary value data. This lack of understanding by the vendor obviates any thorough knowledge and understanding by analysts and leaves the analyst to perform considerable testing to determine and illustrate how various artifacts originated on the system.

Although considerable work has been performed and documented in this area, the awareness that this work is possibly incomplete persists. As new versions of the operating system are developed, locations and formats for storing data in the

Registry change, as well, and some keys or values may be added, moved, modified, or simply removed. Very little is known and documented about what actions cause various keys to be modified; while some testing has been done for a very small number of keys, new questions are being posed all the time that would, quite honestly, require access to the source code to the operating system in order to completely answer. Being closed source, the way Windows is, having complete access to the source code isn't likely to happen anytime soon.

Several years ago, Cory Altheide (whom I used to work with at IBM and is now a responder for Google) and I conducted some research into tracking the use of USB devices across Windows systems. After we were done, we published our findings, confident that we'd figured out a way to determine when a USB device was last connected to a system. More recently, Rob Lee (of consulting firm Mandiant and SANS fame) conducted additional testing and determined that what Cory and I had determined was really the first time that the device had been connected during the current (or most recent) boot session, meaning that if the system was running for several days and the USB device connected and disconnected several times, the best we could hope to show (with just the data we'd found) was when the device had first been connected during that boot session. Additional information is available in Windows Vista and Windows 7, but there simply is no comprehensive listing of actions by a user or within the operating system that would affect particular Registry keys.

## MALWARE AND THE WINDOWS REGISTRY

Most of the time, when looking for indications of malware remaining persistent on a system, I'll go right to the Registry. Not only is this a popular location for malware to use to maintain persistence, but very often new persistence locations in the Registry are also discovered by analyzing a new bit of malware that's been found. The reason is that many malware authors will become aware of these locations and how to use them well before anyone else, including antivirus vendors and malware analysts.

Analyzing the Registry for new bits of malware can often be a game of catch-up, as some new means of persistence may have been discovered by the bad guys and not yet commonly known by responders and incident analysts.

To make matters worse, not only do malware authors make extensive use of the Registry so that their creations will remain persistent on systems across reboots and logins, but some have even gone so far as to place entire Windows executables files into binary value data!

The other challenge of Registry analysis is the fact that while the binary structure of the Registry remains the same across versions of Windows (that is, the core binary structure of the Registry is very much the same between Windows 2000 and Windows 7, inclusive), important keys and values change between versions, often very drastically. In many cases, this applies to the base operating system as well as to new and even existing applications. This can make it very difficult for an analyst who figures out and documents some specific Registry keys and values, based on a particular version of an application and operating system, only to find those settings null and void when an updated version of the application or the operating system is released.

One example of these changes is how user search terms are maintained within the Registry. With Windows XP, you could find various search terms under a key named "ACMru." Subkeys beneath this key pertained to particular form fields that a user could submit terms to when performing searches. With Windows Vista, search terms were recorded in a file, but not in the Registry. With Windows 7, search terms are again stored in the Registry, but under an entirely different path, beneath a key named "WordWheelQuery." These keys are discussed in greater detail in Chapter 4, "Case Studies: Tracking User Activity."

It is not the goal of this chapter or even this book to provide a comprehensive listing of all similar changes that occur between various versions of the Windows operating system; rather, it is enough to understand that these changes can and do occur, and it is incumbent upon analysts to keep up-to-date on analysis techniques and procedures, particularly, as they pertain to the Windows Registry.

# Tip

Something that is very important to keep in mind when considering whether to engage in live response activities (as opposed to acquiring an image of the hard drive and conducting postmortem analysis) is that while your actions do have an effect on the system (processes loaded into memory, files created on the system as a result of your actions, and so on), so does your *inaction*. Think about it. A live system is running, with things going on all the time. Even though a system just sits there, processes are running and actions are occurring on the system. With Windows XP, simply wait 24 h and a System Restore Point will (by default) be automatically created. Wait 3 days and the system will conduct a limited defragmentation. Also consider the fact that if someone is exfiltrating data from your systems, then while you wait and do nothing, they continue to take more data. So the question of live response really comes down to (a) do I do nothing or (b) do I take the correct actions to protect my organization as best I can under the circumstances?

# What Is the Windows Registry?

So far we've talked about Registry analysis, but what is the Windows Registry? According to Microsoft Knowledge Base (KB) article 256986 [4], the Windows Registry is a "central hierarchal database" intended to store information that is necessary to configure the system for one or more users, applications, and hardware devices. In short, the Windows Registry is a binary data structure meant to replace the configuration and initialization (.ini) files used by previous versions of Windows (okay, Windows 3.1). For a normal Windows user and for most administrators, this is pretty transparent and means very little to them. Most users and administrators do not interact directly with the Registry; instead, they interact with it through some sort of *graphical user* interface (GUI), such as the Registry Editor that is distributed with most Windows installations. Figure 1.1 illustrates the Registry Editor on Windows XP.

As you can see in Figure 1.1, the Registry Editor provides a user or administrator with an easy means to navigate the Registry by providing a layer of abstraction. There may be times when even an administrator doesn't go as far as using the Registry Editor, as most interaction with the Registry may be through application installation (that is, launching the installation process, which then adds and modifies Registry entries) or removal.

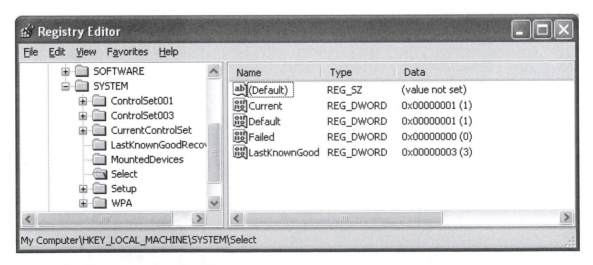

**Figure 1.1** Registry Editor on Windows XP

> ## Note
>
> Graphical tools are primarily intended to make a task easier for the user and to protect the users from themselves. The GUI prevents the user from seeing what happens "under the hood." However, that's exactly where malware authors and attackers go … under the hood. The best source of information regarding autostart locations in the Registry is the anti-virus vendors; as they receive new malware samples to analyze, they begin to see what methods and autostart locations (and persistence mechanisms) these folks are using. Neither Microsoft nor application vendors provide such a breadth of information. Further, relying on antivirus vendors to let us know what they're seeing is reactive, not proactive.

Many of the instructions and Knowledge Base (KB) articles available from Microsoft that deal with interacting with the Registry do so by having the reader interact with a GUI component of the Windows Explorer shell or through another application. For example, a user wouldn't directly access the Registry to delete keys and values created when an application is installed; instead, they would likely use the Add/Remove Programs Control Panel applet. In those instances where Microsoft does identify specific Registry keys, there is always a stern warning against directly modifying the Registry, as to do so might leave the system inoperable.

## Purpose of the Windows Registry

Microsoft tells us that the Registry maintains configuration information about the system, but what does this really mean? It's one thing to say that the Registry replaces the text-based .ini files of old and is a database that maintains configuration information about the system and applications that run on it, but what does that really mean to the incident responder and forensic analyst? We're not so much interested in what this means to a user or to an administrator; instead, what we'd like to know is, what does that mean to those of us who would need to delve into this resource? Well, what it means is that there's a lot of information in the Registry that tells the operating system and applications what to do, where to put things, and how to react to certain stimulus. There are a lot of little nuances that can have a significant effect on incident response and forensic analysis that are all managed through the Registry. For example, one Registry value tells the operating system to clear the page file when the system is shut down, and another setting tells the operating system whether or not to enable the use of a hibernation file, whereas yet another value disables the updating of last access times within the file system. When you think about it, all of these values can have a significant impact on a wide range of incident response activities and digital forensic analysis.

Devices that have been connected to the system are tracked through the Registry. Information about devices is maintained in the Registry so that the devices are recognized and presented as they were previously when they're reconnected to the system; as such, this information can be extremely valuable to a forensic analyst when attempting to track the use of an iPod, digital camera, or thumb drive on a system or across several systems.

The Registry also tracks a great deal of information about a user's activities. This can be very beneficial to a forensic analyst. Let's say you sit down to play a game of Solitaire on your Windows system, and the first time you run the application, you get the default settings, with respect to how many cards are dealt and how the game is timed and scored. You change most of these settings to something else and then resize and reposition the game window. When you're done playing, you close the window and shut down the system. The next day, you come back and launch the game again, and all of your settings are still there, having persisted across a log out and reboot. This is due to the fact that the settings are recorded in the Registry so that the next time you launch the application or game, your most recent and preferred settings are read, and the application window is presented in the location, size, and shape that you left it.

The Registry also tracks a number of other user actions, such as clicking through the **Program** menu to start an application, as well as keeping track of recently accessed files that are associated with various applications, such as MS Word, Excel, Windows Media Player, and so on. The user will generally see these files on the Recent Documents portion of the Program menu, or as part of a drop-down menu specific to the application, as illustrated in Figure 1.2.

# Warning

Not all applications create a presence in the Registry. For example, some peer-to-peer (P2P) sharing applications are cross-platform and Java-based, and as such, don't rely on the Windows Registry to store information. Instead, they use configuration files in order to make cross-platform coding easier.

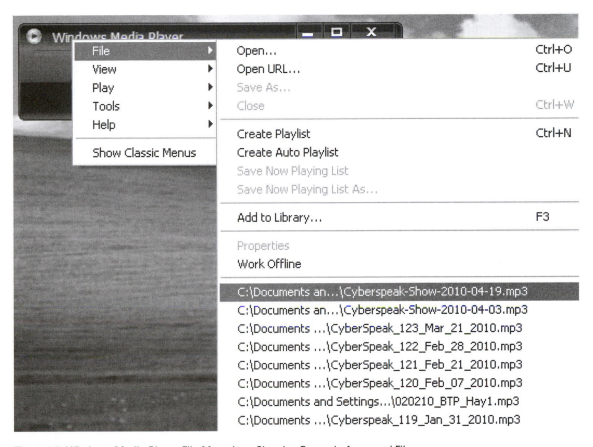

**Figure 1.2** Windows Media Player File Menu Item Showing Recently Accessed Files

Much of the information tracked in the Registry can be associated with a time value of some sort, and as such, the Registry becomes something of a log file. As will be addressed later in this chapter, all Registry keys maintain a property called their "LastWrite time." Whenever a Registry key is modified … created, values or subkeys are created or deleted, or a value is modified … the key's LastWrite time is updated to reflect that change. This value is analogous to a file's last modification time (although, as of yet, I have been unable to locate an accessible *application programming* interface, or "API," that allows for the arbitrary modification of LastWrite times as it is with file MAC times). However, this is not the only place that time stamps are maintained in the Registry. Many values contain time and date information and, often, in different formats. In this way, the Registry can be considered in many respects to be a log file.

## Tip

While analyzing a system to determine if a user had looked at images or videos (as opposed to a virus or worm putting those files on the system), I ran across the use of the Window Washer application, which is intended to "clean up" behind a user. In this case, the application maintained the last date and times that it had been run in its own Registry values, which I was able to correlate to other, similar data. There were two separate values, one for date and one for time, maintained as strings.

## Location of the Windows Registry on Disk

From a forensic analysis perspective, an analyst does not generally interact with the Registry through the Registry Editor. An analyst will most likely interact with Registry hive files directly, through a commercial forensic analysis application, or as a result of extracting them from a file system or from an acquired image. There are a number of such tools available, several of which will be discussed in Chapter 2, "Tools." However, it is important for the analyst to know where these files exist on disk so that they can be retrieved and analyzed. The main, core system Registry hive files (specifically, SAM, Security, Software, and System) can be found in the Windows\system32\config directory, as illustrated in Figure 1.3.

**Figure 1.3** Registry Hive Files in the Windows\System32\Config Directory

# Note

With Windows NT and 2000, there was actually a limit to the maximum size of Registry file, per MS KB 124594 [5]. This restriction was removed as of Windows XP and 2003 [6].

The hive files themselves, illustrated in Figure 1.3, are referred to as "hive" files, as the files contain the binary database structures or "hives." These are the hive files that maintain configuration information about the system, such as operating system version and settings, local user account information, installed software and components, and so on.

On Windows Vista and above systems, there is another hive file in the system32\config directory named "Components." Although there are a number of keys and values listed in this hive file, as of this writing, I have yet to find anything significant from a forensics or incident response standpoint; however, this may change in the near future. Also beginning with Windows Vista, the boot environment for Windows systems was completely re-engineered. The result is that in the C:\Boot directory, you will find a file called "BCD" (the "boot configuration data" file) which contains information maintained in the same structure as Registry hive files. A detailed discussion of the BCD architecture is beyond the scope of this book, and the file itself is mentioned here (and in Chapter 3) only because it shares the Windows Registry structure along with the other Registry files.

Information specific to individual users is maintained in the NTUSER.dat hive file that is located in the User Profile. For Windows 2000, XP, and 2003, the User Profiles are found in the Documents and Settings directory at the root of the system drive, whereas for Vista and later versions, the User Profiles are found in the "Users" directory. There is also another user hive that is merged with the NTUSER.dat hive file when a user logs in, allowing for a unified presentation of the information from both hives. This is the USRCLASS.dat hive, located in the User's Profile, in the Local Settings\Application Data\Microsoft\ Windows folder. The information maintained in this hive file can vary between operating system versions. With Windows 7, some entries normally found in the user's NTUSER.dat hive file have been moved to the USRCLASS.dat hive; this will be addressed later in this book.

## REGISTRY REDIRECTION AND VIRTUALIZATION

With more modern versions of Windows, Microsoft has implemented redirection and virtualization with respect to the Registry. Registry redirection [7] essentially means that on 64-bit versions of Windows, some Registry calls by 32-bit applications are redirected to another portion of the Software hive. What this means to an analyst is that some 32-bit application information (that is, those keys that are not identified as being shared between 64- and 32-bit applications) will appear in the HKEY_LOCAL_MACHINE\Software\Wow6432Node key path, rather than in the HKEY_LOCAL_MACHINE\Software key path. Similar redirection does not occur within the Software key in the user's hive. Microsoft KB article 896459 [8] provides a list of shared keys. Note that Registry reflection for synchronization has been disabled as of Windows 2008 and Windows 7.

Registry virtualization is a bit different and impacts an examiner's analysis differently. Microsoft describes Registry virtualization [9] as, beginning with Windows Vista, "an application compatibility technology that enables registry write operations that have global impact to be redirected to per-user locations." What this means is that Registry modifications (writes, anything to create keys or values) that have a global impact on the system will be written instead to a "virtual store" (HKEY_USERS\<*SID*>_Classes\VirtualStore\Machine\Software\key path), which translates to the USRCLASS.dat hive file mentioned above.

Portions of the Windows Registry visible through the Registry Editor are "volatile," meaning that they are populated when the system is booted or when a user logs in and do not exist on disk when the system is shut down. This is extremely important for first responders and forensic analysts to understand, as there may be valuable data that does not exist within an acquired image and *must* be collected while the system is still running.

One example of volatile data is the HKEY_CURRENT_USER hive. When viewed through the Registry Editor, you can clearly see this hive, and after a little exploration, you'll find that the information in this portion of the Registry pertains specifically to the logged-on user. However, when you shut the system down and analyze an acquired image, you won't find an HKEY_CURRENT_USER hive or any file by that name. That's because this hive is populated by using the hive of the user who's logged into the system.

For the currently logged-in user, the HKEY_CURRENT_USER\SessionInformation key contains a value named Program Count that keeps track of the number of programs you have running on your desktop. This is the count you see when you lock your workstation. However, this value doesn't exist in the user's NTUSER.dat file when the system is shut down.

# Note

When performing postmortem analysis of the Registry, it is a straightforward process to determine which ControlSet had been mounted as the CurrentControlSet on the live system. Simply open the System hive in a viewer and locate that Select key. Beneath that key, you will find a value named "Current," whose data is a number. If the data is "0 × 0001," the ControlSet mounted as the CurrentControlSet is ControlSet001 [10].

Another example of volatile Registry keys and values is the HKEY_LOCAL_MACHINE\Hardware key and its subkeys. This key stores information regarding the devices connected to the system (CPU, keyboard, mouse, hard drive, and so on) and their assigned resources, and is populated when the system boots up.

If you open the Registry Editor and navigate to the HKEY_LOCAL_MACHINE\System hive, you'll see a key named "CurrentControlSet," and most likely, two others whose names begin with "ControlSet00" and end in a number. The CurrentControlSet doesn't exist when the system is shut down and is populated at boot time from one of the available ControlSets.

Yet another example of a volatile portion of the Registry is the HKEY_CLASSES_ROOT key. When the system is booted, this key is populated with the contents of the HKEY_LOCAL_MACHINE\Software\Classes key, and when a user logs in, the HKEY_CURRENT_USER\Software\Classes key contents are added and, according to Microsoft, take precedence of the entries from HKEY_LOCAL_MACHINE entries [11].

What's important to keep in mind is that there are portions of the Windows Registry that only exist in memory. Thanks to folks like Aaron Walters and Brendan Dolan-Gavitt (both of Volatility memory analysis fame), this information can be accessed, retrieved, and analyzed; the necessary tools for collecting this data will be discussed later in this book.

## Nomenclature

When working in the incident response and digital forensics field, as with many other fields, it is necessary to have and observe specificity of terminology. Basically, this is just a fancy way of saying that we all need to agree on what different things are called and then call them that. When I took one of my first vendor-specific training courses for a commercial forensic analysis application, the instructor spent the first hour or more

## Tip

Understanding the version of Windows that you're analyzing can have a significant impact on your examination. For example, Windows XP creates and maintains System Restore Points by default, which means that depending on the system being used you may have access to a great deal of historical data. Portions of the Registry are maintained in System Restore Points (that is, not all portions of the hives are stored, as it wouldn't do well to reset a user's password to an older one when restoring a system to a previous state) and can be easily accessed during analysis. Also, keep in mind that System Restore Points are created for a number of reasons, such as driver installations, as well as simply being created every 24 hours. More recent versions of Windows (Vista, Windows 7) use Volume Shadow Copies to maintain backups of files, and accessing those Volume Shadow Copies can give you a view into the Registry in an earlier state. Understanding System Restore Points and Volume Shadow Copies can provide a view into Registry data that isn't accessible through any other means.

Finally, Windows 7 includes the ability to run XP Mode, a specific Windows XP installation intended to provide backward compatibility to run older applications. Users can install applications that have trouble running in Windows 7 into the XP Mode Virtual PC installation and access them via the Windows 7 desktop. This also means that on any Windows 7 system with XP Mode installed, there is a second source of potentially valuable Registry hive files.

explaining what a "CPU," "hard drive" or "disk," a "computer system" really were. As someone with an electrical engineering degree, if you ask me to go into a room with a computer and retrieve a "CPU," I'm going to open the computer, go to the motherboard and extract that little black square thing with all of the pins coming out of it, so I really hope that you aren't expecting the entire computer.

In short, it's important that when talking about parts of the Registry, we all must have and use a consistent understanding of what it is we're referring to so that we can communicate clearly and avoid (as much as possible) confusion and misunderstanding. Figure 1.4 illustrates the various components of the Registry, specifically keys, subkeys, values, and data. We'll go into more depth regarding the details of the binary structure of these components.

From the Registry Editor view illustrated in Figure 1.4, "keys" and "subkeys" are the folders displayed in the left-hand pane of the editor. This is an apt metaphor, in that keys can contain or point to other keys (that is, subkeys) as well as values. Keys also contain very valuable information from a forensic perspective (their LastWrite time) within their binary structure. Values, in the right-hand pane in Figure 1.4, are much simpler and contain data of a specific type, be it a string value, multiple string values, binary, or DWORD, which is just a 32-bit binary value.

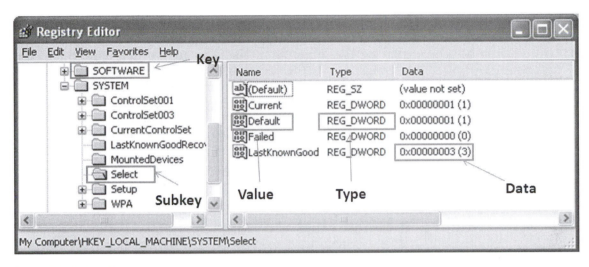

**Figure 1.4** Registry Nomenclature

More importantly, we now have a frame of reference for discussing the Registry and Registry analysis throughout the rest of this book and a common understanding of what a "key" is and what a "value" is, and how they relate to each other. Many times in such discussions, consistent terminology may be reversed or simply not used, and confusion ensues.

## Registry Structure

Now that we've seen where the Registry "lives" within a live system, and subsequently within an acquired image, it's important to take that one step further and understand the structure of the Registry itself, as we may find vitally important information in places other than within Registry hive files. For example, we may find Registry data within unallocated space from an acquired image, or within the hive file itself (yes, Registry hive files do contain "unallocated space"!). We may also find Registry data and indeed entire hives within a memory dump from a live, running system, or within the Windows page file.

## Tip

Brendan Dolan-Gavitt has done considerable work with respect to locating and accessing Registry information within Windows memory dumps and has contributed plugins to the Volatility project for accessing this data.

Regardless of where Registry data (keys, values) are found, it is important to understand the binary structure of the Registry so that we can understand what Registry viewing applications are showing us. Whether we're viewing a Registry hive file via a commercial forensic analysis application or a hive file viewer, understanding the structure of the Registry helps us understand what we're seeing, as well as what we aren't seeing. Remember that the viewer provides a layer of abstraction, representing to the analyst what the data should look like; as such, some data may not be apparent or easily read and understood because of shortcomings in the viewer, the nature of the data, and so on.

## REGISTRY HIVES AND SEARCHES

When performing PCI data breach investigations, one of the things I needed to do was search across the entire hard drive for what could be credit card data, including both the numbers themselves, as well as track data. In one particular instance, my search revealed a number of hits within Registry hive files, specifically an NTUSER.dat hive in one User Profile and within the Software hive file. Viewing the data around the search hits within the hive files, I did not see anything that resembled a Registry key or value; likewise, opening the hive files in a viewer and searching for the search hits provided no indications that the hits were key or value names, or in Registry data. As it turned out, the search hits were actually located in file slack, something that we were able to determine through an understanding of the binary structure of the Registry.

Thankfully, the binary structure of the Registry itself has remained fairly consistent across the various versions of the Windows operating system, from Windows NT all the way to Windows 7. This means that a viewer application that understands the structure of the Registry will, for the most part, work equally well on hive files from all versions. What's changed, however, are the names and locations of various keys and values … where data is stored and what format it is in will differ between versions of the Windows operating system. Windows XP, for example, maintains information about wireless access points (WAPs) that have been connected to (connections that were managed by Windows, rather than a third-party utility) in a binary data structure within values beneath a specific Registry key. Vista and Windows 7 use an entirely different format for similar information and add some additional information … all of which is located beneath a different Registry key. A great place to start in developing an understanding of the hive file structure is Mark Russinovich's "Inside the Registry" article in Windows NT Magazine (available online at http://technet.microsoft.com/

en-us/library/cc750583.aspx). This article provides an excellent overview of the structure of the Registry, identifying the various cell types (key, value, subkey list, value list, and so on), bins, and the cell map relationships between them.

When I initially began looking into the structure of the Registry from a programming perspective, I relied heavily on Peter Nordahl's work with his offline NT Password and Registry Editor [12] in order to understand the binary structures that comprise a Registry hive file. Peter's utility allows you to boot a Windows system (originally from a disk, there's now a version that runs on a boot CD) and, for one, modify any password. When you reboot the system, you can then log into the system using the user account you select and the new password you created. I used an early version of this utility to access Windows XP systems turned in by departing users in a corporate environment, and I have used the boot CD version more recently when booting an acquired image through VMWare. Although the utility itself has been extremely useful, what I was looking for was the source code, which Peter provides. Within the source distribution archive is a file called "ntreg.h," which contains constant values and definitions for various structures within the Registry. Within the source archive, you will also find a file named "WinReg.txt," which has a bit of a summary of what's in the ntreg.h file, including descriptions of some of the structures without as much detail as the header file. Using this information, along with a hex editor, I was able to start writing my own binary Registry hive file parser in Perl, allowing me access the information stored within the files and obtain as much detail as I wanted. As I began developing this hive file parser, I ran across the Parse::Win32Registry Perl module (available online at http://cpan.uwinnipeg.ca/dist/Parse-Win32Registry) written by James Macfarlane. This module provides an easy-to-use *object-oriented* (OO) interface for accessing various structures within the hive files. I should point out that this is an entirely different module from the Win32::TieRegistry module that ships with ActiveState's Perl distribution, in that the Win32::TieRegistry module allows a Perl programmer to interact with a *live* Registry (on a running system, as may be the case during incident response), not directly with the hive files, as is the case with James' module.

In the spring of 2008, Jolanta Thomassen asked me if I would act as her sponsor for her graduate thesis, which involved understanding the structure of the Windows Registry with a specific focus on locating deleted keys and values within the hive file itself. This topic had intrigued me for quite some time (as a reference for her, I provided a link to a UseNet post I'd made in

2001 asking about unallocated space in hive files), and Jolanta did a fantastic job not only in understanding what deleted keys and values "look like" but also how to recover them and present them in an easy to understandable format. The result of her work is a utility called *regslack*, the Windows portable executable (PE) version of which I use quite regularly, and I have to say, effectively.

In February 2009, Peter Norris posted his master's thesis regarding *The Internal Structure of the Windows Registry* online at http://amnesia.gtisc.gatech.edu/~moyix/suzibandit.ltd.uk/MSc/. Peter's work goes into considerable detail regarding the binary structure of the Windows Registry and also referenced Jolanta's work. It is beyond the scope and focus of this book to review Peter's work in detail, and such a review is left as an exercise to the reader.

Mark Russinovich's "Inside the Registry" article, mentioned earlier in this chapter, describes a number of Registry cell or "record" types. Of those, we are primarily interested in and will be focusing on the key and value cells/records, as these provide the vast majority of information of interest to forensic analysts. Other cell types (subkey list, value list, and so on), while significant, are beyond the scope of this book, and a detailed examination of those cell types is left as an exercise to the reader. These cell types are simply pointers to lists of subkeys or values and do not contain key or value structures themselves.

Registry hive files are made up of 4-KB sections or "bins." These bins are meant to make allocation of new space (as the hive file grows), as well as the maintenance of the hive file itself, easier. The first four bytes of a normal hive file starts with "regf" (or 0×66676572 in hexadecimal). From there, as you traverse through the hive file on a binary level, as with a hex editor, every 4096 bytes you should see "hbin" (0×6E696268, in hex). Per Peter Norris' thesis work, various cells within the hive files do not cross hbin sections; that is, a key cell will not be split between two adjacent hbin sections, overlapping the border between them. As such, the hbin sections can be considered self-contained.

The first hbin marker is very important, as this is the base location for offset values listed with the key and value cells throughout the rest of the hive file. What this means is that when you're reading values within a key cell structure (which we'll be looking at shortly) and you read an offset that value is the offset from the first hbin marker. For example, as we'll see shortly, each key cell contains a value for the offset to its parent key, which essentially points back to that key. That offset, in bytes, is measured from the beginning of the first hbin marker,

## Tip

As with other types of files, allocation of new space for hive files, as the Registry grows, can pose something interesting challenges for a forensic analyst. When a new hbin section is required, that 4-KB section is, in many cases, allocated from previously used space within the file system, space that at one time may have contained valid data. During one examination in particular, I ran a search for credit card numbers and received several hits "in" Registry hive files. Closer examination of the data indicated that the discovered credit card numbers were not part of the "live" Registry (not contained in key or value names, nor in value data), and the most likely explanation was that the numbers had resided in sectors that had previously comprised another file (possibly a database) which had been deleted.

which itself is 4096 bytes from the beginning of the hive file. On the surface of this, you may be wondering how this information is useful. Several open-source tools that assist the analyst with locating and extracting (that is, "carving") data from unallocated space within an image allow the analyst to designate a header and footer for locating data or to designate a header or marker (also known as a *magic number*) and then read in a set number of bytes. These data carving tools can be used to search unallocated space or similar unstructured data such as the Windows page file or a hibernation file for Registry "hbin" sections.

## Registry Key Cells

The Registry "hbin" sections are made up of several types of cells, but for our purposes, we're going to focus on the key and value cells. Key cells (or "keys") are very important to forensic analysts as they contain time-based information within their structure, in the form of their LastWrite time. The LastWrite time is a 64-bit FILETIME structure, marking the number of 100-nanosecond intervals since midnight of January 1, 1601 [13]. A key cell (without the name) is 80-bytes long and starts with a 4-byte (in Microsoft parlance, a "DWORD") value indicating its size, followed by the node identifier, node type, the offset to the key's parent, the number of subkeys, the offset to the subkey list, the number of values, the offset to the value list, the offset to the security identifier, and the length of the key name (begins immediately after the key structure). Note that this is not a comprehensive list of the values within the key cell structure but rather an overview of the values that are of great interest. Figure 1.5 illustrates the binary structure of a Registry key (viewed in a hex editor) with the node identifier (ID) and LastWrite time values of the structure highlighted.

As illustrated in Figure 1.5, the node ID is "6E 6B" (0×6B6E in little endian format), or "nk," and is followed by the node type of 0×2C, which indicates a root node (0×20 indicates a "normal" key node). Immediately following the node type is the LastWrite time, which is a 64-bit FILETIME object.

Table 1.1 lists the key cell structure details, illustrating the elements of that structure that are of primary interest to forensic analysts.

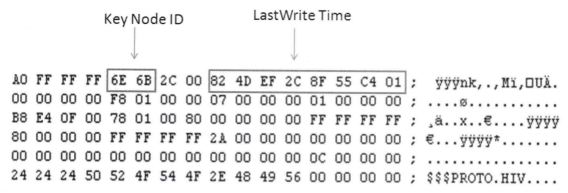

**Figure 1.5** Registry Key Structure with Node ID and LastWrite Time

## Table 1.1  Registry Key Cell Structure Details

| Offset (bytes) | Size (bytes) | Description |
| --- | --- | --- |
| 0 | 4 | Size |
| 4 | 2 | Node ID ("nk", or 0x6B6E) |
| 6 | 2 | Node Type (0x2C or 0x20) |
| 8 | 8 | LastWrite time |
| 20 | 4 | Offset to this key's parent |
| 24 | 4 | Number of subkeys |
| 32 | 4 | Offset to the list of subkey records |
| 36 | 4 | Number of values |
| 44 | 4 | Offset to the value list |
| 48 | 4 | Offset to security identifier record |
| 76 | 2 | Length of the key name |

Table 1.1 should not be considered all-inclusive, as it details those structure elements that are most important to forensic analysts. Again, the size of the structure detailed in Table 1.1 is 80 bytes, and the first four bytes of the structure contain the size of the key cell, which includes the key name and any necessary padding. Therefore, the total size of a Registry key is the 80-byte header, name, and padding; for the key illustrated in Figure 1.5, the total size is 96 bytes.

The size value (the first four bytes or "DWORD") is an important aspect of the key structure of which to take notice. When read as an unsigned integer, the size is "4294967200," and we know that a single key would not usually be expected to be on the order of 4 GB in size. However, when read as a signed integer value, those four bytes equal "−96." Again, the key "header" itself is 80 bytes, and the actual name of the key begins immediately after the key structure. The name of the key illustrated in Figure 1.5, "$$$PROTO.HIV," is 12 bytes and there are an additional four bytes of padding, rounding out 16 bytes. That makes the total size of the key itself 96 bytes. This is important, as Jolanta (and others) had determined that for normal, allocated Registry keys, the size is a negative value when read as a signed integer value. However, when a key is "deleted," the size value is made positive. If the key in Figure 1.5 was deleted, the size would be changed to "60 00 00 00," or 0×60. This, along with some other checks, is how deleted keys can be located within unallocated space within the hive file.

## Registry Value Cells

The other type of cell that we want to take a close look at is the value cell. Remember, Registry keys can contain subkeys and values; actually, as we've seen, a key doesn't actually contain this information, as it instead has offsets to pointers to subkey and value lists. Value cells, on the other hand, are much simpler, as

## Note

Time-based information is maintained in the Registry (and on Windows systems, in general) in a number of formats. There are values whose data consists of (in part or entirely) a 32-bit UNIX epoch time format, whereas the LastWrite times of keys, as well as data of some values, consist of 64-bit FILETIME objects. Still other time-based data is maintained as 128-bit SYSTEMTIME objects [14], and others are simply maintained as strings (for example, the Skype application has a value named "LastUpdatedDate" in the user's NTUSER.dat file with string data of "01/10/2009").

they don't contain pointers to any other cells. They are important as they do contain value names and point to the data that, in many cases, we're interested in knowing and understanding. Figure 1.6 illustrates the binary structure of a value cell, with the value node identifier and value type highlighted.

Table 1.2 provides the relevant value cell structure details. As with the key cell, the first four bytes of a value cell (as illustrated in Figure 1.6) contain the size of the cell.

Notice that although value cells contain some specific information, something that they do not contain is a FILETIME object, nor any other reference to a time stamp of any kind. Again, as with the key cell, not all of the value cell structure elements are listed, and Table 1.2 should not be viewed as all-inclusive. For example, immediately after the "value-type" element is a 2-byte element called *flags*, and as of this writing, I have neither been able to locate an available description of this element nor of its use.

Registry values can point to data of a variety of types. Table 1.3 lists the available Registry value types, along with their names and descriptions. This information is also available from Microsoft [15].

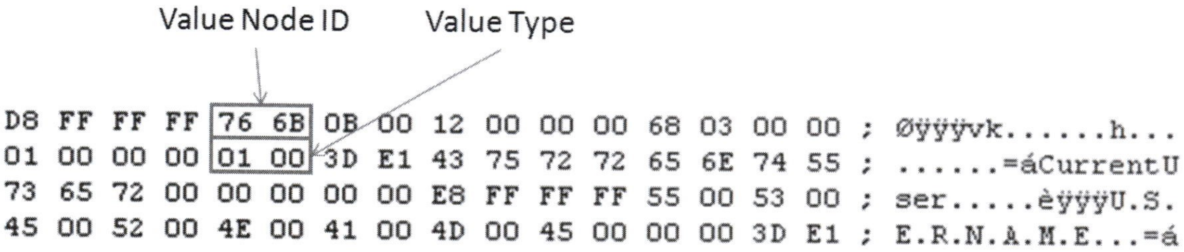

Value Node ID          Value Type

```
D8 FF FF FF 76 6B 0B 00 12 00 00 00 68 03 00 00 ; Øÿÿÿvk......h...
01 00 00 00 01 00 3D E1 43 75 72 72 65 6E 74 55 ; ......=áCurrentU
73 65 72 00 00 00 00 00 E8 FF FF FF 55 00 53 00 ; ser.....èÿÿÿU.S.
45 00 52 00 4E 00 41 00 4D 00 45 00 00 00 3D E1 ; E.R.N.A.M.E...=á
```

**Figure 1.6** Registry Value Structure with Node ID and Value Type

## Table 1.2 Registry Value Cell Structure Details

| Offset (bytes) | Size (bytes) | Description |
| --- | --- | --- |
| 0 | 4 | Size (as a negative number) |
| 4 | 2 | Node ID ("vk", or 0 × 6B76) |
| 6 | 2 | Value name length |
| 8 | 4 | Data length |
| 12 | 4 | Offset to data |
| 16 | 4 | Value type |

## Table 1.3  Registry Value Types

| Type | Name | Description |
|------|------|-------------|
| 0 | REG_NONE | No value type |
| 1 | REG_SZ | Unicode null-terminated string; can be Unicode or ASCII |
| 2 | REG_EXPAND_SZ | Unicode null-terminated string with environment variables/references |
| 3 | REG_BINARY | Binary data (no set length or structure) |
| 4 | REG_DWORD | 32-bit number |
| 5 | REG_DWORD_BIG_ENDIAN | 32-bit number |
| 6 | REG_LINK | Unicode symbolic link |
| 7 | REG_MULTI_SZ | Multiple Unicode strings, each '\00' terminated |
| 8 | REG_RESOURCE_LIST | Resource list (resource map) |
| 9 | REG_FULL_RESOURCE_DESCRIPTOR | Resource list (hardware description) |
| 10 | REG_RESOURCE_REQUIREMENTS _LIST | A series of nested arrays that store information about device drivers |
| 11 | REG_QWORD | 64-bit number |

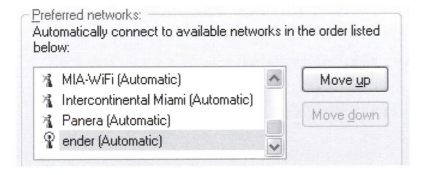

**Figure 1.7** Windows XP Wireless Network Connection Preferred Networks

Additional descriptive information about the various Registry value types can be found in Microsoft Knowledge Base (KB) article 256986 [4]. These types are important because there's considerable information available that may appear in easily readable text when presented in a GUI, but actually exists within the Registry in a binary format. For example, when Windows XP is used to manage wireless network connections on a laptop, the list of preferred networks can be viewed in the Wireless Networks tab of the Wireless Network Connections Properties page, as illustrated in Figure 1.7.

The list of wireless access point names and their preferred settings (automatic, manual), illustrated in Figure 1.7 (along with a number of other settings) are contained in binary data within specific Registry values discussed in Chapter 3, "Case Studies: The System," of this book. Other information may be stored in Unicode format, as opposed to ASCII text, and still other information (specifically, time stamps) will be stored in a binary format that must be extracted and translated before it is easily understood.

## Summary

In this chapter, we've taken a look at what the Windows Registry is, on a variety of levels. By now, you should have a basic understanding of not only what the Registry is and its purpose but also where the Registry "lives" on disk and where to look for Registry files within an acquired image. This is extremely important from a forensic analysis perspective, as it allows the analyst to understand issues that may develop through the use of commercial forensic analysis applications. Also, we've addressed more detailed information, going so far as to outline the binary structure of key and value cells. This information allows the analyst to search for and recognize these structures, not only within Registry hive files but also within other data sources, such as the Windows page file, memory dumps, and hibernation files, as well as unallocated space on disk.

## Frequently Asked Questions

**Q:** What is the Registry?

**A:** Microsoft describes the Registry as a "hierarchal database" used to store, maintain, and manage configuration and user activity data. The Registry is a core aspect of the Windows operating system, and significant modifications to specific portions of the Registry can render the system unbootable. However, there is a significant amount of data, much of it associated with time stamps that can be extremely valuable to incident responders and forensic analysts. In many respects, the Windows Registry can also be considered to be a log file, of sorts, in that much of the information in a hive file can be associated with a time stamp, as well as some event that impacts the data or the time stamp.

**Q:** Where should I look for Registry files?

**A:** The primary location for the core Windows Registry hive files is in the Windows\system32\config directory. Registry hives specific to users will be found in the User Profile: "C:\Documents and Settings" for Windows 2000, XP, and 2003 and "C:\Users" for Windows Vista and later versions. Due to back and recovery technologies used by the various versions of the Windows operating systems, you can also find Registry hive files within XP System Restore Points, as well as previous versions of hive files in Volume Shadow Copies on Windows Vista and later systems.

**Q:** What are the primary differences between the Registry hive files on the different versions of Windows?

**A:** From a binary perspective, there are no significant differences between hive files from Windows 2000 and XP systems, all the way up to Windows 7 systems. However, with each version of Windows, there are some changes to what information can be found in the Registry, where that information can be found (that is, the key path), and in what format (that is, string, binary, and so on). For example, on Windows XP, if a user performed a search by clicking **Start | Search | For Files and Folders**, information about the search would appear in a Registry key called *ACMru*. With Windows Vista, search information was no longer maintained in the Registry. However, with Windows 7, information about a user's searches is maintained in a Registry key named *WordWheelQuery*. There's nothing really unusual about this; although it is outside the scope of this book to describe all of the various changes between versions of Windows, others do exist. With Windows Vista, User Profiles were moved to the "C:\Users" directory, and the Task Scheduler logged to an EVTX file, rather than a flat text file (Schedlgu.txt) as with Windows XP and 2003. Again, listing all of the differences between the various versions of Windows isn't something I want to do in this book; rather, I will point out where there are significant differences that will impact incident response and forensic analysis activities.

# References

[1] Windows NT contains file system tunneling capabilities. Microsoft Support. N.p., n.d. http://support.microsoft.com/kb/172190 (accessed 28.07.10).

[2] How to disable the Prefetcher component in Windows XP. Microsoft Support. http://support.microsoft.com/kb/307498 (accessed 29.03.07).

[3] Support for Windows Server 2003 SP1 on Windows Storage Server 2003-based server appliances. Microsoft Support. http://support.microsoft.com/kb/894372 (accessed 31.03.07).

[4] Windows registry information for advanced users. Microsoft Support. http://support.microsoft.com/kb/256986 (accessed 04.02.08).

[5] Understanding and configuring registry size limit (RSL). Microsoft Support. http://support.microsoft.com/kb/124594 (accessed 20.02.07).

[6] Registry size limit functionality has been removed from Windows Server 2003 and from Windows XP. Microsoft Support. http://support.microsoft.com/kb/292726 (accessed 28.12.07).

[7] Registry redirector. Microsoft Developer Network. http://msdn.microsoft .com/en-us/library/aa384232(VA.85).aspx.

[8] Registry changes in x64-based versions of Windows Server 2003 and in Windows XP Professional x64 edition. Microsoft Support. http://support .microsoft.com/kb/869459 (accessed 21.04.08).

[9] Registry virtualization. Microsoft Developers Network. http://msdn .microsoft.com/en-us/library/aa965884(VS.85).aspx.

[10] What are ControlSets? What is CurrentControlSet?. Microsoft Support. http://support.microsoft.com/kb/100010 (accessed 01.11.06).

[11] File types. Microsoft Developers Network. http://msdn.microsoft.com/ en-us/library/cc144148(VS.85).aspx.

[12] Offline NT password & registry editor. http://pogostick.net/~pnh/ntpasswd.

[13] Info: working with the FILETIME structure. Microsoft Support. http:// support.microsoft.com/kb/188768 (accessed 23.01.07).

[14] SystemTime structure. Microsoft Developer Network. http://msdn .microsoft.com/en-us/library/ms724950%28VA.85%29.aspx.

[15] Registry value types. Microsoft Developer Network. http://msdn.microsoft .com/en-us/library/ms724884.aspx.

# 2

# TOOLS

INFORMATION IN THIS CHAPTER
- Live Analysis
- Forensic Analysis

## Introduction

Analysts faced with extracting and analyzing data from the Windows Registry may be required to do so in a number of different scenarios. During troubleshooting or incident response scenarios, administrators may want to query multiple systems for Registry data, or an analyst may want to examine Registry hives extracted from an acquired image for indications of an intrusion or violations of acceptable use policies. Regardless of the data to be extracted and reviewed, an analyst is going to use some sort of tool to collect that data and possibly even analyze it. In this chapter, we'll address some of the possible scenarios that an analyst may encounter and present some tools that may be used in those, and other, situations.

In this chapter, we will be focusing on the use of open source and freely available tools. There are a couple of reasons for this, the first being that such tools are generally accessible to a much wider audience than commercial forensic analysis applications. Second, I feel that it's important for analysts to understand the mechanics of what they're trying to achieve and to understand what's going on "under the hood" before using the commercial forensic analysis applications. Third, there are a number of tools available that provide functionality, either in and of themselves or through process, that commercial forensic analysis applications do not provide. Finally, I simply cannot afford to purchase all of the forensic analysis applications, and while writing this book, I only had access to one of the commercial forensic analysis applications available on the market.

The list of tools presented and discussed in this chapter should not be considered a comprehensive list of such tools. These are simply the tools I have used or encountered (mostly used) myself, and do not indicate a preference either way. Are there other, better tools? Possibly! However, the point I'm trying to make isn't which is the best tool but to demonstrate what we're trying to accomplish so that you, the reader, will be able to make a decision as to which will be the best tool for you. There may be tools available for Linux or Mac platforms, but I will be sticking to the Windows platform; the tools discussed all run on Windows systems. Some of the tools discussed later in this chapter will, in fact, work on platforms other than Windows, which does not restrict an analyst to a particular analysis platform.

## Live Analysis

In Chapter 1, "Registry Analysis," we looked at some information about the Windows Registry structure, going into a deep, detailed view of the binary structure of Registry key and value cells. However, we also mentioned that in many cases, users and administrators do not interact with the Registry at such a deep level. In fact, the majority of interaction by most users and administrators occurs either through some abstraction mechanisms, be it a viewer, an installation routine, or through some kind of graphical wizard. In many cases, a user or an administrator may not even realize on running an application or installation routine that she's extracted data from or modified entries in the Windows Registry.

However, there will be times when administrators and responders need to go beyond a simple viewer application and collect information from the Registry of a live system. For example, administrators may need to proactively scan the infrastructure for specific settings, in order to track application versions for licensing, or to determine the location of some applications that are installed.

### SCANNING FOR APPLICATIONS

While working as a security engineer at a financial services company several years ago, I was tasked with creating a report of all installed IM applications on all systems within the infrastructure, as well as their versions. I did this by first enumerating all active systems within the domain and then connecting to each one to query the Registry for the pertinent information.

Responders may need to scan systems across the enterprise once they've determined some key artifacts of an incident, and shutting down and acquiring an image from each system simply isn't cost effective (or possible). Fortunately, there are tools and mechanisms available, which allow administrators and responders alike to collect and correlate just about any Registry information they may need.

## Querying a Live Registry

There are a number of ways to interact with and extract data from a Registry on a live Windows system. In Chapter 1, we mentioned the Registry Editor (regedit.exe), a native GUI application resident on Windows systems.

However, using regedit.exe can be cumbersome. For example, you can only view the Registry on the system you're currently logged into and accessing. In the case in which multiple systems need to be queried quickly, regedit.exe is not particularly a viable, or scalable, solution. Also, regedit.exe does not allow the analyst to see some data, such as Registry key LastWrite times (also discussed in Chapter 1, "Registry Analysis"). So, while you can look and search for keys, and traverse through the Registry in the GUI, you're still somewhat limited in what you can do, what information you can retrieve, and how quickly you can go about collecting information from multiple systems across the infrastructure. This can be particularly detrimental during a number of incidents, such as potentially widespread malware infections, as well as intrusions.

### Reg.exe

Reg.exe is a native, command line-based Registry console tool that ships with Windows, starting with Windows XP. This native utility has the ability to manipulate the Registry, not only reading information from it but also adding, deleting, and modifying Registry keys and values.

The easiest way to get started using reg.exe is to open a command prompt and simply type **reg /?**. You'll see that there are a number of operations available; to get more information about a particular operation, type **reg <operation> /?**. For example, typing **reg query /?** provides information on the options that are available via the query operation.

In order to query information from the Run key (that is, get a listing of the subkeys and values pointed to by the key), you would type the command:

```
Reg query HKLM\Software\Microsoft\Windows\CurrentVersion\Run
```

In order to query for a specific value, you would add **/v** to the command, and if you wanted to query all subkeys and values, you would add the **/s** switch to the command. In order to run the above command on a remote system, you would type the following command, adding the reference to the remote system:

```
Reg query \\Machine\HKLM\Software\Microsoft\Windows\
    CurrentVersion\Run
```

In this case, "Machine" would be the name or IP address of the remote system; this, of course, assumes that the user account being used to run the command has the necessary privileges to access the remote system and that network connectivity between the administrator's system and remote system permits access to the appropriate ports (that is, firewalls are not blocking connectivity, and so on.). In many incident response scenarios, this is perhaps the biggest impediment to rapid remote response.

The benefit of using a console tool such as reg.exe is that it can very easily be included in batch files, allowing for a range of remote processing options. For example, an administrator can run a batch file to query the contents of the Run key across a wide range of systems within the infrastructure, using redirection operators at the command line (that is, ">" or ">>") to direct the output of the command to files rather than simply displaying the output at the console. Those files can then be searched from specific entries, looking for installed applications, or perhaps malware.

However, a limitation of reg.exe is that other key information, such as a key's LastWrite time, is not available. Using reg.exe on a remote system is also limited, as only the keys and values under the HKEY_LOCAL_MACHINE and HKEY_USER hives are available.

# Warning

In the spring of 2010, the Microsoft Malware Protection Center (MMPC) had a reference to a worm named *Win32/Verst,* which had reportedly been found on the microSD cards installed in new Samsung Wave phones, in a specific geographic region of Europe. This worm reportedly did not affect the phone, but instead infected the Windows PC that it was connected to and created an entry in the Run key in the Software hive as its persistence mechanism (which will be discussed in more detail in Chapter 3, "Case Studies: The System"). This illustrates that malware can come from anywhere, even some of the most unlikely infection vectors, and that persistence mechanisms, which have been used and well known to responders and analysts for years, are still in active use.

*Autoruns*

Autoruns.exe [1] is a tool written by Mark Russinovich of Microsoft, formerly SysInternals. Autoruns is a great GUI tool that allows you to see a *lot* of the various locations on a system, where various programs can be run automatically, with little to no user interaction. Figure 2.1 illustrates the GUI for Autoruns, version 10.02, run on a Windows XP system.

Figure 2.2 illustrates the Autoruns GUI when the tool is run on Windows 7. The most notable addition to GUI is the available tab named *SideBar Gadgets*.

Figures 2.1 and 2.2 shows that there are a number of locations, many of which (albeit not all) are found in the Registry, that allow programs to start automatically, often with no more interaction from the user than booting the system or logging into the system. Autoruns is a very useful tool for troubleshooting

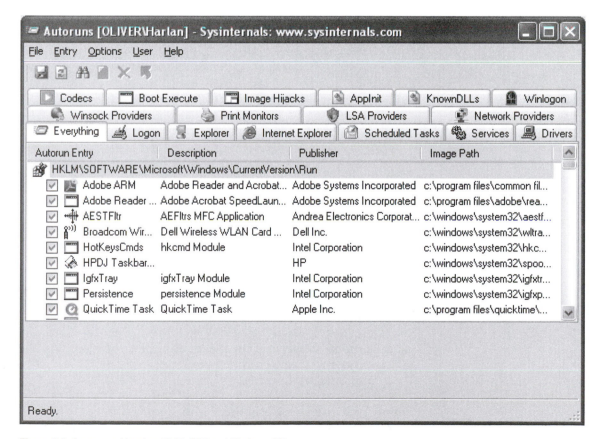

**Figure 2.1** Autoruns, Version 10.02, GUI on Windows XP

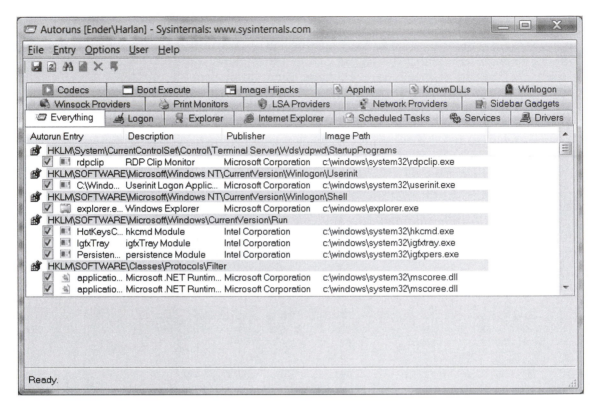

**Figure 2.2** Autoruns, Version 10.02, GUI on Windows 7

systems, as well as for locating malware and suspicious applications, during incident response. In fact, Autoruns comes with a command line companion tool called *autorunsc.exe* (not the addition of the "c" in the filename), both of which are intended to be run on live systems. Incident responders can include this tool in batch files used for collecting information from systems and gain a considerable amount of insight into what may be happening on the system. This tool can also be deployed remotely by responders using the Psexec.exe (remote command execution tool) also available from Microsoft. As of version 10, Autoruns includes the capability to analyze off-line Registry files; the administrator simply selects the appropriate locations via the "Offline System" dialog box illustrated in Figure 2.3.

To examine off-line files using autorunsc.exe, use the "-z" switch. To see other available options for use with autorunsc.exe, simply type **autorunsc /?** at the command prompt.

Although both of these tools are extremely thorough in the locations from which they extract data, there are a couple of

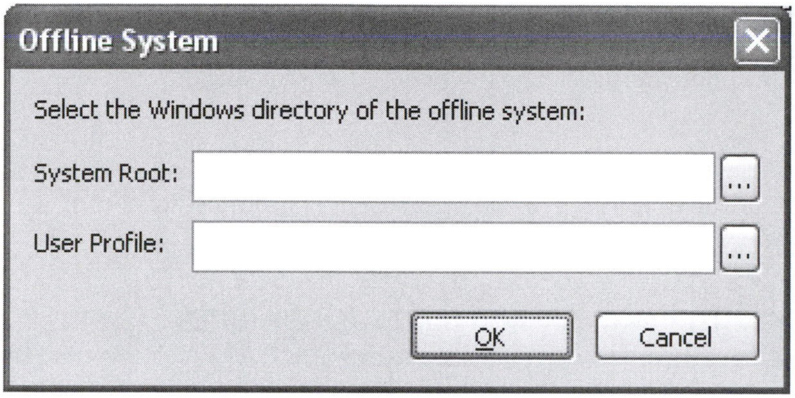

**Offline System**  ⊠

Select the Windows directory of the offline system:

System Root: [                    ] [...]

User Profile: [                    ] [...]

[ <u>O</u>K ]  [ Cancel ]

**Figure 2.3** Autoruns "Offline System" Dialog Box

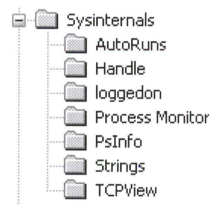

- Sysinternals
  - AutoRuns
  - Handle
  - loggedon
  - Process Monitor
  - PsInfo
  - Strings
  - TCPView

**Figure 2.4** Excerpt from RegEdit Illustrating Microsoft SysInternals Tool Keys

things to consider when deploying these tools. First, none of the tools collects Registry key LastWrite times. Registry key LastWrite times can be extremely valuable when conducting incident analysis or building a timeline of activity from affected systems. Second, all the entries are simply presented, and there's very little explanation as to what many of the tabs refer to or how the information they provide can be used, particularly by less experienced analysts. In short, this can provide an analyst with considerable amounts of data which she has no idea how to use. Finally, these tools all employ an end-user license agreement (EULA) that must be agreed by the user before the tool will run for the first time on the system. When the tool is run and the EULA is accepted, a Registry key is created for the tool, as illustrated in Figure 2.4.

In order to run autorunsc.exe successfully on a system for the first time during incident response, a command line similar to the following, accepting the EULA, should be used:

```
autorunsc -v -a /accepteula
```

The "/accepteula" switch will automatically accept the EULA; if this is not used, a dialog box will appear and will wait for user interaction to accept the EULA before proceeding.

### AUTORUNSC.EXE AND DIGITAL SIGNATURES

The "-v" switch used with autorunsc.exe tells the tool to verify digital signatures of files. There are a couple of things that analysts need to keep in mind when using this switch and viewing the output of the tool. First, in order to verify a file's digital signature, it has to be opened and accessed, modifying the last accessed time of the file. Second, around June 2010, I began to notice an increase in the number of articles in the media where malware files were found to use legitimate, albeit stolen digital signatures. I would not suggest that this is when it started; more accurately, this is when I first started to notice more articles in the media. Specifically, the malware known as *Stuxnet* was reported to use legitimate digital signatures from RealTek Semiconductor Corp.and JMicron.

The point of mentioning these three items is not, say, that you shouldn't use autorunsc.exe; rather, the point is to educate the user of what to expect when using the tool. As I mentioned, these two tools are very thorough and collect a great deal of valuable data. However, using these tools on a system will leave the artifacts described above.

## Windows Scripting

Windows Management Infrastructure (WMI), Windows Script Host (WSH), and Windows PowerShell are all native Windows scripting interfaces that can be used to query information from the Registry. Providing an introduction to any of these facilities is beyond the scope of this book but suffices to say that a great deal of useful information can be found at the Windows Script Center [2]. Essentially, I'm mentioning these scripting interfaces here for completeness, although I have never used them myself.

## Perl

Anyone who knows me and has read any of my previous books is probably surprised that it took me this long to mention Perl! Although not native to Windows systems, Perl is freely available

## Tip

While working as a security engineer at a financial services company, I put together a process to help me identify and address systems that appeared to be infected with malware. Using Perl, I would run a script that would export a list of all active systems on the network to a file. Then, through another Perl script, I would read that file and query the Run key within the Software hive on all of the systems. Initially, I got a lot of information back, much of it being legitimate entries in this key. In relatively short order, I was able to validate the legitimate entries so that I could run the script on a weekly basis and only get a relatively short list of possibly malicious entries. I have since used or recommended similar approaches during and following incident response activities.

from ActiveState.com and, particularly when it comes to Windows systems, is an extremely powerful and versatile tool.

For accessing the Registry on live systems, Perl has the Win32::TieRegistry module available, which installs by default as part of the ActiveState Perl distribution (called *ActivePerl*). This module is specific to and will only run on Windows systems, as it relies on the underlying Windows application programming interface (API) to function properly.

The following Perl code uses the Win32::TieRegistry module to query the contents of the Run key on the local system and to present that information in an easy way to view format:

```perl
#! c:\perl\bin\perl.exe
# Perl script to demonstrate extracting data from the Run key
  on a
# live system
use strict;
use Win32::TieRegistry(Delimiter=>"/");

my $reg;
my $r = "SOFTWARE/Microsoft/Windows/CurrentVersion/Run";

if ($reg = $Registry->Open("LMachine",{Access=>0x20019})) {
 if (my $run = $reg->Open($r,{Access=>0x20019})) {
 my %info = $run->Information();
 my $lastwrite = getTime(unpack("VV",$info{"LastWrite"}));
 print "LastWrite: ".gmtime($lastwrite)." Z\n";
 my @vals = $run->ValueNames();
 if (scalar @vals > 0) {
  foreach my $v (@vals) {
    my $data = $run->GetValue($v);
    printf " %-30s %-30s\n",$v,$data;
  }
 }
```

```
  else {
  print $r." has no values.\n";
  }
 }
}


#------------------------------------------------------------
# getTime()
# Get Unix-style date/time from FILETIME object
# Input : 8 byte FILETIME object
# Output: Unix-style date/time
# Thanks goes to Andreas Schuster for the below code, which he
# included in his ptfinder.pl
#------------------------------------------------------------
sub getTime() {
  my $lo = shift;
  my $hi = shift;
  my $t;
  if ($lo == 0 && $hi == 0) {
   $t = 0;
  }
  else {
    $lo -= 0xd53e8000;
    $hi -= 0x019db1de;
    $t = int($hi*429.4967296 + $lo/1e7);
  };
  $t = 0 if ($t < 0);
  return $t;
}
```

There are a couple of interesting things to consider about Perl scripts, such as the one listed above. For one, using a scripting language such as Perl (you should note that this applies to other scripting languages, as well) allows the administrator to add quite a bit of error checking and handling to the script. For example, what happens if the name of the key (or in the case of accessing remote systems, the name of the remote system) is spelled improperly or not fully known? The administrator can add appropriate checking in place to write error messages that are useful and meaningful or can have the script search (via Perl's *grep()* function) for key or value names that contain certain sequences of characters.

Another interesting aspect of the above script is the ability to define the level of access to the Registry using the *Access* keyword. In this case, the hex value 0×20019 is used instead of the keyword "KEY_READ," which, according to Microsoft [3], allows read (not write or modification) access to the Registry. This is very important when accessing portions of the Registry that may only allow administrators read access.

Finally, notice the *getTime* subroutine utilized in the script. This is a subroutine originally developed by Andreas Schuster [4] to translate 64-bit FILETIME objects into equivalent 32-bit UNIX time values. For most purposes, this presents a key's LastWrite time without any significant loss in granularity with respect to time, in that the translated time value is presented to the second (FILETIMEs have a granularity of 100 ns). Another interesting thing to notice here is code reuse; if you get a piece of Perl code or a snippet of a script working that's very versatile or useful (such as Andreas' code), all that's required to reuse that code is cut and paste.

In the late fall and winter of 2008, we (incident responders) were seeing issues with some new network worms. These worms were running rampant on customer networks, as they were utilizing standard business functionality to spread. One of the telltale artifacts of these worms (Conficker/Downadup, and so on) was a randomly named Windows service used as a persistence mechanism, allowing the worm to continue functioning across reboots (Windows services within the Registry will be addressed in greater detail in Chapter 3, "Case Studies: The System"). But how does an administrator, using the native Windows tools, reach across the enterprise to determine all of the randomly named services? One way to do this would be to create a batch file using reg.exe, but would you be able to query the information you needed? Most likely, you'd end up with a lot more information than you needed, and probably not much of what you really needed, leaving you to sort through all of it. This being the case, how fast could you actually respond?

Another option is to use a script similar to the one below, called *regscan.pl*. An administrator can run the script from a central location and reach out to query information from remote systems.

```
#! c:\perl\bin\perl.exe
#---------------------------------------------------------
# regscan.pl
# Retrieves data from Windows Service Registry keys;
  LastWrite times,
# ImagePath value (if avail.), Parameters\ServiceDll value
  (if avail),
# and lists all entries sorted based on LastWrite times.
#
# usage: regscan.pl <system_name>
#
# Output:
# LastWrite Time|ServiceName|ImagePath|ServiceDll
# - values are "|" separated
#
```

```perl
# Copyright 2010 Quantum Analytics Research, LLC
#---------------------------------------------------------
use strict;
use Win32::TieRegistry(Delimiter=>"/");

my $server = shift || Win32::NodeName;
my $regkey = "HKEY_LOCAL_MACHINE\\System\\CurrentControlSet\\
  Services\\";
$regkey =~ s/\W/g;
$regkey = "//$server/".$regkey;

my %svcs;
my $remote;
eval {
 $remote = $Registry->Open($regkey, {Access=>0x20019});
};
die "Error occurred connecting to Registry: $@\n" if ($@);

# If connected to the key, dump a list of subkeys
my @subkeys = $remote->SubKeyNames();
foreach my $s (@subkeys) {
 my $str = $s;
 my %info = $remote->Information();
 my $lw = getTime(unpack("VV",$info{"LastWrite"}));

eval {
 my $k = $remote->Open($s,{Access=>0x20019});
 $str .= "|".$k->GetValue("ImagePath");
};
$str .= "||" if ($@);

eval {
 my $k = $remote->Open($s."\\Parameters",{Access=>0x20019});
 $str .= "|".$k->GetValue("ServiceDll");
};
$str .= "||" if ($@);
my $type;
eval {
 my $k = $remote->Open($s,{Access=>0x20019});
 $type = $k->GetValue("Type");
};
print " ERROR: ".$@."\n" if ($@);
push(@{$svcs{$lw}},$str) if ($type eq "0x00000010" || $type
  eq "0x00000020");}

foreach my $t (reverse sort {$a <=> $b} keys %svcs) {
 foreach my $item (@{$svcs{$t}}) {
  print gmtime($t)."Z"."|".$item."\n";
 }
}
```

```
#--------------------------------------------------------------
# getTime()
# Get Unix-style date/time from FILETIME object
# Input : 8 byte FILETIME object
# Output: Unix-style date/time
# Thanks goes to Andreas Schuster for the below code, which
  he
# included in his ptfinder.pl
#--------------------------------------------------------------
sub getTime() {
 my $lo = shift;
 my $hi = shift;
 my $t;
 if ($lo == 0 && $hi == 0) {
  $t = 0;
 }
 else {
  $lo -= 0xd53e8000;
  $hi -= 0x019db1de;
  $t = int($hi*429.4967296 + $lo/1e7);
 };
 $t = 0 if ($t < 0);
 return $t;
}
```

Regscan.pl takes one argument: to query the name of the system. If no name is provided, the local system (that is, the system that the script is being run on) is queried. The script connects to the (remote) Registry and enumerates through the services, looking specifically for those that are "own" and "share" processes, as opposed to kernel or file system drivers. It then sorts the services based on Registry key LastWrite times and displays information about each of the services, such as the LastWrite time, service DisplayName value, ImagePath value, and ServiceDll value, if applicable. All of these values are pipe ("|") separated, but this can easily be changed.

MS KB article 962007 [5], "Virus Alert about the W32/Conficker Worm," provides a description of the worm, as well as how the ServiceDll value is used as a persistence mechanism by the worm. This persistence mechanism is also used by various other worms and malware.

Running the regscan tool (the Perl script and a "compiled" Windows executable are provided on the accompanying CD) is pretty simple, but how would you use or deploy something like this within an infrastructure, particularly during incident response activities? Well, some of the issues we've seen have been with Windows services with random names that are loaded as part of the svchost.exe process. The malware is actually a Windows dynamic-linked library (DLL), and as such, when created as a Windows service, it will include a "ServiceDll" value beneath the "Parameters" subkey within the Registry. To use regscan tool to see if the local system is infected, we can use the following simple command line:

```
C:\tools> regscan | find "svchost" /i
```

It would probably be much easier to analyze and correlate this information across multiple systems if we redirected the output of the command to a file, but this command shows how we can use custom, open-source tools to collect very specific information, particularly when native or commercial tools don't particularly do the trick. The "compiled" version of regscan tool can easily be included in a batch file without having to install Perl on any systems, and run against multiple systems across the infrastructure.

Again, by providing an executable version of the tool, you do not need to install Perl on your system. You can, if you choose to do so, install ActivePerl and use the Perl script provided along with the "compiled" tool. This will allow you to see what the script/tool does and modify it to meet your needs.

More than anything else, using scripting languages such as Perl (or Python, and so on) allows for a greater, more granular level of control when accessing Registry data. The ability to access key information (that is, LastWrite time, number of values, and so on) allows the administrator to add the necessary program flow in order to implement decisions. This allows for complex, repetitious tasks to be automated, increasing efficiency and accuracy.

# Tip

There are a number of tools that I've written and made available, and those mentioned in this book and that are included on the accompanying CD were written in Perl and "compiled" for distribution with Perl2Exe. By providing an "executable" version of the tool, you do not need to install Perl on your system, or any other system for that matter; instead, you simply copy the tool to your system or run the tool from the CD. However, if you choose to make use of tools such as regscan.pl, you only need to install Perl on your system; you do not need to install Perl on every system within your infrastructure.

## LIVE RESPONSE

Something that is very important to keep in mind when considering whether to engage in live response activities is that as your actions do have an effect on the system (processes loaded into memory, files created on the system as a result of your actions, and so on), so does your *inaction*. Think about it. A live system is running, with things going on all the time. Even while a system just sits there, processes are running and actions are occurring on the system. With Windows XP, simply wait for 24 hours and a System Restore Point will (by default) be automatically created. Wait 3 days and the system will conduct a limited defragmentation of the hard drive. Also, consider the fact that if someone is exfiltrating data from your systems, then while you wait and do nothing, they continue to take more data. So, the question of live response really arises: do I do nothing? or do I take the correct actions to protect my organization as best I can under the circumstances?

## Monitoring the Registry

Often, an analyst wants to conduct Registry analysis by first monitoring the Registry while conducting some sort of action, such as launching an exploit against a live system, or when installing an application or launching malware on a system. Rather than querying the Registry for specific values, the analyst wants to observe changes that occurred to the Registry, by either using before-and-after snapshots of the Registry or monitoring the Registry throughout the activity to observe keys that may be read, as well as keys and values that may be deleted, modified, or created.

Each of these options has their own particular strengths and weaknesses. For example, comparing snapshots taken before and after an atomic action (an "atomic action" refers to doing only one thing, performing one step) can provide a succinct view of what happened, but there may be a lot going on "under the hood," and as such, there may be nothing that differentiates what process made the observed changes. When monitoring a live system throughout some activity, it is possible to determine which process may have made a change to the Registry (that is, added, deleted, or modified keys or values), but a great deal of activity occurs on a live system, and the analyst may be overwhelmed with the shear amount of available data.

Monitoring tools are most often used in testing scenarios. For example, analysts performing malware reverse engineering may launch their malware sample in a controlled test environment and monitor that malware as it executes in order to see what interaction it has with the Registry. In many cases, malware may create or modify an entry in the Registry in order to maintain persistence on the system, enabling it to survive users logging out or the system being rebooted. Similarly, application installations may be monitored in order to determine if they modify Registry entries, and if so, which ones.

I have used monitoring tools during dynamic malware analysis and when conducting testing of new versions of Windows. When Windows 7 became available, one of the things I did was install monitoring tools so that I could perform normal user actions (that is, run searches across the system, and so on) and then see what effect those actions had on the Registry.

### Regshot

Regshot is a tool for determining changes made to the Registry, which is available on SourceForge.net [6]. Regshot is a Registry compare/diff utility that allows you to take snapshots of the Windows Registry on a live system and compare them in order to determine the changes undergone. With such testing tools, it's always a good idea to snapshot the Registry before and after an atomic action, meaning that you perform a single task (that is, installing an application, launching a program, and so on). This way, the changes you observe are kept, as much as possible, free of extraneous information. For example, set up your test environment to launch a program and snapshot the Registry. Then, launch the program, and as soon as you get an indication that the program launch has completed, immediately create the second snapshot. Again, this is to minimize, as much as possible, the extra information that appears in your comparison report that has nothing to do with our analysis. Figure 2.5 illustrates the Regshot user interface when you first launch the application.

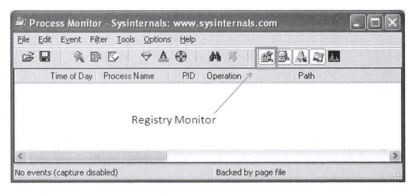

**Figure 2.5** First Stage of Regshot 1.8.2

Clicking the "1ˢᵗ shot" button brings up a context menu with three options: shot, shot and save, and load. These options allow you to create a snapshot, create and save a snapshot, or load a snapshot. If you choose the "shot and save" option, once the snapshot is created, a "Save As" dialog box will appear and you can provide a path and filename to save the snapshot (file extension is ".hiv" by default).

Once the first snapshot has been created, the "1ˢᵗ shot" button becomes subdued, and the "2ⁿᵈ shot" button is highlighted. Clicking that 2ⁿᵈ shot button, you get the same options; if you're doing some sort of extensive testing, it may be a good idea to go with the "shot and save" option, documenting (of course) the name and status of the snapshot for later use.

After the second snapshot has been created and saved, you can click on the "Compare" button, which will run a comparison between the two selected snapshots and create a text (unless you chose HTML) report. Just running two snapshots while writing this section created and modified entries in my user hive related to accessing the files and file extensions involved in the test process I was describing. It's beyond the scope of this chapter to address those changes here, but it is suffice to say that when used under the appropriate conditions, Regshot can be a very valuable tool. I had used an earlier version of the tool when I was documenting changes made to the Registry on Windows XP when running searches (**Start | Search | For Files and Folders** . . .), and I had used more recent versions of the tool when researching similar changes on Vista and Windows 7 systems.

Again, snapshot comparison tools such as Regshot are most useful in a stringent testing environment, when snapshots can be made before and after a single atomic action. One thing to keep in mind about this tool is that it only snapshots the Registry, so file system changes are not included. However, in a testing environment where virtualized systems are used, a snapshot comparison test can be run for just the Registry, the system itself can be reverted to a previous state, and then snapshot comparisons can be run separately for the file system.

### RegMon

RegMon, or Registry Monitor, is a live monitoring tool that was originally available through SysInternals.com and is now incorporated into the Microsoft Process Monitoring tool [7]. Even though it is part of the overall ProcMon tool, we can refer to the Registry monitoring functionality as *RegMon*. Figure 2.6 illustrates the Process Monitor UI, with the Registry Monitor function indicated.

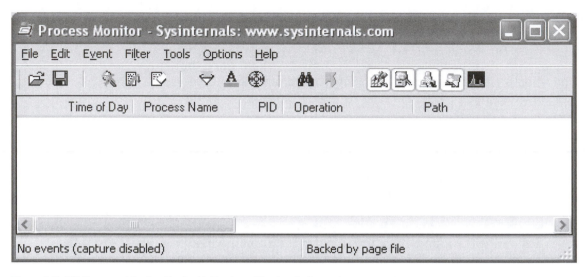

**Figure 2.6** MS Process Monitor Tool with Registry Monitor Indicated

To run ProcMon, simply download the archive and extract the executable file, then double-click the icon. The UI illustrated in Figure 2.6 appears, without the added text or highlighting, of course. When conducting Registry testing, I usually halt all monitoring (click on the magnifying glass icon so that a red *X* appears over it, as shown in Figure 2.6) and uncheck the various monitoring functionality, leaving only the Registry monitoring enabled.

Once you're ready, in order to enable monitoring of Registry activity, simply click the icon of the magnifying glass with the red *X*, and monitoring will start. You'll see the user interface quickly fill up with events, even before you do anything. Quickly perform the action that you want to monitor and then click the icon of the magnifying glass to stop monitoring. Once monitoring stops, be sure to save the contents of the UI to a file and begin your analysis. One of the useful functions of the UI is that you can filter activities based on a variety of criteria, such as process names.

Keep in mind, however, that not all pertinent activity occurs specifically with the application or process in question. The example I like to use to demonstrate this is to run the Solitaire card game (something that is, at the same time, harmless and very visual) that ships with Windows systems. Open a command prompt and type **sol**, and you will see the Solitaire card game open. Close the game and prepare ProcMon to capture data. Start the capture and then launch Solitaire via the command prompt.

| | | | |
|---|---|---|---|
| cmd.exe | 3868 | RegOpenKey | HKLM\Software\Policies\Microsoft\Windows\Safer\CodeIdentifiers |
| cmd.exe | 3868 | RegQueryValue | HKLM\SOFTWARE\Policies\Microsoft\Windows\Safer\CodeIdentifiers\LogFileName |
| cmd.exe | 3868 | RegCloseKey | HKLM\SOFTWARE\Policies\Microsoft\Windows\Safer\CodeIdentifiers |
| cmd.exe | 3868 | RegOpenKey | HKLM\Software\Microsoft\Windows NT\CurrentVersion\Image File Execution Options\sol.exe |
| csrss.exe | 960 | RegOpenKey | HKCU |
| csrss.exe | 960 | RegOpenKey | HKCU\Software\Policies\Microsoft\Control Panel\Desktop |
| csrss.exe | 960 | RegOpenKey | HKCU\Control Panel\Desktop |
| csrss.exe | 960 | RegQueryValue | HKCU\Control Panel\Desktop\MultiUILanguageId |
| csrss.exe | 960 | RegCloseKey | HKCU\Control Panel\Desktop |

**Figure 2.7** Cmd.exe Accessing the "Image File Execution Options" Key

Solitaire opens quickly, so immediately go back to ProcMon and stop capturing data. An interesting activity, an attempt to open a subkey beneath the "Image File Execution Options" key, is highlighted in Figure 2.7.

The attempt to access the key highlighted in Figure 2.7 is standard Windows activity and is in fact provided as a means for debugging Windows services, as described in MS KB article 824334 [8]. MS KB article 892894 [9] describes how to use this key to disable the Windows Update service. However, malware authors also like to use this as a persistence mechanism for their applications; I should know, as I've seen this employed "in the wild."

ProcMon provides some very useful functionality, but it also provides a *lot* of data! It may behoove you to run several tests and then look for commonalities among them, or to start by using tools such as Regshot to develop some initial information and then expand on that using ProcMon.

### REGISTRY HIVES IN MEMORY

Although Windows memory collection and analysis is beyond the scope of this book, it is worth mentioning that Registry hives can be extracted from memory dumps. Thanks to Aaron Walters' development of the Volatility Project (found on the Web site www.volatilesystems.com/default/volatility) for interacting with Windows XP memory dumps, and to Brendan Dolan-Gavitt (a.k.a. "moyix," a developer who works on the Volatility project) for developing Volatility plug-ins for collecting and parsing Registry hives, which can be found on the Web site http://moyix .blogspot.com/search?q=registry.

## Forensic Analysis

When I first began writing this chapter, I called this section "Postmortem Forensic Analysis," but then I realized that in some cases, the same tool (or tools) used to access Registry hive files extracted from an acquired image could be used in other scenarios, such as via F-Response. Hence, I changed the name of this section to "Forensic Analysis" because the "Postmortem" scenario was simply too limited. Compared with the earlier section, in this section, we're taking steps to limit the changes to the system and data.

One of the first things we need to do in order to collect information from Registry hive files is to determine how we plan to access those files, and we will look at two ways to do this in a manner that minimizes the changes to the data in those files. One way is to acquire an image of the system and extract the files from the image via applications such as FTK Imager Lite [10] or ProDiscover [11]. The second way is to access the drive locally using FTK Imager Lite, or remotely via F-Response, which can be found on the Web site www.f-response.com.

Figure 2.8 illustrates an excerpt of the File Listing pane from FTK Imager Lite 2.9.

Figure 2.8 shows clearly several of the Registry hive files (specifically the SECURITY, SOFTWARE, and SYSTEM files). At this point, all the analyst needs to do is to highlight, right-click, and export the files to a convenient location, and begin analysis.

You can also use ProDiscover in a similar manner. After loading the image file into the project, the analyst can expand the Content View of the project until the *Windows* directory is visible, then navigate to the *system32\config* directory, and manually export the Registry hive files from the project. The analyst would then need to follow the same process with the hive files from the user profiles. Another method for extracting

| | | | |
|---|---|---|---|
| SecEvent.Evt | 64 KB | Regular File | 1/18/2008 12:53:41 AM |
| SECURITY | 256 KB | Regular File | 1/18/2008 12:54:00 AM |
| SECURITY.LOG | 1 KB | Regular File | 1/18/2008 12:53:46 AM |
| SECURITY.LOG.FileSlack | 1 KB | File Slack | |
| software | 8,192 KB | Regular File | 1/18/2008 12:54:00 AM |
| software.LOG | 1 KB | Regular File | 1/18/2008 12:53:46 AM |
| software.sav | 588 KB | Regular File | 6/18/2004 9:04:47 AM |
| SysEvent.Evt | 64 KB | Regular File | 1/18/2008 12:53:41 AM |
| system | 2,560 KB | Regular File | 1/18/2008 12:54:00 AM |

**Figure 2.8** Excerpt of File Listing Pane from FTK Imager Lite 2.9

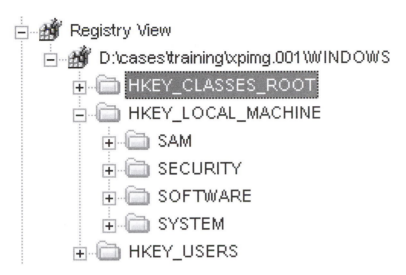

**Figure 2.9** ProDiscover v6.5 Project with Registry View Populated

the hive files involves creating and using a ProDiscover's ProScript, which is ProDiscover's scripting functionality based on Perl. A properly crafted ProScript would allow the analyst to load an image and then run the ProScript to export all of the necessary hive files to an appropriate location.

An alternative method for extracting not the hive files themselves but specific data from the hive files involves the use of ProDiscover's Registry Viewer. Figure 2.9 illustrates the populated Registry View in a ProDiscover v6.5 project.

After loading an image file into a ProDiscover project and opening the file structure in the Content View, the analyst then right-clicks on the *Windows* directory and chooses "Add to Registry Viewer." ProDiscover will locate the hive files in the *system32\config* directory, as well as those in the user profiles, and populate the Registry View with the appropriate information. Once this has been completed and the project saved, the analyst can use ProScripts to extract specific information from the Registry. Several such ProScripts were provided on the CD that accompanies *Windows Forensic Analysis*, Second Edition.

### F-Response

Earlier in this chapter, I mentioned using an application called *F-Response*, which we can use to get access to Registry hive files on live remote systems. Figure 2.10 illustrates the F-Response

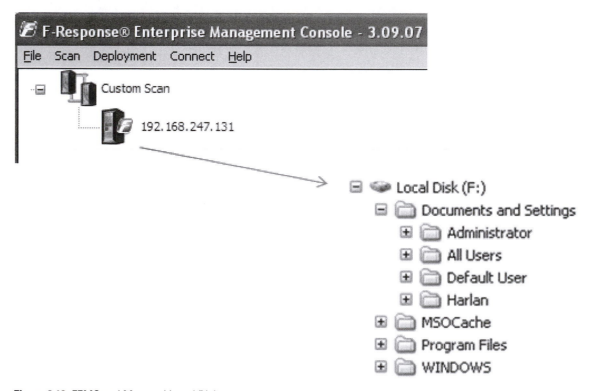

**Figure 2.10** FEMC and Mounted Local Disk

Enterprise Management Console (FEMC) open and connected to a system and the corresponding mounted local disk (drive F:\).

The setup and use of F-Response is beyond the scope of this book, and best addressed and understood by visiting the Web site www.F-response.com, purchasing the appropriate F-Response product and viewing the provided videos. F-Response provides a means for accessing disks, volumes, and even memory on remote Windows (and other operating systems, although memory isn't supported in all cases) systems in a read-only manner. This capability is extremely useful when you need immediate response to remote systems or for surreptitious acquisitions as there is no user interaction required on the remote system (if you're using F-Response Enterprise Edition). Once you access the remote system, you can perform any task that is necessary, from identifying and copying files to using tools such as FTK Imager Lite to acquire an image of the drive. For our purposes, simply accessing the mounted local disk (F:\ in our example above) and copying the Registry hive files of interest, through manual or automated means, are all that need to be done.

There is a Perl script provided on the CD that accompanies this book called *grab.pl* (an EXE version of the script, compiled with Perl2Exe, is also provided), which allows an analyst using F-Response to mount volumes from remote systems as local disks to automate the copying of files, in particular Registry hive files. The script is a command-line interface (CLI) tool, so to view the options, simply type **grap.pl –h** (or "grab –h" if you choose to use the "compiled" version) at the command prompt. You can use this script after you've installed F-Response on a remote system and mounted the C:\ volume as a local drive on your system (F:\ in the above example). Once you've done that, you can run the script with the –d switch to identify the drive letter in question, and grab.pl will read a list of files to collect from the remote system (default is "files.txt"; however, the analyst can create separate files specific to various incidents). Grab.pl reads in the list of files (and their paths), and if it finds each file, it calculates a hash for the file, copies it to a local directory, and then compares the hash of the copied file to ensure that no changes have occurred to the file. The script also logs all of its activity, so you can see the actual hashes that were generated for each file and the results of the hash comparison. Grab.pl can also be used when an acquired image file is mounted locally using a tool such as ImDisk [12] or SmartMount [13]. This kind of automation increases efficiency and reduces mistakes that can occur when performing repetitive tasks, such as connecting to a large number of systems (via F-Response) and copying the Registry hive files. Scripts like this are also more efficient than batch files that simply copy all files in selected directories as many of the files may not be required, and it takes a great deal of time to copy all of these unnecessary files. If you open grab.pl in an editor, you'll see that it has code that allows it to locate user profiles and copy just the NTUSER.DAT files, rather than copying the entire contents of all profiles.

Scripts and tools such as grab.pl are used to obtain the necessary files for analysis rather than to conduct the actual analysis. Once you have the files that you need, you can then use other tools to perform the appropriate analysis.

### MiTeC Registry File Viewer

Once the hive files have been extracted, they can be loaded into a viewer application such as the MiTeC Windows Registry File Viewer (listed as "Registry Viewer 2.0" at www.mitec.cz/Data/XML/data_downloads.xml), as illustrated in Figure 2.11.

The Registry File Viewer (RFV) is an extremely useful tool, which allows the analyst to view and navigate through a hive file

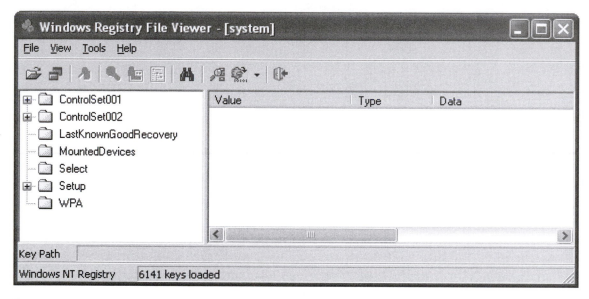

**Figure 2.11** MiTeC Windows Registry File Viewer UI

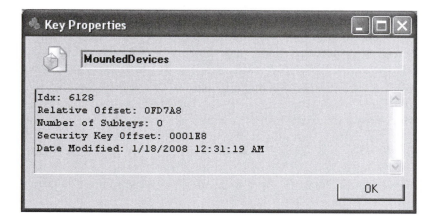

**Figure 2.12** Key Properties Dialog

just as they would as if they were using RegEdit, with the notable exception that the hive files being viewed are not "live." Clicking on keys in the left-hand pane causes the values to appear in the right-hand pane. Right-clicking on a key and choosing Key Information from the drop-down dialog box causes the Key Properties dialog to appear, as illustrated in Figure 2.12.

As illustrated in Figure 2.12, the analyst can quickly see the relative offset of the key, as well as the LastWrite time of the key, identified in the "Date Modified" entry.

RFV also provides the capability to search through the hive file. When hits are found, double-clicking that hit takes you directly to that specific item in the main view of the application. In addition to searching, if you click on **Tools** from the menu bar, you'll see "Spy & Analyze" in the *drop-down* menu, with four additional entries: UserAssist, StreamMRU, SAM, and Windows.

With the appropriate hive file loaded, choosing any of these will provide some interesting parsing capabilities. For example, if you open a **SAM** hive file in RFV and choose **SAM** from the *Spy & Analyze* choices, the application will parse through the SAM and provide the embedded information in an easily readable format. Once you've done this, right-click in the display and choose **Save File** to save the parsed output.

Figure 2.13 illustrates the results of running the UserAssist Spy & Analyze function with a user's hive file opened in RFV. You can see the raw values listed with their binary data, and immediately

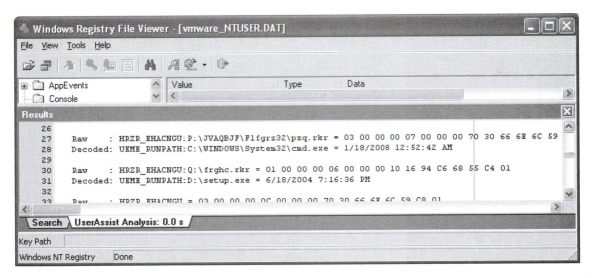

**Figure 2.13** RFV Showing Results of Spy & Analyze UserAssist

# Note

The usefulness of specific keys and values, such as the UserAssist key contents, the StreamMRU, the SAM hive, and the ACMru key mentioned later in this chapter, will be discussed in detail in Chapters 3 and 4 of this book. For now, these keys and values are being mentioned here in order to demonstrate the functionality of specific tools.

following each entry, the translated (via ROT-13 decoding) value name, with the last time the application was launched is listed. As we will see in Chapter 4, "Case Studies: Tracking User Activity," the time stamp listed is extracted from the binary data of the value.

### RegRipper

Like many of the tools I write and use, RegRipper was a tool born out of necessity. During analysis of Windows systems, I found myself accessing the Registry hive files over and over again, sometimes looking for the same keys and values in case after case. Like many, I started out with a list of keys and pertinent values and wanted to make things easier on myself, so I wrote a couple of scripts, all of which did very similar things, such as open a hive file, locate a key or value, and then print out what was found (if anything). I then found that I was running the same script over and over on the same sorts of hive files (Software, NTUSER.DAT, and so on), so I decided to "bind" the scripts together in a batch file so that all I had to do was point the batch file at a file, and all of the scripts would be run.

This seemed like a good approach at the time. However, it wasn't very flexible or scalable. What I really wanted was a scanning engine that would take a plug-in, or a series of plug-ins (as a "profile"), and run them across a Registry hive file, giving me the results and an audit log of activity. From this, RegRipper (GUI illustrated in Figure 2.14) was born.

RegRipper has proved to be extremely useful and flexible. In short, the RegRipper GUI illustrated in Figure 2.14 is an interface to an "engine" of sorts. Behind the scenes, RegRipper processes sets of instructions listed in plug-ins files. This is similar to tools such as Nessus (a popular vulnerability scanner based on a plug-in architecture, found on the Web site www.nessus.org/nessus/), which consists of a scanning engine and a series of plug-ins that contain instructions. The RegRipper plug-ins files are kept in the "plug-ins" subdirectory within the directory where RegRipper is installed, and each plug-in tells the RegRipper engine to which hive file the plug-in applies, which key(s) or value(s) to look for, and what to do once they've been found. For example, plug-ins can be very simple and can simply look for a Registry key, and then list a single value, if found, or all values beneath that key. Or a plug-in can contain several keys, the contents of which are correlated, and a consolidated view of the data provided by the plug-in.

Plug-ins can also provide specific output formats. One method I have found very valuable in processing Registry information is to collect a good bit of time-stamped information (that is, Registry

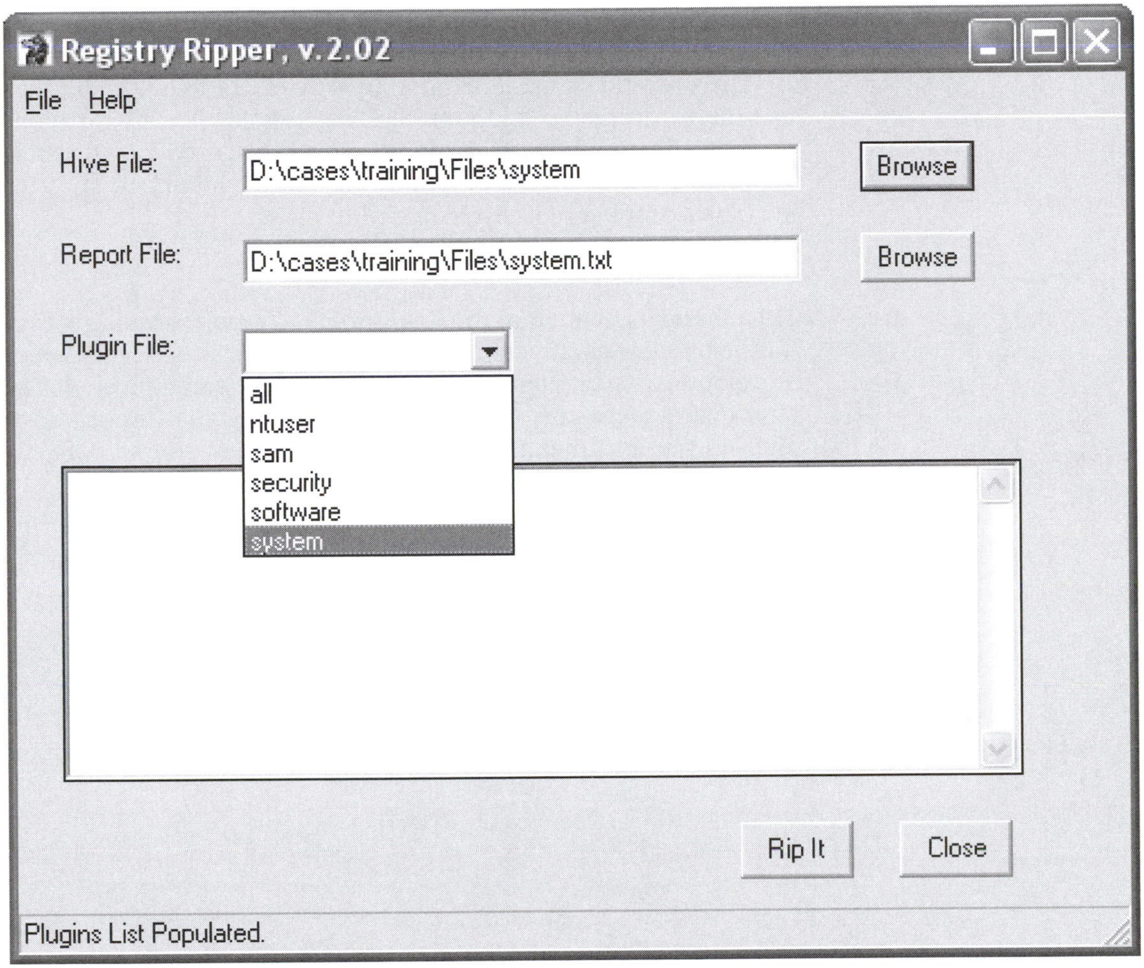

**Figure 2.14** RegRipper GUI Interface

key LastWrite times, time stamp data collected from value data, and so on) and then to sort that information, listing it in the output based on the most recent time first. This has been very helpful not only in visualizing what happened but also in determining when an incident may have occurred, and what activities may have occurred following that date/time. There are also a number of binary values (as we'll see in Chapters 3 and 4) within various Registry keys whose structure contains specific pieces of information, and that binary data need to be parsed in a specific and often a unique manner. Plug-ins can make use of the code provided by the overall application itself, but also parse those unique structures and provide the analyst with easy to read and understand information.

The drop-down list illustrated in Figure 2.14 tells which plug-ins file or profile (a "plug-ins file" or "profile" is a list of plug-ins) the RegRipper engine should run. This drop-down list is populated when the RegRipper application is launched and can include a number of user-created plug-ins files.

### Rip.pl

Rip.pl is a CLI version of the RegRipper GUI tool, something that I developed originally for testing purposes. It was very easy when developing a new plug-in to keep running the same plug-in over and over against the same hive file, tweaking the performance and output and making other necessary adjustments as I went along.

Typing just **rip.pl** at the command line (or "rip.pl –h") provides the syntax information for the tool, which is shown below:

```
C:\Perl\tools>rip.pl
Rip v.20090102 - CLI RegRipper tool
Rip [-r Reg hive file] [-f plugin file] [-p plugin module] [-l]
   [-h]
Parse Windows Registry files, using either a single module, or
   a plugins file.
All plugins must be located in the "plugins" directory;
   default plugins file
used if no other filename given is "plugins\plugins".

 -r Reg hive file...Registry hive file to parse
 -g ...............Guess the hive file (experimental)
 -f [plugin file]...use the plugin file (default: plugins\
       plugins)
 -p plugin module...use only this module
 -l ...............list all plugins
 -c ...............Output list in CSV format (use with -l)
 -h................Help (print this information)

Ex: C:\>rip -r c:\case\system -f system
   C:\>rip -r c:\case\ntuser.dat -p userassist
   C:\>rip -l -c

All output goes to STDOUT; use redirection (ie, > or >>) to
   output to a file.

copyright 2008 H. Carvey
```

As you can see from the syntax/usage information for rip.pl/ .exe, there's some considerable functionality in this tool. I use

# Tip

Sometimes during an examination, I'll need to determine the likelihood of a user profile having been logged into the system or accessed during a specific timeframe. In some cases, a good way to get a "feel" for this is to run rip.pl against a user hive, using the UserAssist or RecentDocs plug-ins; reviewing the time stamps from the Registry keys and values can provide an indication of when the user account was logged in by illustrating user activity that occurred during that time. Again, the specifics of these keys will be discussed in Chapter 4, "Case Studies: Tracking User Activity"; they are mentioned here simply to demonstrate the use of rip.pl to collect information that may be of interest to a specific examination.

rip.pl quite often for both testing of newly developed plug-ins, running individual plug-ins, and for running plug-ins that may take some time (a few minutes or more) to run, as I don't want to try to run them as part of the RegRipper GUI and have the interface appear to hang or stop functioning. Also, there are just times when I may only want specific information for an examination, such as the contents or LastWrite times of the UserAssist or the RecentDocs subkeys. It's simply much faster and more efficient for me to run one or two specific plug-ins via rip.pl than it is to run all of the plug-ins in a profile via RegRipper, and then open the output file and find the specific bits of information that I'm looking for.

Also, as you can see, rip.pl does have the "-f" switch that allows you to run entire plug-ins files against a specific hive file, as opposed to running one plug-in at a time. To do so, simply run a command similar to the following:

```
C:\tools>rip.pl -r d:\cases\training\files\software -f software
```

The above command line provides the same functionality as using RegRipper to run the "software" plug-ins file against the specified hive file, except that the output in this case goes to the console. You may want to pipe the output through "more" (that is, append "| more" to the command) to see the output scroll by one screen at a time or redirect the output to a file, appending "> *file*" to the command. This capability can be used to automate the collection of Registry information from hive files extracted from an image or from an image mounted as a drive letter (read-only, of course) on your analysis system. For example, create a batch file called *regrip.bat* in the same directory as RegRipper and include the following lines:

```
@echo off
Echo Scanning Software hive. . .
```

```
rip -r %1\software -f software
Echo Scanning System hive. . .
rip -r %1\system -f system
Echo Scanning SAM hive. . .
rip -r %1\sam -f sam
Echo Scanning Security hive. . .
rip -r %1\security -f security
```

To run this batch file, use a command line similar to the following if you've extracted the hive files out of an acquired image and put them into a case-specific "files" directory:

```
C:\tools>regrip.bat d:\cases\training\files
```

The output of the commands within the batch file will be displayed in the console (that is, STDOUT) of the command prompt window, so if you want to keep the output, be sure to redirect it to a file.

To run this batch file if you've mounted the acquired image as a read-only drive letter (that is, H:\) on your analysis system, you can use a command line similar to the following:

```
C:\tools>regrip.bat H:\Windows\system32\config > D:\cases\
  files\regrip.txt
```

In both cases, the batch file assigns the single command line argument provided (which is the path to the directory where the hive files are located, provided without a trailing slash) to the variable "%1" and uses that to populate the variable throughout the included commands. In each instance, rip.exe runs the specified plug-ins file against the appropriate hive file and redirects the output to a text file. All of this is done automatically, and works very well, assuming that the hive files are where they should be. Admittedly, the provided batch file is very simple and does not include a great deal of feedback or error checking, but it can be used quite effectively in a number of analysis scenarios. Analysts familiar with batch file programming (or willing to search Google for hints) can extend the batch file to meet their needs.

Another use for rip.pl is to get a listing of the available plug-ins. For example, running rip.pl with just the "-l" switch (see the syntax information listed above) will tell the script to go to the hard-coded plug-ins directory (that is, the "\plugins" subdirectory located within the current working directory) and list all of the available plug-ins. An excerpt of the output of this command appears as follows:

```
162. winver v.20081210 [Software]
  - Get Windows version
```

```
163. winzip v.20080325 [NTUSER.DAT]
 - Get WinZip extract and filemenu values

164. win_cv v.20090312 [Software]
 - Get & display the contents of the Windows\CurrentVersion
   key

165. wordwheelquery v.20100330 [NTUSER.DAT]
 - Gets contents of user's WordWheelQuery key

166. xpedition v.20090727 [System]
 - Queries System hive for XP Edition info
```

As you can see, the output includes the number of plug-ins, which is a count maintained by the script; plug-ins themselves are not numbered. You can also see the name and version of the plug-in, as well as the hive for which it is intended, and the short description of what the plug-in does. You can also get this information in .csv format by using the "-l" and "-c" switches together. An excerpt of the output of this command appears as follows:

```
winver,20081210,Software,Get Windows version
winzip,20080325,NTUSER.DAT,Get WinZip extract and filemenu
  values
win_cv,20090312,Software,Get & display the contents of the
  Windows\CurrentVersion key
wordwheelquery,20100330,NTUSER.DAT,Gets contents of user's
  WordWheelQuery key
xpedition,20090727,System,Queries System hive for XP Edition
  info
```

Redirecting the output of the command (that is, rip.pl –l –c > plugins.csv) will allow you to open the list of plug-ins in Excel or some other spreadsheet software. From there, you can sort on third column in order to group the plug-ins together by their target hives, and so on.

Another means for managing the plug-ins listing at the command line is to use the *find* command. For example, to list those plug-ins for the Software hive, you can easily use the following command:

```
C:\tools>rip.pl —l —c | find "Software"
```

Now, this command will print out all lines that include the word "Software," but it is relatively easy to tell which plug-ins are intended to be run against which hive files.

Rip.pl also includes the -g switch, which at the time that the functionality was written was a pretty experimental bit of functionality. Over time, and with testing, the functionality has proven to be very accurate. The idea is that the switch allows rip.pl to guess the type of hive file that it's looking at; it does this by looking for specific core sets of Registry keys that should exist in specific hive files. In order to use this functionality, all you would need to do is run the following command:

```
C:\tools>rip.pl —r D:\cases\test\software —g
```

The above command returns "software = 1"; this isn't all that surprising, considering that the hive file is named "Software." However, Adam James and Matt Churchill used this code to modify RegRipper so what it could be run against images mounted on an analysis system as a drive letter [14].

Rip.pl isn't the only tool available for managing plug-ins; shortly, we'll discuss the Plugin Browser, which provides a GUI for plug-in management.

### RipXP.pl

RipXP is a unique version of rip.pl/.exe that was written specifically for Windows XP. One of the things I had wanted to do, and something Rob Lee once said, "hey, wouldn't it be cool if you could . . .," was to run a single plug-in against not only a specific hive file on a Windows XP system but also to have that same plug-in run automatically against the hive files stored in any and all available Windows XP System Restore Points. For that purpose, I developed ripXP.pl, and the "XP" in the name referring to the fact that it is intended only for Windows XP, as that is the Windows operating system that maintains System Restore Points in the format accessed by the tool. The syntax information for ripxp.pl appears as follows:

```
C:\Perl\tools>ripxp.pl
RipXP v.20090818 - CLI RegRipper tool
RipXP [-r Reg hive file] [-p plugin module][-d RP dir][-lgh]
Parse Windows Registry files, using either a single module
  from the plugins folder. Then parse all corresponding hive
  files from the XP Restore Points (extracted from image)
  using the same plugin.

 -r Reg hive file...Registry hive file to parse
 -g ...............Guess the hive file (experimental)
 -d RP directory....Path to the Restore Point directory
 -p plugin module...use only this module
 -l ...............list all plugins
 -h...............Help (print this information)

Ex: C:\>ripxp.pl -g
  C:\>ripxp.pl -r d:\cases\ntuser.dat -d d:\cases\svi
    -p userassist
```

```
All output goes to STDOUT; use redirection (ie, > or >>) to
  output to a file.
```

There's a little work required in order to run ripxp.pl (or the
.exe version) correctly. System Restore Points are maintained in
the "System Volume Information" directory, and NTFS permissions prevent even Administrators from directly accessing that
directory. The least complicated way to handle this issue when
your analysis system is running Windows is to open your acquired
image in FTK Imager (or the Lite version, both of which are freely
available from AccessData) and to extract the Restore Point directories to a directory structure on your analysis system, as illustrated in Figure 2.15.

Once you've extracted the Restore Point directories in a manner
similar to what's illustrated in Figure 2.15, be sure to also extract
the "live" Registry hives from the image as well. In the example

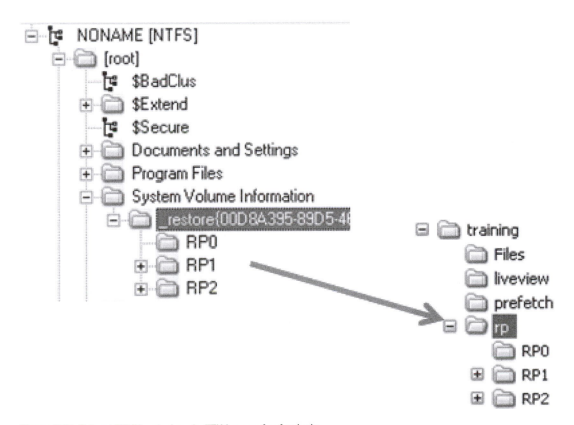

**Figure 2.15** Extract RP Directories via FTK Imager for Analysis

illustrated in Figure 2.15, I extracted the files to the "training\Files" directory. Now, to run ripXP against the "live" System hive and the corresponding System hives in the Restore Point directories, simply use the following command:

```
C:\tools>ripxp -r d:\training\Files\System -d d:\training\rp
  -p mountdev
```

It should be easy to see that ripXP is best used with plug-ins that extract data that may have changed over time. In the case of the above example, as various external devices are attached to the system, we would expect some of the values to change, particularly those that begin with "\DosDevice\." Another plug-in that may be useful to run across the System hives in the Restore Points is shares.pl; this may provide you with information about shares that were available at some point in the past, when a Restore Point was created, but has since been removed or "unshared."

Another example where this would be extremely valuable would be to run the userassist.pl plug-in against a user's NTUSER.DAT hive (found in the root of the user profile, as described in Chapter 1, "Registry Analysis"), as well against all those hives available in the System Restore Points, using the following command:

```
C:\tools>ripxp -r d:\training\Files\ntuser.dat -d d:\training\
  rp -p userassist
```

The value of the contents of the UserAssist key will be addressed in greater detail in Chapter 4, "Case Studies: Tracking User Activity," but it is suffice to say at this point that there may be a great deal of information available, particularly on a heavily used system. Over time, some keys and values may be updated, modified, or even deleted, and being able to see what was available at some point in the past can be (and believe me, has been) of great value to an analyst.

A tool like this can also be used to great effect when Registry keys or values have been deleted. There are tools that will delete certain keys; for example, Window Washer (version 4.7) would delete the user's RecentDocs (also discussed in detail in Chapter 4, "Case Studies: Tracking User Activity,") key. We will discuss in some detail later in this chapter how deleted keys and values can be recovered from unallocated space within a hive file, but having the ability to retrieve historical data from the Registry can be extremely valuable. Not only can we retrieve deleted keys, but being able to go back in time and get historical information about key and value contents from points in the past can be extremely valuable.

One final point about this tool: ripXP is not intended to be used to analyze Registry hives from Volume Shadow Copies. This is a completely different backup technology employed on Windows Vista systems and beyond and does not operate or provide data in a manner similar to Windows XP System Restore Points.

### Plugin Browser

Earlier in this chapter, we discussed plug-in usage and management via the command line using rip.pl/.exe. I've also written a tool called the *Plugin Browser* that allows you to manage plug-ins via a graphical user interface, which is illustrated in Figure 2.16.

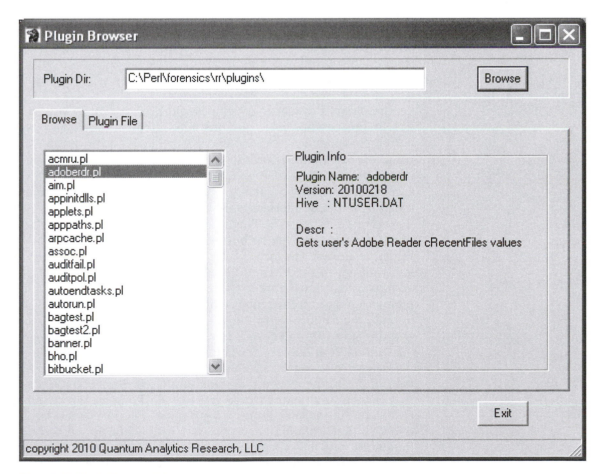

**Figure 2.16** Plugin Browser UI

## Note

Within RegRipper, the plug-ins directory is hard coded so that all plug-ins are maintained in the "\plugins" subdirectory within the current working directory where RegRipper (and rip.pl/.exe, as well as ripxp) are kept. Looking toward future developments for tools such as RegRipper, I opted to allow the analyst to select the plugins directory; RegRipper is open-source, and given some of the modifications that have been made to it thus far, I wouldn't be surprised if someone developed a version where the plug-ins directory could be selected by the analyst.

The Plugin Browser is fairly straightforward and simple to use. At the very top of the UI is where you can select the plug-ins directory. Once you select the directory, all of the plug-ins are read by the browser and used to populate the list box in the Browse tab. When you select a **plug-in** in the list box, information about the plug-in (that is, the same information extracted by rip.pl) is displayed to the right. This allows you to easily browse through the various plug-ins, checking versions and seeing what each does (based on the short description).

The Plugin Browser also has a Plugin File tab, which you can use to create your own plug-ins files. Remember, RegRipper parses plug-ins files (several of which are included with the distribution of RegRipper on the CD that accompanies this book), which contain lists of plug-ins to be run against a hive file. Clicking on the Plugin File tab in the Plugin Browser UI provides a slightly different interface, as illustrated in Figure 2.17.

Figure 2.17 shows the Plugin File tab that provides a number of different options via the buttons in the middle of the window. From the Browse tab, you can locate various plug-ins of interest and then go to the Plugin File tab and click the >> button to add that plug-in to a plug-ins file. The "<<" button allows you to remove a plug-in from a plug-in file. The Open button allows you to open a current plug-in file in the editor window to the right, and the Save button allows you to save the contents of the editor window to a plug-in file. This allows you to customize plug-ins files for your own use, based on your goals and needs, for any type of examination you may be conducting. For example, you may have examinations where you would like to see everything that all of the available plug-ins for the Software hive can extract, but for other examinations, you may only want to see certain things. By creating specific plug-ins files, you can focus your analysis and look for those items of interest for that particular examination.

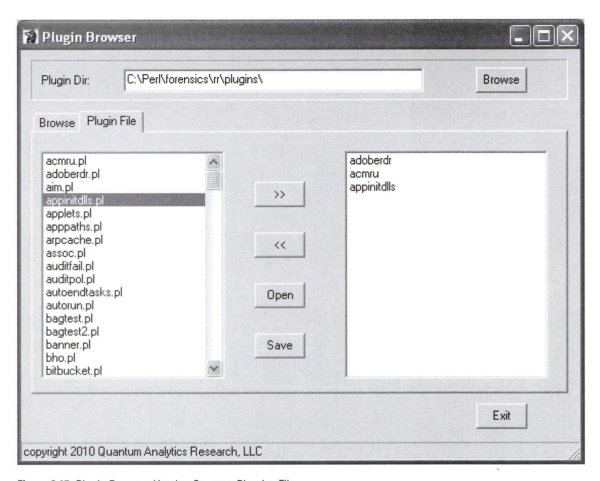

**Figure 2.17** Plugin Browser Used to Create a Plug-ins File

Keep in mind, however, that this is not the only way to create plug-ins files. Notepad or any other editor can be used to create a plug-ins file. Simply create a file with no extension (that is, "notepad ntuser2") in the plug-ins directory, add any comments you would like (comments are lines that start with "#"), and then list the plug-ins you would like to run in the order that you would like to run them. If the order doesn't matter, just add plug-ins!

### Writing Plug-ins

Right up front, I'll say it, writing RegRipper plug-ins requires some programming knowledge, particularly Perl. However, it's not an absolute requirement, as some very simple, albeit useful plug-ins can be (and have been) written simply by copying code out of or modifying existing plug-ins to meet specific needs. This approach is a lot more immediate (and responsive) than contacting an outside source for assistance. There are a number of plug-ins available that determines if a key or value exists, queries specific values, retrieves all values from a key, and even query and correlate the content of multiple keys. There are plug-ins that parse value data to retrieve specific information, as well as translate value names, and even use Perl data structures and built-in functions to organize collected data into something understandable. Given the various techniques employed in the available plug-ins, I would think that there would be very little that couldn't be done using the existing code base as examples.

RegRipper was provided as an open-source project, and even though I provided Windows .exe files, this was done simply to make the tools easier for folks who didn't want to install Perl in order to use the tools. This proved to be effective, and providing the actual Perl code allowed anyone who was interested to take a peek at it or even to take a crack at modifying it. Since the code was made available, there have been a number of minor changes that folks have sent, or simply posted to lists or to their own blogs. There have also been requests and recommendations for larger, more encompassing changes, and although some of those will likely be included in a future version of the RegRipper tools, some of them will be left to the user. After all, RegRipper is open source.

Speaking of open source, in October 2008, Jason Koppe posted to his blog [15] that he'd modified James Macfarlane's regview.pl code to create a simple plug-in generator script. In his blog post, Jason discusses how he modified the regview.pl script (provided with the Parse::Win32Registry module) to create a simple plug-in generator script. Jason provides several images in his post, one of which illustrates the output of a plug-in created with the plug-in generator.

Don Weber, author of the Security Ripcord blog (and a former Marine and good friend of mine), has used his familiarity of programming to create several RegRipper plug-ins, which he has made available through his blog [16]. Don specializes on programming in Python, and I greatly appreciate the fact that he stepped over to "the dark side" to dabble in a little Perl. Hey, it was for a good cause!

Don's not the only one to have written his own plug-ins. Chris Pogue, whom I used to work with on at IBM and is now working for TrustWave, has let me know that one of the members of his team had written a plug-in or two to meet their own needs, based on things they were seeing on engagements. At the end of August 2010, Michael Hale Ligh (who describes himself as "a [malware] reverse engineer who specializes in vulnerability research and malware cryptography") sent me a chapter of his upcoming book, *Malware Analyst's Cookbook and CD: Tools and Techniques for Fighting Malicious Code* (to be published by Wiley Publishing; as of this writing, there is no release date available), to review; in that chapter, he described the use of RegRipper in malware detection efforts and wanted to be sure that his description was technically accurate. Michael also described several plug-ins that had been written to enumerate persistent routes, "ShellExecute" hooks, and pending file deletions, to name a few, from the appropriate Registry hives. Esten Rye, of the *RyeZone. net* blog, wrote his own plug-in in March 2010, based on already-available plug-in, to extract the home page loaded by Internet Explorer when a user launches the browser. This shows that creating your own plug-in is simple enough, and some folks who have little to no programming experience have done so, simply due to their own needs.

## REQUESTING PLUG-INS

When I first released RegRipper, I recognized that not everyone has the ability (or interest) to program, and as such, I have offered to write plug-ins for people who needed them. However, I have made one consistent request: be clear and concise about your request and provide a sample hive file. I say this because most times, analysts will see something in another tool, and think, "hey, it would be great to have that in RegRipper," without knowing what goes on under the hood. I've had requests for plug-ins to parse Registry keys and values used by specific applications that, to be honest, I may not have access to; I've also been asked to parse values from keys that may appear to be part of every Windows installation, but simply aren't. When someone has provided a clear, concise request, and a sample hive file, I've been able to turn it around in as quickly as 20 min. The longest time it has ever taken me to provide the plug-in was about 4 h, and that was only because I wanted to tweak the output to make it a bit easier to read.

So, given all of this, how do you write a plug-in? Well, to start with it helps to keep the framework provided by RegRipper in mind. If you're running RegRipper (or rip.pl/.exe) as a Windows executable, most of the necessary Perl modules have already been provided for you, bundled along with the executable. If you're running the tools as Perl scripts, you'll need to make sure that you've already installed the required modules. Fortunately, ActiveState's ActivePerl distribution has a nice little tool, the Perl Package Manager (PPM), which makes this a really easy job. Fortunately, RegRipper itself (rr.pl) only relies on two modules: Win32::GUI and Parse::Win32Registry. These modules can be easily installed using the following commands:

```
C:\Perl>ppm install parse-win32registry
C:\Perl>ppm install win32-gui
```

Running these commands from the command line will install the necessary modules and dependencies for you. The other tools, rip.pl and ripxp.pl, only require the use of the Parse::Win32Registry module.

In order to begin writing a plug-in, you'll need an editor. I prefer UltraEdit that can be found on the Web site www.ultraedit .com because it does syntax highlighting (Perl functions and key words are displayed in colored text, making it easy to find misspelled keywords), provides line numbering in the editor (makes it easy to track down coding errors), does auto-indenting when you're writing functions or subroutines, and it is a great hex editor for troubleshooting. There are other editors available, such as Open Perl [17], EPIC [18], and PADRE [19], but even something as simple as Notepad (or even the old DOS "edlin"; how's that for "carbon dating"?) will work for very basic coding needs.

Now that we're ready to write a plug-in, we'll walk through one of the current plug-ins to use as an example. One very simple plug-in is acmru.pl, a plug-in that lets us retrieve information about searches run on Windows XP systems when the user clicks **Start | Search | For Files and Folders**. The name of the plug-in is derived; in this case, from the name of the Registry key of interest, which is "ACMru." So the name of the plug-in file itself is "acmru.pl." The first thing I generally like to put in the beginning of the file is a comment header section, which are all ignored by the Perl interpreter when the script is run because they're just comments. While we don't put code we want executed in this section (each line starts with "#"), we can put things here like the name of the person who wrote the plug-in, the version, any references or special items that someone can use later to better understand what the plug-in is attempting to achieve.

As this is a plug-in, the next thing we need is a package name. In the case of the RegRipper plug-ins, the package name is the same as the plug-in file name, without an extension: "acmru." After that, there is a Perl hash that contains configuration information: %config. The settings in this hash can be accessed (just read) by RegRipper and other tools through functions provided by the plug-in. The configuration hash has a number of standard keys that refer to the hive file that the plug-in is written for (that is, SAM, Software, System, and so on), and the version, which is essentially the date that the plug-in was written in YYYYMMDD format. This configuration information can be accessed by external tools once the plug-in is loaded by calling the *getConfig()* function of the plug-in. Other functions (or subroutines) can provide similar access to the plug-in for the exchange of information.

So far, this is what the contents of our plug-in looks like:

```
# Comments here
package acmru;
use strict;

my %config = (hive      => "NTUSER\.DAT",
        hasShortDescr => 1,
        hasDescr      => 0,
        hasRefs       => 0,
        osmask        => 22,
        version       => 20080324);
sub getConfig{return %config}
sub getShortDescr {
  return "Gets contents of user's ACMru key";
}
sub getDescr{}
sub getRefs {}
sub getHive {return $config{hive};}
sub getVersion {return $config{version};}

my $VERSION = getVersion();
```

You'll notice that we have a couple of subroutines (*getDescr()*, and so on) that don't seem to do anything, and they don't. They're provided as part of a template I developed early on when I was writing plug-ins so that I didn't have to keep writing everything over again from scratch each time I wrote a plug-in. You can see that the *getShortDescr()* subroutine simply returns a string that provides a brief description of what the plug-in is supposed to do, but it doesn't provide any details as to how the plug-in functions. These subroutines provide a means by which the plug-in can provide information to the calling program (RegRipper, rip, or ripxp). For example, whichever program is running a plug-in can call *getVersion()* to get the version of the plug-in being run so that information can be logged as part of the overall examination documentation.

At this point, we're ready to have the plug-in actually do some work. All of the core work performed by the plug-in is in the *pluginmain()* function of the plug-in, and every plug-in has a *pluginmain()* function. When RegRipper parses the plug-ins file (or profile) and loads the first plug-in, it calls the *pluginmain()* function of the plug-in to get the work done. *Pluginmain()* takes one argument, the path to the hive file

## Note

Rip.pl, provided with RegRipper, contains code that allows it to guess the type of hive file being accessed. This was experimental at the time that it was written but has proven over time to be very reliable. However, in the version of RegRipper provided on the CD that accompanies this book, that functionality is not fully available in the entire suite of tools.

## Tip

RegRipper also provides a *getTime( )* function, which can be used to translate 64-bit FILETIME objects into 32-bit Unix epoch time, which can then be presented in human-readable format using built-in Perl functions, such as *gmtime()*.

to be accessed. In our case, the ACMru key only exists in the NTUSER.DAT hive file on Windows XP systems; that is, you won't find an ACMru key in the System or Security hives on Windows XP.

Now, RegRipper does provide some services or functionality to the plug-ins. For example, there has to be a way to log information about what happens within the plug-in, as well as report the plug-in's findings if everything goes well. RegRipper provides a couple of functions that the plug-ins can use to provide this information; specifically via the *logMsg( )* and *rptMsg( )* subroutines. The *logMsg( )* subroutine allows the plug-in to send messages to the log file maintained by RegRipper so that the analyst can troubleshoot any issues that occur, and the *rptMsg( )* subroutine allows the plug-in to report its findings to the report file illustrated in Figure 2.14; the log file is automatically generated in the same directory where RegRipper lives). The plug-ins then call these functions using *::logMsg( )* or *::rptMsg( )*, providing the strings that should appear in the appropriate file.

Rip.pl and ripxp.pl also provide these functions (they must, in order to use the plug-ins), but provide different functionality. Rip. pl doesn't maintain a log file of its activity, so its own *logMsg( )* subroutine is an empty shell that does absolutely nothing with the string that's sent to it. The *rptMsg( )* subroutine, on the other hand, simply prints whatever is sent to it to the console (that is, STDOUT) rather than to a file. This allows the analyst to use redirection to send the output to a file.

At this point, we've covered the basics of writing RegRipper plug-ins. The rest of what's required is based on basic Perl programming and reading the documentation that is installed with the Parse::Win32Registry module. RegRipper and its companion tools rely on the Parse::Win32Registry module and use the functions provided by that module such as *get_list_of_subkeys( )* and *get_list_of_values( )*, both of which return Perl lists (or arrays). These functions are used to navigate through "live" portions of the Registry hive file in order to retrieve the required data. For example, some applications (MS Office, in particular) list their active keys beneath a specific key that identifies the current version of the application installed, and previously installed versions are considered defunct. Therefore, when searching for the appropriate keys and values, you'll first have to navigate to one specific key path, list all of the subkeys, determine which is most recent, and then continue navigating beneath that key to get the data in which you're most interested.

Returning to the acmru.pl plug-in, we first get the list of values beneath the ACMru subkey of interest, using the aforementioned *get_list_of_values()* subroutine. From there, we step through each available value, getting the name and its data, and placing that information into a Perl hash, using the value name as the key. The code that does this appears as follows:

```
my %ac_vals;
foreach my $v (@vals) {
 $ac_vals{$v->get_name()} = $v->get_data();
}
```

Beneath these subkeys, the value names appear as 0000, 0001, 0002, and so on. When displaying these values and their data, it looks better when they appear in order, so to do that, we can use code that appears as follows:

```
foreach my $a (sort {$a <=> $b} keys %ac_vals) {
 ::rptMsg("\t".$a." -> ".$ac_vals{$a});
}
```

The code on the "foreach" line essentially tells Perl to sort the keys of the Perl hash (%ac_vals), listing them with the smallest value first. Each entry is printed with the Registry value name, and arrow ("→") and the value data, on one line.

When it comes to providing output, particularly for reporting, there are a number of different techniques you can use. For example, you can simply build a string like we did above with the values within the quotes or you can make them a bit more descriptive. If you have data that is easier to understand if it's formatted neatly or in a particular manner, you can use Perl's

# Tip

Perl hashes can be very valuable when it comes to establishing uniqueness and reducing duplicates. In 1999, while I was working at a consulting company, a friend gave me a little tidbit that I've used ever since. In a Perl hash, if you make the items you're interested in the key of the hash and set the value to 1 (that is, $hash{key} = 1), you will eliminate duplicates because every time that key is encountered, no matter how many times, the value will always be 1.

built-in *sprint()* function to provide that formatting. There are a variety of ways to format the data, and it's best to choose which one makes the most sense for what you're trying to achieve.

Plug-ins can be written as in a simple or complex manner as you need. I know of some who have written plug-ins to extract log-in banner information, and others who've written plug-ins to extract information about a particular software package found during a number of data breach investigations. If I find the need to correlate information from multiple Registry keys, I sometimes find it best to just perform that correlation in the plug-in rather than extract the data from the various keys and then perform the correlation and analysis later. Regardless of the approach, there are a number of plug-ins available (on the accompanying CD), which can be used as examples in creating your own plug-ins.

## Toolkits

Overall, RegRipper and its associated tools (rip.pl, ripxp.pl) have proven to be extremely useful and every effective. Since the tools were released in 2008, I've received comments from folks who've used the tools, saying such things as the tools have reduced days or weeks worth of work to mere minutes. In fact, the tools have become popular enough to be included in other toolkits. For example, the Revealer Toolkit [20] includes the RVT_regripper plug-in (written by Jose Navarro, a.k.a Dervitx) within its framework, which relies on rip.pl. RegRipper is included in the SANS SIFT (SANS Investigative Forensic Toolkit) Workstation distribution [21] and in the PlainSight [22] open-source forensic environment.

RegRipper has proven useful enough that others have put forth the effort to get it installed into their platform of choice or modify it to meet their needs. A post to the Grey Corner blog [23] provides instructions on how to install RegRipper on Linux systems, specifically Ubuntu. Going back to the Windows platforms, RegExtract [24] is based on RegRipper and provides some additional functionality. Matt Churchill and Adam James first modified RegRipper to run against mounted drives and then extended RegRipper and it's plug-in-based approached to what they refer to as "WindowsRipper" [25], providing a more comprehensive framework to analyzing acquired Windows images.

### Regslack

In the spring of 2008, Jolanta Thomassen contacted me about providing an idea (and being a sponsor) for her dissertation for work at the University of Liverpool. I pointed her to an old (circa 2001) post on the Internet, asking about unallocated space within a Registry hive file. Not long after, Jolanta produced regslack, a Perl script that combs through a hive file and locates deleted keys and unallocated space. If you remember from Chapter 1, "Registry Analysis," when a key is deleted, the first four bytes (DWORD) of the key, which is the length of the key, is changed from a negative value (as a signed integer) to a positive value. For example, if the "live" key had a length of –120 as decimal value, then the deleted key length is 120.

Regslack is a command-line tool and is very easy to use. Simply open a command prompt and pass the path to the Registry file in question to the program:

```
C:\tools>regslack.pl d:\cases\test\software
```

Regslack sends its output to the console (that is, STDOUT), so be sure to redirect it to a file (that is, "> file"), as in some cases there can be quite a lot of information. Regslack has proven quite useful during a number of examinations. For example, if you find indications of a user account being active on a system, but can't find that account listed in the SAM hive, try running regslack against the hive file. In one instance, I found indications of a user account with the name "Owner" and a RID of 1003 in the Event Logs on the system, but no indication of such an account within the SAM hive. Running regslack, I found the following:

```
SAM\SAM\Domains\Account\Users\Names\Owner
Offset: 0x3c70 [Fri Jun 18 17:03:22 2004]

SAM\SAM\Domains\Account\Users\000003EB
Offset: 0x3d08 [Fri Jun 18 18:59:27 2004]
```

The second key (Users\000003EB) had two values (F and V) associated with it, just as you'd expect for a local user account. The V value included the name "Owner." Thanks to regslack, I'd found the user account, as well as the time when the account had been deleted. With a little more work, using Perl code that I've already written (as part of RegRipper), I could extract and translate that binary data from those values into something a bit more understandable.

## Tip

Jolanta's dissertation is available online at the SentinelChicken Web site http://sentinelchicken.com/data/ JolantaThomassenDISSERTATION.pdf.

I have also used regslack to great effect to recover deleted keys and values from a user's hive file, in particular after the user had run an application called *Window Washer* on their system. I researched the version of the application and found that it reportedly did delete certain keys when run. Sure enough, the key was not visible in the allocated (or "live") space within the hive file, but it was fairly easy to recover using regslack. There were indications that Window Washer had been run several times, so I suggested to the customer that we extract the user hive files from the System Restore Points and see if we could find anything of value within them.

During another incident, I had run searches for sensitive data and received several hits within two hive files. Closer examination of those hits, and the hive files, revealed that the hits were not "in" the hive files, in that they were not contained in keys or values, rather they were within unallocated space in the hive files. It turned out the hits were part of the hive files as a result of file initialization issues, as described by Eoghan Casey at cmdLabs (found on the Web site http://blog.cmdlabs.com/?p=157).

As of version 0.51, the Parse::Win32Registry module also has the ability to extract deleted keys and values from within a hive file. One of the scripts that James provided with the distribution of the module, regscan.pl, includes code that references checking whether a found entry is allocated (that is, *$entry->is_allocated*). Modifying the code slightly to skip over and not display allocated entries allows us to see just the deleted keys and values. The documentation that James has provided for the module includes a section on lower level methods for processing hive files and refers to the entry object methods that allow for a lower level of access to entries within the hive file. This can allow us to walk through a hive file and locate deleted keys and values.

## Summary

There are a number of very useful tools and techniques available for extracting data from Registry hive files during both "live" (interacting with a live system) and "forensic" (interacting with hive files extracted from a system or acquired image) analysis. The tools or techniques you employ depend on how you engage and interact with the Registry, as well as the goals of your interaction and analysis. You can opt to use a viewer application, such as RegRipper that extracts and parses specific keys and values based on plug-ins or regslack that parses unallocated space within a hive file. In my opinion, tools such as those discussed in this chapter have the advantages of not only being freely available but the open-source tools I've written and provided were written by someone actively involved in a wide range of analysis; I've not only been engaged in data breach investigations (most commonly associated with the theft or exposure of credit card data), but I've analyzed malware outbreaks, intrusions (including those associated with the advanced persistent threat, or APT), and I've assisted law enforcement in dealing with potential "Trojan defense" issues. As I mentioned in this chapter, the RegRipper suite of tools (which includes the rip.pl and the Plugin Browser) was developed to meet and service my needs and the needs of my analysis. These tools were not developed in a manner that resulted in having to modify my analysis to meet the needs or limitations of the tools. Ultimately, the goal has always been to provide my customers with timely accurate results, and the tools discussed in this chapter have helped me deliver on this.

Regardless of which approach is taken, as described in Chapter 1, "Registry Analysis," your actions and analysis should be thoroughly documented in a clear, concise manner.

## Frequently Asked Questions

**Q:** Under what circumstances should I use Regshot?

**A:** Regshot, and any snapshot-based tool like it, is best used when you simply want to know the changes that occur to the Registry as the result of a single atomic action. Due to background processes, no action is truly "atomic" (that is, nothing occurs on a Windows system completely in the absence of another action), but tools like Regshot allow you to make snapshots before and after a single action and then compare the two. Situations that benefit from this sort of tool include launching malware, installing or upgrading tools or applications, and so on.

**Q:** What are some of the differences between "live" and "forensic" analysis?

**A:** First, "live" analysis is performed when the system is still running; the live Registry can be queried, data extracted, correlated, and interpreted. However, the data that you have access to varies from that of "forensic" analysis, which for our purposes involves extracting the raw hive files themselves, either from a live system (via FTK Imager, F-Response, or some other means) or from an image acquired from a system. When interacting with a live system, you're subject to the privileges of the user account you're using and the access control lists (ACLs) on various portions of the Registry, in particular the SAM hive. When performing forensic analysis, you can access the raw data in the hive files without worrying about permissions and privileges. A benefit of live analysis is that you have access to volatile data that does not exist when performing forensic analysis.

**Q:** What is the best tool to use for Registry analysis?

**A:** The question of "best" generally takes us back to the goals of our analysis. I tend to choose tools best suited to my needs and recognize that not all tools are useful in all cases. Obviously, I prefer RegRipper and its associated tools, as I wrote those tools out of necessity and in an attempt to solve the challenges I faced during my own analysis. When I suspect that there may be value in examining the contents of unallocated space within a hive file, I will look to RegSlack. If I suspect that there may be keys or values for which I have yet to write a plug-in, I will open the hive file in a viewer such as the one included in ProDiscover or I will use the MiTeC Registry File Viewer. Many times, I will also use tools to add data from the output of RegRipper to a timeline in order to add context to that information. Overall, in my humble opinion, the "best" tools for Registry analysis are the curiosity of the analyst and whatever method they use to document what they do (that is, Forensic CaseNotes, Microsoft Word, Notepad, and so on).

# References

[1] AutoRuns for Windows v10.02. Microsoft SysInternals site. http://technet .microsoft.com/en-us/sysinternals/bb963902.aspx (accessed 22.07.10).
[2] Script Center Home Page. Microsoft. http://technet.microsoft.com/en-us/ scriptcenter/default.aspx.
[3] Registry key security and access rights. Microsoft. http://msdn.microsoft .com/en-us/library/ms724878(VS.85).aspx.
[4] A. Schuster, Computer Forensic Blog. http://computer.forensikblog.de/en.
[5] Virus alert about the Win32/Conficker worm. Microsoft Support. http:// support.microsoft.com/kb/962007 (accessed 8.07.10).
[6] Browse regshot Files on Sourceforge.net. SourceForge.net. http:// sourceforge.net/projects/regshot/files.
[7] Process Monitor v2.92. Microsoft SysInternals. http://technet.microsoft .com/en-us/sysinternals/bb896645.aspx.
[8] How to debug Windows Services. Microsoft Support. http://support .microsoft.com/kb/824344 (accessed 2.07.10).
[9] How to turn off Windows Update feature in Windows XP. Microsoft Support. http://support.microsoft.com/kb/892894 (accessed 25.01.10).

[10] AccessData Product Downloads. http://www.accessdata.com/downloads .html.

[11] Technology Pathways – Computer Forensics, Digital Discovery, Auditing, Incident Response. http://www.techpathways.com/DesktopDefault .aspx?tabindex=3&tabid=12.

[12] Tools and utilities for Windows. ImDisk Virtual Disk Driver. http://www .ltr-data.se/opencode.html#ImDisk.

[13] ASR Data – Smart Mount. http://www.asrdata.com/SmartMount.

[14] Binary Intelligence: Run RegRipper against a mounted drive. http://www .binint.com/2010/05/run-regripper-against-mounted-drive.html (accessed 14.05.10).

[15] NSSA Documentation: RegRipper, RegView, and Bluetooth Registry Settings. Blog post, 7 Oct 2008, http://nssadoc.blogspot.com/2008/10/regripper-regview-and-bluetooth.html.

[16] Security Ripcord >> Scripts and Tools. http://www.cutawaysecurity.com/ blog/scripts-and-tools.

[17] Open Perl IDE. http://open-perl-ide.sourceforge.net.

[18] EPIC – Eclipse Perl Integration. http://www.epic-ide.org.

[19] Padre, the Perl IDE. http://padre.perlide.org.

[20] Revealer Toolkit. Google Code. http://code.google.com/p/revealertoolkit.

[21] SANS Computer Forensics Community. SANS Portal. https://computer-forensics2.sans.org/community/siftkit.

[22] PlainSight. http://www.plainsight.info.

[23] The Grey Corner: Running RegRipper on Linux. http://grey-corner.blogspot .com/2010/04/running-regripper-on-linux.html (accessed 25.04.10).

[24] RegExtract: woanware. http://www.woany.co.uk/regextract.

[25] Turning RegRipper into WindowsRipper. MattChurchill.net blog, 1 Jun 2010, http://mattchurchill.net/2010/06/windowsripper.

# 3

# CASE STUDIES: THE SYSTEM

## Introduction

When I sat down to write this book, I was aware that for most folks, providing spreadsheets, tables, and lists of Registry keys and values would not be an entirely effective means of communicating and sharing information about Registry analysis. In fact, after writing the first edition of *Windows Forensic Analysis* (Syngress Publishing, published in 2007, a.k.a., *WFA*), it was pretty clear to me that listing Registry keys and files wasn't as effective as providing examples of Registry analysis, and of how all of these could be used together. When I began writing the second edition of *WFA*, I specifically included a chapter on just "case studies," in hopes of demonstrating how I and others have used various data sources from a Windows system, in incident response and forensic analysis scenarios, to gather information and build an overall picture to solve the challenges we were facing. Talking with others, I can see how this can be an effective approach … leaving someone with stacks of lumber and roofing shingles and some tools and nails does not help his or her build a house. However, showing someone how a house can be built, with some of the various places where modifications can be made, is more of a "teach a man to fish" approach, and it can lead to more involvement in Registry analysis, in particular, and Windows forensic analysis as a whole.

In short, this chapter (and the one after it) will not be a comprehensive list of all possible Registry keys and values that would be of interest to an analyst, mapped against various types of examinations. Rather, we will take a look at some use cases, as well as some scenarios that I and others have run across, and problems that we've encountered and solved. My overall goal is to demonstrate how easily data from the Registry can be extracted, and how it can be used to further an examination.

## Security and SAM Hives

The first hives we'll look at are the Security and SAM hives, in part, because they have perhaps the least amount of data available ("pound for pound," so to speak) compared with the System and Software hives. These hives contain some useful information, and there's no question that what they can provide can be extremely valuable during an examination, but the data in the other two hives, in my experience, is both considerably more expansive and fluid.

### Data from the Security Hive

At the time of this writing, I am aware of little data that might be relevant to an examination that has been discussed publicly; however, there are a few keys and values that are of interest. One such Registry key is "PolAcDms," which was mentioned in the Wikipedia page on security identifiers [1]. The "Default" value within this key contains the security identifier (SID) for the system (or "machine"), which is a unique name that identifies an object, and in this case, the system. As we will address later in this chapter, this information can be used to determine which users on a system are local users, and which users are domain users, which is something that can be very useful with respect to a domain-connected (as opposed to standalone) system and, in particular, a system with multiple domain trusts. Parsing the SID from the binary data is not an arduous task, and is included in the RegRipper polacdms.pl plug-in, the output of which (when run against a Security hive extracted from a Vista system) is shown as follows:

```
Launching polacdms v.20100531
PolAcDmS
Policy\PolAcDmS
LastWrite Time Fri Aug 31 15:14:53 2007 (UTC)
```

```
Machine SID: S-1-5-21-3831915772-716441274-3601324335
PolPrDmS
Policy\PolPrDmS
LastWrite Time Thu Nov 2 12:48:01 2006 (UTC)
Primary Domain SID: S-1-5-
```

Not only does this plug-in extract and parse the machine SID from the PolAcDmS key, but it also extracts and parses the domain SID (for the domain to which the system was connected) from the PolPrDmS key. In this example, the Security hive was extracted from a standalone system used by a home user. In instances where the system was connected to a domain, the primary domain SID can be parsed from the "Default" value of that key, and it will be visible following "Primary Domain SID:". Later in this chapter, we'll discuss local user accounts found in the SAM hive, as well as the ProfileList key from the Software hive, and see how an analyst can use this information.

The other key that is of use and interest to analysts from the Security hive is the "PolAdtEv" key. Parsing the binary data retrieved from this value is not a trivial task. However, our understanding of how this data can be parsed and understood can be helped along with Microsoft (MS) KnowledgeBase (KB) article 246120 [2]. As stated, this article applies to Windows NT 4.0, and there are only seven areas of auditing listed in the article. However, Windows XP has nine areas of auditing, as illustrated in Figure 3.1.

**Figure 3.1** Audit Policy through Local Security Settings (Windows XP)

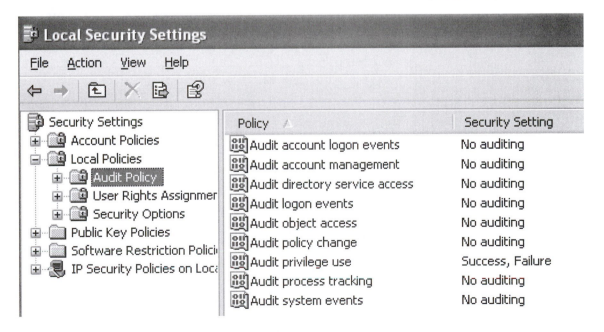

In order to view the information illustrated in Figure 3.1, all we need to do is open the Administrative Tools Control Panel applet and select the **Local Security Policy** shortcut. Another way to view this information (one that is useful during live response, as it can be added to a batch file) is to run auditpol.exe; running it on that same live system, the following can be observed:

```
D:\tools>auditpol

Running ...

(X) Audit Enabled
System              = No
Logon               = No
Object Access       = No
Privilege Use       = Success and Failure
Process Tracking    = No
Policy Change       = No
Account Management      = No
Directory Service Access = No
Account Logon       = No
```

Okay, so that's how we can extract the information from a live system, but what about from an acquired image? Using MS KB article 246120 as a basis and toggling various settings on and off, we can see what modifications affect which areas of the data, and develop an extrapolation of the data to our Windows XP system. Or, the RegRipper plug-in auditpol.pl can be used to extract and parse the necessary information, either as part of a plug-ins file or run individually through rip.pl (or rip.exe), as shown below:

```
Launching auditpol v.20080327
auditpol
Policy\PolAdtEv
LastWrite Time Mon Jul 12 18:09:46 2010 (UTC)

Auditing is enabled.
    Audit System Events    = N
    Audit Logon Events     = N
    Audit Object Access    = N
    Audit Privilege Use  = S/F
    Audit Process Tracking = N
    Audit Policy Change    = N
    Audit Account Management  = N
    Audit Dir Service Access = N
    Audit Account Logon Events = N
```

This information can be very valuable as it tells us a lot about the state of auditing on the system at the time that an image was acquired. First, the LastWrite time of the key lets us know when the settings were last modified (the time is listed in Universal Coordinated Time, or UTC). This can be very helpful in understanding why we see, or don't see, certain events in the Event Log, as well as provide an indication of when the audit policy was changed. There've been a number of examinations where I've created a time line and seen clearly when the incident occurred, and seen that as a result of response and remediation actions taken by local IT staff, antivirus scans have been run and the audit policy has been updated, just before an image was acquired from the system.

Next, we see whether or not auditing is enabled, and if so, which events are audited. This will also provide us with some indication of what we can expect to see in the Event Log. For example, if auditing of successful logon events isn't enabled, then we wouldn't expect to be able to see when someone logged into the system using a user account, either legitimately or as a result of compromised credentials. I have used this information during examinations quite extensively; during one instance, I used the fact that auditing for both successful logins and failed log-in attempts were both enabled, but there were no indications of remote logins through the Remote Desktop Protocol (RDP), to further illustrate that a particular user account had been accessed locally and used to view illegal images.

It is important to note that while this key and value exist on Windows Vista and 7 systems, there has yet to be extensive testing on these systems. Figure 3.2 illustrates the audit policy on a Windows 7 Ultimate system.

As you can see from Figure 3.2, there are nine areas of auditing listed, just as there are with Windows XP. In fact, the audit policies in Figures 3.1 and 3.2 look very similar. However, the "Default" value for the PolAdtEv key on Windows XP contains data that is 44 bytes long, whereas on available Windows Vista and 2008 systems, the data is 136 bytes long, and 138 bytes on available Windows 7 systems. So again, considerable testing

# Tip

If successful, use of privilege events are being audited (i.e., Audit Privilege Use = S) on a Windows XP system, and a user modifies the system time through the "Date and Time" Control Panel applet (this can also be done by right-clicking on the time display on the Task Bar and choosing "Adjust Date/Time"), an event ID 577 appears in the Security Event Log, indicating the use of the "SeSystemtimePrivilege" privilege.

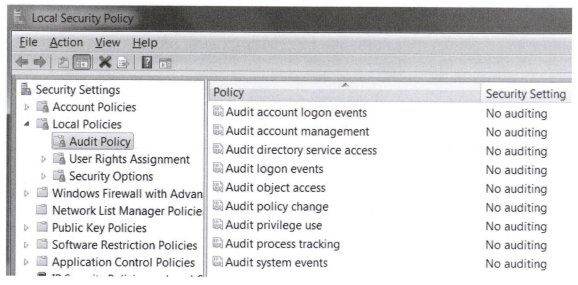

**Figure 3.2** Audit Policy on a Windows 7 Ultimate System

needs to be performed in order to create a version of the audit-pol.pl plug-in that works for Vista, as well as Windows 2008 and Windows 7.

## User Information from the SAM Hive

Most administrators and analysts are aware that information about local users on a system is maintained in the SAM "database" or hive file. In corporate environments, the SAM hive may not have a great deal of useful information, but for environments where the users will access systems using local accounts (home users, laptops, and so on), this hive file can provide a great deal of valuable data. We'll also see, later in this chapter, how the SAM hive can be used in other ways.

---

# Tip

Although information about user accounts local to the system are maintained in the SAM hive, the Software hive contains the ProfileList key (HKLM\Software\Microsoft\Windows NT\CurrentVersion\ProfileList), which is a list of all the profiles on the system. This can show you remote or domain users who have logged into the system. We will discuss the ProfileList key later in this chapter.

The samparse.pl plug-in extracts both user and group information from the SAM hive. Most of the information specific to each user is available beneath the SAM\Domains\Account\Users\*RID* key for each user, where *RID* is four zeros followed by the user's relative identifier (RID) in hexadecimal format. For example, the Administrator account has an RID of 500, which would appear as 000001F4 in the SAM, as illustrated in Figure 3.3.

The key for each user contains at least two values, F (contains several time stamps, and so on) and V (contains user name, comment, and so on), which are binary data types and contain information about the user account. I have relied heavily on the source code for Peter Nordahl–Hagen's ntpasswd utility [3] to understand and decode this data into something usable. Sometimes within the user's key, you will also find a value name

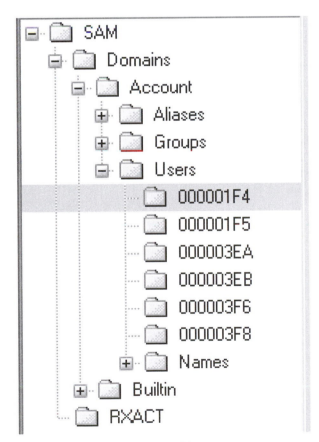

**Figure 3.3** Windows XP SAM Keys through RFV

"UserPasswordHint," which contains a string value if a user has entered a password hint.

An excerpt of the user information extracted from the F and V values in the SAM hive by the samparse.pl RegRipper plug-in appears as follows:

```
User Information
------------------------
Username        : Administrator [500]
Full Name       :
User Comment    : Built-in account for administering the
  computer/domain
Account Created : Tue Sep 11 14:26:13 2007 Z
Last Login Date : Fri Aug 31 15:52:42 2007 Z
Pwd Reset Date  : Thu Nov 2 13:09:52 2006 Z
Pwd Fail Date : Never
Login Count     : 4
 --> Password does not expire
 --> Account Disabled
 --> Normal user account

Username        : Guest [501]
Full Name       :
User Comment    : Built-in account for guest access to the
  computer/domain
Account Created : Tue Sep 11 14:26:13 2007 Z
Last Login Date : Never
Pwd Reset Date  : Never
Pwd Fail Date : Never
Login Count     : 0
 --> Password does not expire
 --> Account Disabled
 --> Password not required
 --> Normal user account

Username        : Harlan [1000]
Full Name       :
User Comment    :
Account Created : Tue Sep 11 14:26:01 2007 Z
Password Hint   : usual plus a bit more
Last Login Date : Mon Jan 12 12:41:35 2009 Z
Pwd Reset Date  : Tue Sep 11 14:26:02 2007 Z
Pwd Fail Date : Fri Jul 11 19:54:07 2008 Z
Login Count     : 16
 --> Password does not expire
 --> Password not required
 --> Normal user account
```

As you can see, a great deal of information is available in the user's keys within the SAM. This information can be used to demonstrate activity on the system (i.e., Last Login Date, Login Count values) for a specific user account, as well as tell you a number of other things, such as if the Guest account has been enabled and used. Another tell-tale sign of unusual activity would be if accounts such as the support or HelpAssistant accounts have been enabled.

Note that in the output excerpt above, the "Harlan" user account has an extra field that the other two do not; specifically, "Password Hint." Many Windows systems (including Windows XP) allow the option to add a password hint to the user account, as illustrated in Figure 3.4.

**Figure 3.4** Add a Password Hint to a Windows 7 User Account

# Tip

Of particular note in the output of the samparse.pl plug-in is the entry for "Password not required." In some cases, analysts have taken this flag value to mean that the account does not have a password, and that is not the case. Rather, it means that password policies (length, complexity, and so on) applied to the user accounts on the system do not apply to those accounts for which the "Password not required" flag is set. I had posed the question to someone knowledgeable in this area, and had been informed, "That specifies that the password-length and complexity policy settings do not apply to this user. If you do not set a password, then you should be able to enable the account and logon with just the user account. If you set a password for the account, then you will need to provide that password at logon. Setting this flag on an existing account with a password does not allow you to logon to the account without the password." This is somewhat supported by MS KB article 305144 [4], which indicates that enabling the flag means that a password is not required.

There have been several cases where a somewhat careless user has added something odd to his or her password hint, and it has turned out to be the user's password!

## THE CASE OF THE DISAPPEARING USER ACCOUNT

I was examining an image sent to me, looking for indications of malicious activity. As is often the case, I neither had a really good idea of the specific activity of interest, nor of the time frame in question. I had created a time line of activity on the system, using the file system metadata, Prefetch file metadata, Event Log record data, and so on, as sources, and had started to see some unusual activity. In one instance, I found that a particular user account had logged in about a year before the image had been acquired, but I didn't find any indication of that user account in the SAM. I used regslack.exe to extract deleted keys and values, and unallocated space from the SAM hive, and found an account with the same RID as the account I was interested in, but in the deleted data, the key had a different user name associated with it. I also noted that the LastWrite time on the deleted key was very close to the time that the image of the system had been acquired. As it turned out, a system administrator had logged into the system, changed the name on the account when he or she heard that "someone was coming to acquire the system," and then deleted the account. This was confirmed by that same system administrator.

The samparse.pl plug-in will also extract information about local groups from the SAM hive, including the group name, comment, and the SIDs for the users in the group. An excerpt of this output from a Windows XP system is illustrated below:

```
Group Name   : Users [4]
LastWrite : Thu Sep 13 12:35:14 2007 Z
Group Comment : Users are prevented from making accidental
  or intentional system-wide changes. Thus, Users can run
  certified applications, but not most legacy applications
Users :
 S-1-5-4
 S-1-5-21-2096504233-719092796-1279470122-513
 S-1-5-11
 S-1-5-21-11123406-2312686674-711150868-1003

Group Name   : Guests [1]
LastWrite : Fri Jan 19 00:58:18 2007 Z
Group Comment : Guests have the same access as members of the
  Users group by default, except for the Guest account which
  is further restricted
Users :
 S-1-5-21-11123406-2312686674-711150868-501
```

```
Group Name   : Remote Desktop Users [0]
LastWrite : Mon Apr 4 18:34:48 2005 Z
Group Comment : Members in this group are granted the right
  to logon remotely
Users  : None

Group Name   : Administrators [6]
LastWrite : Thu Sep 13 12:35:14 2007 Z
Group Comment : Administrators have complete and unrestricted
  access to the computer/domain
Users :
 S-1-5-21-11123406-2312686674-711150868-500
 S-1-5-21-2096504233-719092796-1279470122-512
 S-1-5-21-2096504233-719092796-1279470122-2003
 S-1-5-21-11123406-2312686674-711150868-1016
 S-1-5-21-2096504233-719092796-1279470122-3560
 S-1-5-21-2096504233-719092796-1279470122-37504
```

As you can see from the sample output from the samparse.pl plug-in, there are a number of users (both local and domain users) in the Administrators group, while other groups (i.e., Guests) have few users, and still others (i.e., Remote Users) have none. This information can be very helpful in determining the level of access that a particular user account had on a system at the time that system was acquired, in order to determine what actions that user could take on the system, such as submit Scheduled Tasks (which is one way that a user could obtain elevated privileges), and so on.

Also, the samparse.pl plug-in is very convenient as it allows you to obtain and view a great deal of local user and group information from a system, all in one easy-to-reference location.

## Cracking User Passwords

There are a number of times during investigations when you would want to determine a user's password. For example, in a number of examinations, law enforcement officials have wanted to know if the user account had a password at all. In most instances, I have seen this sort of query associated with cases where something suspicious (or illegal) is associated with the user account of another family member, and law enforcement officials want to determine if the suspect had free access to that account; an account with no password is extremely vulnerable. In other cases, the "Password not required" flag in the user account settings (mentioned earlier in this chapter) can be very confusing to some analysts, and determining if the user account had a password at all, and attempting to determine what that password is, is paramount to the investigation. Finally, there may be a time

## Tip

There are two types of password hashes stored in the SAM database: LM (LAN Manager [9]) and NTLM (NT LAN Manager [10]). However, administrators can prevent LM hashes from being stored in the Active Directory and local SAM databases [11], as the LM hash has long been known to be relatively weak in comparison with the NTLM hash and is prone to fast brute force attacks in decrypting them. On Windows XP and 2003 systems, setting the NoLMHash value to 1, or creating a password longer than 15 characters, disables storing of the LM hash.

during an investigation where, after you've acquired an image of the system, you may want to boot the system (either the original system or the acquired image, which can be "booted" in a virtual environment through LiveView [5], in order to "see" what the user saw or had access to while he or she had logged into the system.

In order to crack the passwords, the first thing we need to do is to get the hashes. In order to do so, extract the SAM and System hives from the acquired image to a suitable location (as part of my case management, I tend to create specific subdirectories beneath my main case directory just for this purpose). There are a couple of ways to go about obtaining the hashes from these two files (the System hive is required as the passwords are protected with an additional layer of encryption called "SysKey" [6]). To get the hashes, you can use either pwdump7 [7] or Cain [8].

To obtain the password hashes using pwdump7, download and extract the tool files, and then open a command prompt to the directory where the tool is located. It is important to note that running pwdump7 with no arguments will extract the password hashes from your analysis system; this is generally *not* a "good thing." In order to get the password hashes from the System and SAM hive files you extracted from an acquired image, use the "–s" switch:

```
D:\tools>pwdump7 -s <sam_hive> <system_hive>
```

Note that the order of the arguments in the command is important. Also important is to ensure that you use the full and correct paths to the hive files, even if they are located in the same directory as pwdump7.exe, as the program does not prepend the arguments with the path of the current working directory. Not only do you need to do this so that the program knows where the files are located and can open them, but also to ensure that you're using the SAM and System hive files from the same case; mixing the two (using a SAM hive from one case and a System hive from another case) generally results in something not working properly, if at all.

Using the SAM and System hive files from a test case (the "hacking case" available from NIST [12]), we run the following command:

```
D:\tools>pwdump7 -s d:\case\sam d:\case\system
```

This gives us the following output (excerpt):

```
Administrator:500:NO
PASSWORD***********:31D6CFE0D16AE931B73C59D7E0C089C0:::
Mr. Evil:1003:NO
PASSWORD***********:31D6CFE0D16AE931B73C59D7E0C089C0:::
```

In this example, I've removed a couple of the user accounts and only illustrated the ones of most interest to us in this case. As you can see, the output includes the user name, relative identifier (RID), LM hash, and the NTLM hash. This format allows us to easily import these hashes into password-cracking tools; however, as shown in the excerpt, neither of the two accounts has a password. This simple tool can provide a great deal of valuable information to the analyst, particularly, in cases where knowing whether or not an account has a password is pertinent.

There are also a number of free, GUI-based password-cracking tools available, such as Cain & Abel, OphCrack [14], and John the Ripper. There are also for-fee tools such as SAMInside [15], for which there is a limited demo version available. For the "old timers" in the information security industry, L0phtCrack version 6 [16] is also available for a fee, and with a 15-day trial period. It isn't necessary to go through all of these tools, as this is beyond the scope of the book, and the programs are quite easy to use; instead, we'll just take a look at how to use Cain & Abel and OphCrack.

To use Cain (we won't be using the "Abel" functionality), download, install, and launch the program. From the **Tools** menu, select the **Syskey Decoder** entry, as illustrated in Figure 3.5.

## Tip

Booting an image through LiveView (see the appropriate sidebar later in this chapter) can let you verify the finding that a user account has no password. With respect to the NIST hacking case, booting the image in a virtual machine causes it to log directly into the Mr. Evil user account. This is controlled by the DefaultUserName value in the **WinLogon** key, per MS KB article 315231 [13]. In this case, the user account has no password, so there is no DefaultPassword value listed in the Registry. If there were, it would be in plain text, which is why the MS KB article states several times that when using these values, the system itself should be physically secure.

| Tools | Help | |
|---|---|---|
| Processor Info | | Alt+I |
| Disconnect.. | | Alt+D |
| Route Table | | Alt+R |
| Tcp/Udp Tables | | Alt+P |
| Base64 Password Decoder | | Alt+6 |
| Access Database Password Decoder | | Alt+A |
| Cisco Type-7 Password Decoder | | Alt+7 |
| Cisco VPN Client Password Decoder | | Alt+V |
| VNC Password Decoder | | Alt+N |
| Hash Calculator | | Alt+C |
| RSA SecurID Token Calculator | | Alt+S |
| Remote Desktop Password Decoder | | Alt+T |
| Syskey Decoder | | Alt+K |
| WPA PSK Calculator | | Alt+L |

**Figure 3.5** Selecting **Syskey Decoder** In Cain **Tools** Menu

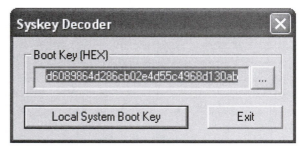

**Figure 3.6** Boot Key Selected

When the Syskey Decoder dialog appears, select the button with the three dots in the "Boot Key (HEX)" box and navigate to the System hive that you extracted from the image. Once the file is selected, click **Open** in the Open dialog, and the "boot key" will appear in the text field, as illustrated in Figure 3.6.

Selected the **boot key** and hit **Ctrl-C**, copying the boot key to the clipboard, and then click the **Exit** key in the Syskey Decoder dialog. Next, in the main Cain window, click the **Cracker** tab, and then highlight "LM & NTLM Hashes" in the left-hand pane, as illustrated in Figure 3.7.

Now, click the blue plus sign that is located directly above the **Sniffer** tab. If the plus sign is grayed out, try clicking on NTLMv2

**Figure 3.7** Cain **Cracker** Tab Selected

**Figure 3.8** "Add NT Hashes from" Dialog in Cain

| User Name | LM Password | < 8 | NT Password | LM Hash | NT Hash |
|---|---|---|---|---|---|
| Administrator | * empty * | * | * empty * | AAD3B435B514... | 31D6CFE0D16A... |
| Guest | * empty * | | * empty * | | |
| HelpAssistant | | | | 211182921697... | BD8C73557C81... |
| SUPPORT_388945a0 | * empty * | * | | AAD3B435B514... | C23FADD57E66... |
| Mr. Evil | * empty * | * | * empty * | AAD3B435B514... | 31D6CFE0D16A... |

**Figure 3.9** Hashes Populating Cracker Pane

Hashes entry in the left-hand pane, and then back on the LM & NTLM Hashes entry. In the "Add NT hashes from" dialog, click the **Import hashes from a SAM database** radio button, and then paste the boot key (from the clipboard) into the "Boot Key" text field. **Click** the button with the three dots next to the "SAM Filename" text field and navigate to the SAM hive, as illustrated in Figure 3.8.

Click on Next in the "Add NT Hashes from" dialog, and the Cracker pane in Cain gets populated with the LM and NTLM hashes for each user account, as illustrated in Figure 3.9.

We used the same SAM and System hive files as we used with the pwdump7.exe example previously in this chapter, so it should be no surprise that the LM Passwords for the Administrator and Mr. Evil user accounts are listed as "*empty*". In fact, this is excellent validation of our previous findings.

At this point, in order to attempt to crack the password for an account, right-click on a user account, and select the type of password-cracking attack you would like to use, as illustrated in Figure 3.10.

Installing OphCrack (version 3.3.1 at the time of this writing) is a bit different and perhaps a bit more involved than using Cain. Download and install the application, and then be sure to follow the application instructions for downloading and installing the necessary rainbow tables (also available from the Sourceforge.net site; other tables can also be found elsewhere on the Internet). For the purposes of this example, the "XP Free Fast" tables were installed.

To begin, open OphCrack and click the **Load** button, and then select the **Encrypted SAM** option, as illustrated in Figure 3.11.

When the Browse for Folder dialog appears, navigate to the directory where the SAM and System hives that you extracted from your acquired image are located. Once you've selected the directory and clicked **OK**, the **Progress** tab will be populated with the password hashes, as illustrated in Figure 3.12.

As you can see, the NTLM hashes for the Administrator and Mr. Evil user accounts are also listed as "empty" by OphCrack.

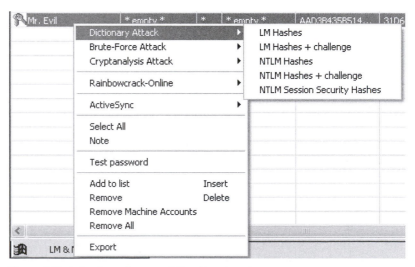

**Figure 3.10** Selecting a Password-Cracking Attack

**Figure 3.11** OphCrack, Load **Encrypted SAM** Option

**Figure 3.12** Password Hashes In OphCrack **Progress** Tab

At this point, if we had user accounts with passwords, and we wanted to attempt to crack them, all we'd need to do is click the **Crack** button (see Figure 3.12).

Again, a detailed discussion of password-cracking attacks or of the Cain or OphCrack applications is beyond the scope of this book. My purpose in providing the information about the tools in this chapter has been to illustrate how freeware tools can be used to derive (and validate) information from Registry hive files; in this case, to illustrate information about user accounts extracted from the SAM database, and to validate whether or not a user account actually has a password associated with it that needs to be typed in by a user. As I mentioned earlier, simply determining whether or not an account has a password has been a very important part of a number of examinations.

### BOOTING AN ACQUIRED IMAGE WITH LiveView

Sometimes during an examination, you may want to "see" what the user saw when they logged into the system. However, if all that is available to you is an acquired image, how can you do this? Well, you can use LiveView to boot the acquired image, but you would still need valid user credentials to log into the system. So, what do you do if you don't have valid credentials for a user account on the system? Actually, it's not all that hard … you just have to be quick.

Before we begin, make sure that you've made a copy of the acquired image … if something should go wrong, we don't want to lose our only source of data. Start by first downloading LiveView, and then downloading the bootable CD release of Peter Nordahl–Hagen's *ntpasswd* utility. As of this writing, the file you're looking for is named "cd100627.zip"; download this file and extract the ISO file from the archive. Follow the LiveView instructions for creating a bootable virtual machine (VM) from the acquired image, and then point the CD player in the VM to the ISO image of the *ntpasswd* utility. Start the VM, and as the system boots, hit **F12** to interrupt the boot sequence. This may take a couple of attempts … the first time I tried it, I didn't successfully access the BIOS until the fourth attempt. Once you do interrupt the boot sequence and access the BIOS, tell the BIOS to boot off of the CD first, save the settings and reboot the system. When it comes back up, follow the *ntpasswd* utility prompts and change the Administrator password. Once you've successfully changed the password, shut the system down, disconnect the CD player in the VM from the ISO, and reboot the system. At this point, you should be able to log into the system with no trouble.

## System Hive

So far in our discussion, we've touched a very little bit on how the System hive can be useful, specifically with respect to extracting password hashes from a SAM hive, in order to determine whether or not a user account has a password, and to attempt to crack it if it does. However, the System hive contains a great deal of configuration information about the system and devices that have been attached to it, so let's take a look at how to derive and interpret some of that data.

Throughout this section, as well as the rest of this chapter, I'm going to be presenting and discussing Registry keys and values that are most often seen, viewed, and accessed during incidents, and subsequently, during analysis. Neither this chapter nor this book is intended to be an all-inclusive listing of Registry keys, as that would be impossible and quite boring. Rather, I'd like to offer up some insight into specific keys and values, and how what you find (or, in some cases, don't find) can be used to further your examination.

## CurrentControlSet

We know that there are portions of the Registry that are volatile, in that they only exist when the system is running. One such key is the CurrentControlSet key in the System hive. Microsoft states that a ControlSet, "contains system configuration information, such as device drivers and services" [17]. When we access the Registry on a live system, we may see two (or more) ControlSet keys (as illustrated in Figure 3.13) in addition to the CurrentControlSet key.

During a postmortem examination, we may need to determine which ControlSet was loaded as the CurrentControlSet when the system was running. In order to do so, all we need to do is view the values within the Select key in the System hive, as illustrated in Figure 3.14.

**Figure 3.13** SYSTEM Hive through RegEdit, Showing the CurrentControlSet

| Name | Type | Data |
|------|------|------|
| (Default) | REG_SZ | (value not set) |
| Current | REG_DWORD | 0x00000001 (1) |
| Default | REG_DWORD | 0x00000001 (1) |
| Failed | REG_DWORD | 0x00000000 (0) |
| LastKnownGood | REG_DWORD | 0x00000003 (3) |

**Figure 3.14** Contents of Select Key in the System Hive

## Note

Most of the RegRipper plug-ins that access the System hive will first check the "Current" value within the Select key, and then extract information from the appropriate ControlSet, based on the value data. This is simply a matter of preference and not a hard-and-fast requirement; plug-ins can be written to access all of the available ControlSets (I have seen System hives with three ControlSets listed) and search for/extract the desired information from each one. This may be useful for comparison, particularly, if the LastWrite times on the keys themselves differ.

Within the Select key, the Current value tells us which ControlSet was loaded as the CurrentControlSet when the system was running. This helps us understand a bit about the system state when it was running; for example, each ControlSet contains a list of Services installed on the system and how they are set to run (i.e., automatically at boot, disabled, and so on).

## Services

Perhaps one of the most referenced and analyzed pieces of information in the System hive, particularly during incident response activities, is the Windows services. Windows services (referred to in the Linux world as "daemons") are programs that run automatically when the system is booted, and are started by the system and with no interaction from the user (however, users with the appropriate privileges can install, start, and stop services). Windows services can be very useful; Web and FTP servers, as well as DNS and DHCP servers, are all Windows services. However, the nature of Windows services (run automatically within no user interaction, as well as with elevated privileges) makes them a target for malware authors, as well, and a great number of bits of malware install as Windows services.

Services on Windows systems can be extremely powerful; they generally run with elevated privileges and start without any interaction from the user beyond booting the system. Is there any wonder why services are targeted so often by malware authors and intruders? Not so much to exploit a vulnerability (yes, that does happen), but instead to use Windows services as a persistence mechanism, ensuring that the malware or backdoor or IRC bot is started each time the system is booted.

In many cases, experienced incident responders will be able to look at a system Registry and "magically" pick out the obscure or malicious services. Some malware creates services with random names, so a quick look at the Registry is all it takes to find

# Warning

Creating services (and other actions, such as submitting Scheduled Tasks) on Windows systems requires Administrator-level privileges; as such, the fact that new services had been created tells you something about the level of access that the malware or the intruder had on the system. Analysts often see partial infections by malware, where the infection process was hindered by the fact that user context that was involved did not have Administrator privileges on the system. So while limiting user privileges can prevent or hamper the effects of a compromise, the flip side is that the artifacts of a compromise that you do find can tell you a lot about what may have happened.

the offending service. Another technique that used to be followed by incident responders and analysts was to look for services that did not have a *Description* value; many legitimate services have descriptions, and some of them can be kind of long, depending on the vendor. The bad guys learned from these techniques, and began using services names that looked a bit more legitimate and began filling in the various values to make the service itself look more legitimate, at least when the values were seen through a Registry viewer. For instance, there have been Description values that appear legitimate, and I have seen others that have had some misspellings (i.e., "down load" spelled as two words) which was enough for me to take a closer look.

Another value beneath a service key that can provide a good deal of context and perspective to an examination is the Start value. A description of the various Start values can be found in MS KB article 103000 [18]. In most instances, you'd expect a Start value of "0x02," indicating that the service is autoloaded, or run automatically. Every now and again, I see malware services that have a Start value of 0x03, which indicates that they're set to start manually, meaning that a user must do something, take some action, for the service to be started. This can be critical when attempting to determine the "window of compromise" for a customer. Basically, if the malware service was installed with a Start value of 0x03, started and run, and then the system shut down, when the system was started again, the service would not start automatically. This may play a significant role in your examination.

RegRipper includes a number of plug-ins for extracting service key information from the System hive, and to be honest, because RegRipper is open-source, there's really no limit to how you present the information. Most of the plug-ins will start off by locating the ControlSet00$n$ marked "Current" in the Select

# Warning

I was performing emergency incident response for an organization that had some issues with malware. The malware wasn't wide-spread, and didn't seem to be infecting systems; in fact, all indications were that the malware was isolated to just a few systems, and the organization simply wanted it gone. Using regedit.exe, I found a service that appeared to be suspicious, deleted it and rebooted the system … but the malware wasn't gone. In this case, the malware used two services for persistence … one that was the malware, and the other that checked for the existence of the malware, and if it didn't find it, installed it.

During another incident response engagement, we had located a malicious service that had a Start value of 0x02 and would dump the virtual memory from credit card back office processing software and collect track data from the memory dump. Using some commercial tools, we found that the service had a *sleep()* function; it used this because when the system is first started, there is no credit card data in memory. Instead, it would read the contents of a register, shift the value to the right four times, and then *sleep()* that number of seconds; based on other artifacts, it appeared at one point to *sleep()* for several days. Under the circumstances, understanding the interaction of the malware on the system, taking all factors into account, helped us provide the customer with a more accurate window of compromise.

In another instance, the first real indicator I'd seen of malicious services was an Event Log record. The source was "Service Control Manager" and the event ID was 7035, indicating that a service had started … even though our findings indicated that the system had been running for quite some time. Further examination indicated that the service was set to start when the system was booted. All other information about the service appeared to be legitimate, even down to the executable file appearing to be a legitimate Windows file.

The point is that it's not always easy to locate a suspicious service or process, particularly when the bad guy is trying really hard to not be discovered.

key of the System hive; however, this is not a hard-and-fast requirement. Plug-ins can be written that will display the same key/value information from all of the available ControlSets, or you can write a plug-in to display the information from both ControlSets if the information itself is not the same in both (or all … I've seen hives with more than two ControlSets) locations. Some of the current plug-ins that retrieve service key information include services.pl, svc.pl, and svc2.pl.

Not long ago, the bad guys were found to be using an even trickier technique to hide and maintain the persistence of their malware or backdoors. Instead of creating a service with an ImagePath value that pointed directly to the malware executable file, they were creating a service that was loaded by the venerable svchost.exe process. Svchost.exe [19] is essentially a "service host," in that multiple copies of svchost.exe can be running, each "hosting" multiple services running from DLLs. When the svchost.exe process starts, it reads through the Registry to see which services it needs to be running, under which instances.

## Note

The Microsoft\Windows NT\CurrentVersion\SvcHost key from within the Software hive can also provide information about services that should be running "under" svchost.exe.

The svcdll.pl plug-in combs through the services keys within the System hive ControlSet identified as "Current" and displays all of those that are loaded by svchost.exe, sorting them based on their key LastWrite times. The svchost.pl plug-in extracts the values and data from the SvcHost key within the Software hive. Because RegRipper and its plug-ins are open-source, anyone with a modicum of Perl programming skill can easily create new plug-ins that perform different functions or display the output in a more meaningful manner.

Services that run under svchost.exe have ImagePath values that contain references to svchost.exe itself, such as:

```
%SystemRoot%\system32\svchost.exe -k netsvcs
```

Then, beneath the service key, there will be a "Parameters" subkey that contains a value named "ServiceDll," which points to the DLL from which the service is run. Conficker is an example of a worm that used this technique for persistence. By creating a service in this manner, it makes the malware a bit harder to find, but not impossible. All we have to do is drop down to the Parameters subkey beneath the malicious service, and the ServiceDll value will point us to the offending malware. Some of the things we'd want to look for with respect to the listed DLL are unusual paths (i.e., the path name includes "temp," and so on), odd looking or apparently names for the DLL itself, and so on. Looking at the referenced DLL itself, misspelled or missing file version information, evidence of the use of a packer to obfuscate the executable code, and so on, are indicators of possibly malicious files.

A side effect of the use of services as a persistence mechanism for malware is that the Windows operating system "does things" that can make an analyst's task of locating the malware, or the initial date that the system was compromised, a bit easier. In particular, when a service or device driver is actually "run," in many cases, an entry beneath the System\CurrentControlSet\Enum\Root appears; specifically, a subkey whose name is "LEGACY_<*service name*>," as shown in Figure 3.15.

Again, these keys appear to be created relatively close to the time that the service is first run. During multiple malware and intrusion examinations involving the creation of services (particularly those that are loaded and run through svchost.exe), there appears to be a correlation between when the file was first

**Figure 3.15** Enum\Root\LEGACY_* keys

created on the system, an Event Log entry indicating that the service was started, and the LastWrite time on the LEGACY_* subkey related to the service. This information can be very valuable when attempting to determine and/or validate the time frame of the initial compromise, or an overall window of compromise.

Beneath each of these LEGACY_* keys, you will often find a subkey named "0000," which also appears to be created and modified in some way when a service is launched. Therefore, the LastWrite time on the LEGACY_*\0000 key for a particular service should closely approximate the last time the service was run. For example, on a Windows XP Service Pack 3 system that I was examining, the Browser service was configured to start automatically when the system booted. The LastWrite time on the Browser service key was 11 August, 2010, at approximately 08:10:28 UTC, and the LastWrite time on the LEGACY_BROWSER\0000 key was 08:11:23 UTC on the same day. As it turned out, the system had last been booted at approximately 08:08 UTC on 11 August, 2010. The LastWrite time on the LEGACY_BROWSER key was 9 May, 2008 at approximately 01:56:17 UTC, which approximates to the time that the system was installed. This same sort of analysis applies to services that are started manually, and should be carefully considered as part of your analysis, including correlating this information with other artifacts from the image, such as Event Log entries, and so on.

During an examination I was working on, not long ago, I found what turned out to be a service installed in conjunction with an incident. I say "an incident" because, as is sometimes the case, when examining a system to determine the root cause of one incident, I run across indications of a previous or multiple

## Note

The legacy.pl plug-in extracts the names of the LEGACY_* subkeys from the Enum\Root key and displays them sorted based on their LastWrite times. Correlating this information with the svcdll.pl and scv2.pl plug-ins (or any others that extract information about services) can prove to be very beneficial in locating malware, as well as establishing the time frame of the initial intrusion.

incidents. In some instances, I've found indications of multiple different bits of malware, as well as one or more intrusions. In this case, I found a service that had been installed, and the file system metadata (i.e., time stamps) for the executable file indicated that it had been created on the system in February, 2009, which was 15 months earlier to the incident I had been asked to investigate. The LastWrite time on both the LEGACY_* and LEGACY_*\0000 subkeys for the service indicated that it had been first launched shortly after the executable file had been created on the system, and that was the only time that the service had been launched. Further analysis determined that the service was not configured to start automatically when the system was booted, but instead was set to be started manually.

Another way that the LastWrite time for the LEGACY_* key can be useful in determining the time frame of an incident or intrusion is when the executable file (.exe or .dll file) itself is subject to "time stomping." That is, there is malware that, when it is installed, the executable file Mac times are modified so that it remains hidden from rudimentary detection techniques, such as searching for new files on a system based on creation dates or creating a timeline of system activity for analysis. In this case, an anomaly may be detected if the creation date for the executable file were sometime in 2004, but the LastWrite time for the service's LEGACY_* key were, say, in 2009.

I, and others, have used this technique to great effect. There have been a number of examinations during which I have found a

## Tip

As noted earlier in this book, there do not appear to be any publicly available APIs for arbitrarily modifying Registry key LastWrite times, as there are with respect to file Mac times (i.e., *SetFileTime()*). As such, a better source of file system metadata that you could correlate to the LastWrite time of the service's LEGACY_* key would be the creation date from the file's $FILE_NAME attribute in the MFT.

suspicious file, or an unusual service referenced in the Event Log, and locating the LEGACY_* entry in the Enum\Root key has led me to other interesting information in my timeline. In most cases, I've seen file creations "nearby" in the timeline that provide me with a clear indication of the initial indicators of the incident.

## USB Devices

Another item of interest to analysts will often be the devices (particularly USB devices) that had been attached to the system. Research into this area has been going on for some time; Cory Altheide and I published some of our joint research in this area in 2005, and some more recent analysis findings have been documented by Rob Lee on the SANS Forensic Blog [20] on 9 September, 2009. In short, the System hive maintains a great deal of information about the devices and when they were attached to the system (some additional information about when the devices were attached will be discussed in Chapter 4, "Case Studies: Tracking User Activity").

In short, when a USB device is connected to a Windows system, the Plug-and-Play (PnP) manager receives the notification and queries the device. Information about the device, extracted from the device descriptor (not part of the memory area of the device) is then stored in the System hive beneath the CurrentControlSet\Enum\USBStor and \USB subkeys. The storage device is then (most often) recognized as a disk device and mounted as a drive letter/volume on the system. As such, additional information related to the device is recorded in the MountedDevices key within the System hive, as well as two subkeys beneath the Control\DeviceClasses key.

Let's take a look at what this looks like in the System hive. First, beneath the Enum\USBStor key, we can find where devices are listed, first by a key known as a device class identifier (ID), and by a subkey beneath the device ID known as the unique instance ID, as shown in Figure 3.16.

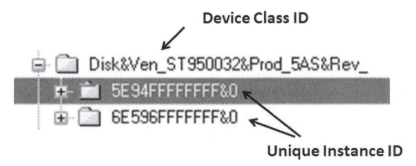

**Figure 3.16** USB Device in the Enum\USBStor Key

**Figure 3.17** Unique Instance ID Assigned by Windows

As you can see in Figure 3.16, the device class ID tells us a little bit about the device itself (in this case, the device is a 500GB Seagate "wallet" drive). Beneath the device class ID, we see two unique instance IDs, which are the device serial numbers extracted from the device descriptor of each device. In each case, the unique instance ID key contains information about the devices within Registry values, including the device "FriendlyName" (in both cases, "ST950032 5A2 USB Drive").

Now, not every USB device has a serial number in its device descriptor. In such cases, Windows will assign a unique instance ID to the device. In order to tell when this is the case, take a look at the unique instance ID for the device, and if the second character (*not* the second to last character, but the second character in the string) is an "&" (as illustrated in Figure 3.17), then the unique instance ID was created and assigned by the operating system, rather than extracted from the device descriptor of the device.

## Mapping Devices to Drive Letters

Once we have information about the USB devices attached to the system, we can attempt to map that device to a drive letter. This may not always be possible, particularly, if multiple devices had been successively connected to the system. For example, I've connected a thumb drive to my system that has been mounted as the drive letter F:\. Later, I disconnect the device, and then at some point connect another device, which is also mounted as the F:\ drive.

Before continuing, we need to understand that Windows treats external USB drives (hard drives in enclosures, such as "wallet" drives) and thumb drives or USB keys differently. Specifically, thumb drives contain a value within their unique

## Note

The usbstor.pl RegRipper plug-in extracts information from the Enum\USBStor key; specifically, for each device class ID, it lists the FriendlyName value (and where applicable, the ParentIdPrefix value) for each unique instance ID (listed as "S/N" for serial number in the plug-in output). The Enum\USB key contains information about all USB devices that had been connected to the system (quite naturally, on some systems, I have entries for "Tableau USB-to-SATA" device), and the usbdevices.pl plug-in will extract this information.

instance ID key called the *ParentIdPrefix*; external drives do not contain this value. I have also seen that neither the storage component of my Motorola MB300 BackFlip smartphone nor a Garmin Nuvi (both the SD card and the flash device) will have a *ParentIdPrefix* value populated beneath the unique instance ID key. The usbstor.pl RegRipper plug-in will display the *ParentIdPrefix* value for those devices that have the value, as illustrated as follows:

```
Disk&Ven_Generic-&Prod_Multi-Card&Rev_1.00 [Sat Jan 2
  12:56:01 2010]
 S/N: 20071114173400000&0 [Sun Aug 1 10:06:03 2010]
  FriendlyName : Generic- Multi-Card USB Device
  ParentIdPrefix: 7&24e8d74f&0
```

However, as indicated, external drives (usually, those in enclosures, produced by Maxtor, Western Digital, and so on) will not have *ParentIdPrefix* values, as illustrated as follows:

```
Disk&Ven_Maxtor&Prod_OneTouch&Rev_0125 [Thu Mar 4 15:50:13
  2010]
 S/N: 2HAPT6RO____&0 [Wed Jun 30 01:27:21 2010]
  FriendlyName : Maxtor OneTouch USB Device
 S/N: 2HAPT6VY____&0 [Thu Jul 8 00:34:48 2010]
  FriendlyName : Maxtor OneTouch USB Device
```

This is important because we may be able to use this information to map a thumb drive or key to a drive letter. I say "may be able to" because it really depends on how soon after the device being connected to the system that an image (or just the System hive) is acquired from the system. As I mentioned earlier, drive letters will very often be reused, so disconnecting one device and connecting another may result in both devices being assigned the same drive letter.

All of the values within the MountedDevices key have binary data. However, different data can mean different things. For instance, Figure 3.18 illustrates an excerpt of values from the

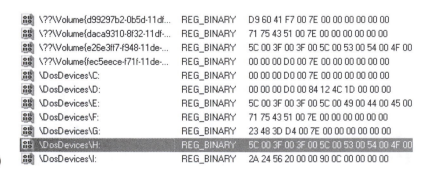

**Figure 3.18** Excerpt of Values from MountedDevices Key (RFV)

| | | |
|---|---|---|
| \??\Volume{d99297b2-0b5d-11df... | REG_BINARY | D9 60 41 F7 00 7E 00 00 00 00 00 00 |
| \??\Volume{daca9310-8f32-11df-... | REG_BINARY | 71 75 43 51 00 7E 00 00 00 00 00 00 |
| \??\Volume{e26e3ff7-f948-11de-... | REG_BINARY | 5C 00 3F 00 3F 00 5C 00 53 00 54 00 4F 00 |
| \??\Volume{fec5eece-f71f-11de-... | REG_BINARY | 00 00 00 D0 00 7E 00 00 00 00 00 00 |
| \DosDevices\C: | REG_BINARY | 00 00 00 D0 00 7E 00 00 00 00 00 00 |
| \DosDevices\D: | REG_BINARY | 00 00 00 D0 00 84 12 4C 1D 00 00 00 |
| \DosDevices\E: | REG_BINARY | 5C 00 3F 00 3F 00 5C 00 49 00 44 00 45 00 |
| \DosDevices\F: | REG_BINARY | 71 75 43 51 00 7E 00 00 00 00 00 00 |
| \DosDevices\G: | REG_BINARY | 23 48 3D D4 00 7E 00 00 00 00 00 00 |
| \DosDevices\H: | REG_BINARY | 5C 00 3F 00 3F 00 5C 00 53 00 54 00 4F 00 |
| \DosDevices\I: | REG_BINARY | 2A 24 56 20 00 00 90 0C 00 00 00 00 |

```
\.?.?.\.S.T.O.R.
A.G.E.#.R.e.m.o.
v.a.b.l.e.M.e.d.
i.a.#.7.&.2.4.e.
8.d.7.4.f.&.0.&.
R.M.#.{.5.3.f.5.
6.3.0.d.-.b.6.b.
f.-.1.1.d.0.-.9.
4.f.2.-.0.0.a.0.
c.9.1.e.f.b.8.b.
}.
```

**Figure 3.19** MountedDevices Key Value Data Showing ParentIdPrefix

MountedDevices key of a System hive file, viewed through the Windows Registry File Viewer (RFV).

As you can see from Figure 3.18, there are two basic types of value names; those that begin with "\DosDevices\" and refer to a drive or volume letter, and those that begin with "\??\Volume" and refer to volumes. These values have data of different lengths; some are 12 bytes long, whereas others are longer. Many of the longer ones are actually Unicode strings that refer to devices, strings that we can read by double-clicking the value (RFV opens a Data View dialog). The contents of the data for "\DosDevices\H:" (highlighted in Figure 3.18) is shown in Figure 3.19.

The Unicode string in Figure 3.19 refers to a removable storage device ("\??\Storage#RemovableMedia#," in this case, a USB device), and the highlighted substring "7&24e8d74f&0" is the *ParentIdPrefix* value for one of the USB devices that had been connected to the system. Therefore, we can use the *ParentIdPrefix* value to map a USB thumb drive from the Enum\USBStor key to a volume identifier within the MountedDevices key, and possibly even to a drive letter. An important factor to keep in mind, however, is that if you plug in one device that is mapped to drive H:\, disconnect it, and then connect another device that is mapped to drive H:\, the previous data for "\DosDevices\H:" is replaced.

## GETTING HISTORICAL INFORMATION

Historical information about drive mappings in the hive files can be found in Windows XP system restore points, as well as within hive files from volume shadow copies on Vista and above systems.

Using the usbstor.pl RegRipper plug-in, we can obtain information about USB removable storage devices attached to the system (note that the key LastWrite times are displayed, but are irrelevant to this example), an excerpt of which is illustrated as follows:

```
Disk&Ven_Generic-&Prod_Multi-Card&Rev_1.00 [Sat Jan 2
  12:56:01 2010]
 S/N: 20071114173400000&0 [Sun Aug 1 10:06:03 2010]
  FriendlyName : Generic- Multi-Card USB Device
  ParentIdPrefix: 7&24e8d74f&0
```

From the mountdev.pl plug-in, we can get information about the values listed in the MountedDevices key, which appears as follows:

```
Device: \??\STORAGE#RemovableMedia#7&24e8d74f&0&RM#{53f5630d-
  b6bf-11d0-94f2-00a0c91efb8b}
    \??\Volume{47042c43-f725-11de-a8a5-806d6172696f}
    \DosDevices\H:
```

So now, we're able to map a USB thumb drive to a drive letter. But what about the USB external drives, such as those in enclosures (i.e., "wallet" drives, and so on)? If you remember from Figure 3.18, several of the values have data that is only 12 bytes long. These are volume identifiers and drive letters that refer to the external drives. In these cases, the first 4 bytes (DWORD) are the drive signature (also known as a volume ID) from the hard drive itself. This signature is written to a hard drive, beginning at offset 0x1b8 (440 in decimal) within the master boot record (MBR) when Windows formats the drive. You can view this value by opening the first 512 bytes of the hard drive (MBR) in a hex editor and navigating to offset 0x1b8. The remaining 8 bytes of the data are the partition or volume offset. In Figure 3.18, we see two drive letters (\DosDevices\C: and \DosDevices\F:) with partition offsets of 0x7e00, which is 32256 in decimal; dividing by 512 byte sectors, this means that the partitions or volumes start at sector 63 on their respective hard drives (note that \DosDevices\C: refers to the hard drive installed in the system, and is used as an example).

What this means is that there is not a direct method for mapping a USB external hard drive listed in the Enum\USBStor key to a drive letter listed in the MountedDevices key.

Although not specifically recognized as a device, per se, the MountedDevices key also maintains information about TrueCrypt [21] volumes that had been mounted on the system, as shown in Figure 3.20.

As you can see, the value name is a bit different from other entries within the MountedDevices key, and the binary data is 16 bytes long and spells out "TrueCryptVolumeU." I have seen other similar values where the data spells out "TrueCryptVolumeT" or

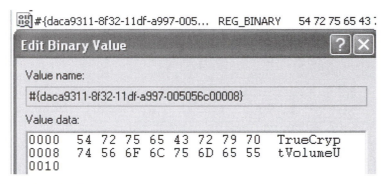

**Figure 3.20** TrueCrypt Volume Listed in the MountedDevices Key

"TrueCryptVolumeS." Although this will give you an indication of a user-accessing TrueCrypt volumes, it does not explicitly tell you where those volumes exist.

## PORTABLE DEVICES

On Vista and Windows 7, even more information is maintained about attached (portable) devices, albeit in the Software hive. Beneath the Microsoft\Windows Portable Devices\Devices key, you will see a number of subkeys that refer to devices. The subkey names can be parsed to get the name of the device and, if available, the device serial number. These subkeys also contain a value named "FriendlyName," which, in many instances, will include the drive letter to which it was mounted, such as "Removable Disk (F:)." Further testing is required, but in some limited sample cases, the LastWrite time for the device subkey seems to correlate closely to the time that the device was last connected to the system. For example, on one Vista test system, a device (DISK&VEN_BEST_BUY&PROD_GEEK_SQUAD_U3&REV_6.15, with serial number 0C90195032E36889&0) had a subkey beneath the Devices key with the LastWrite time of Thu Feb 7 13:26:19 2008 (UTC). The corresponding subkey for the same device, beneath the DeviceClasses subkey (we will discuss this key later in the chapter), had a LastWrite time of Thu Feb 7 13:26:02 2008 (UTC).

When a USB device is first plugged into a Windows system, the PnP manager queries the device to determine information about the device, in order to figure out which drivers to load for that device. On Windows XP and 2003 systems, this information is maintained in the setupapi.log file (for Vista/Windows 7, the file is setupapi.dev.log [22]). Once the device is loaded, two additional keys are created for the device beneath the DeviceClasses key within the System hive. Both of these keys are globally unique identifiers (GUIDs); one refers to disks, and the other refers to volumes, as shown below:

```
Disk GUID - {53f56307-b6bf-11d0-94f2-00a0c91efb8b}
Volume GUID - {53f5630d-b6bf-11d0-94f2-00a0c91efb8b}
```

Both of these GUIDs are defined in the ntddstor.h header file used in Windows. The first GUID, which begins with "53f56307," is defined as GUID_DEVINTERFACE_DISK, or Disk-ClassGUID, and refers to disk devices. An example of what the DiskClassGUID subkeys look like is shown in Figure 3.21.

As shown in Figure 3.21, we see keys whose names begin with "##?#USBSTOR#"; these keys go on to contain device names that look very much like the device descriptor names from the USBStor key mentioned earlier in the chapter. The key name also contains the unique device descriptor or serial number for the device. According to research conducted and published by Rob Lee (of Mandiant and SANS fame), the LastWrite time for this key indicates the first time that the device was last connected to the system during the most recent boot session. What this means is that if the system was booted at 8:30 A.M. and the device was connected to the system at 9:00 A.M., disconnected, and then reconnected later that day, the LastWrite time of the device's subkey beneath the DiskClassGUID key will be 9:00 A.M. This should remain consistent regardless of the number of times the device is disconnected and reconnected to the system.

**Figure 3.21** DiskClassGUID Keys in Windows XP System Hive

# Tip

According to Rob Lee's research, the time that a USB device was last connected to a Vista system can be correlated to the LastWrite time of the ControlSet00*n*\Enum\USB key for the device. For Windows 7 systems, the LastWrite time of the ControlSet00*n*\Enum\USBStor key for the device will tell you when it was last connected to the system.

**Figure 3.22** VolumeClassGUID Keys in Windows XP System Hive

The other GUID is defined as GUID_DEVINTERFACE_VOLUME, or VolumeClassGUID, and refers to volumes. The subkeys beneath this key are associated with volumes that are mounted on the system, as shown in Figure 3.22.

As illustrated in Figure 3.22, the device's key name contains the ParentIdPrefix value for the device, mentioned earlier in this chapter.

## USB DEVICES

According to research conducted and presented by Rob Lee, additional information regarding determining the last time that a USB device was connected to a system is available in the user's NTUSER.DAT hive, specifically beneath the MountPoints2 key. This will be discussed in greater detail in Chapter 4, "Case Studies: Tracking User Activity," but this provides an analyst with two important pieces of information: First one is, of course, the last time that the device was connected to the system. The second one is that by the presence of the key within the user's hive, there is now an association with a specific user. Although a device may have been connected to a system, the analyst will be able to determine the time frame that it was last connected, which may be important when developing a time line of activity on the system, as well as which user account was logged in when the device was connected.

## Printers

There may be times during examinations when you will want to know which printer or printers the system had access to, and may have used. For example, many analysts are familiar with metadata maintained by documents, in particular MS Office Word and Excel documents that use the older OLE/structured storage format (pre-Office 2000 documents), and this information can provide significant information during examinations involving the possible theft of intellectual property. One of the pieces of metadata maintained in some documents is the date that the document was last printed.

## Warning

A lack of awareness of document metadata issues was probably best exemplified by the issues face by the British government in 2003, as shown by the ComputerBytesMan [23].

Knowing which printer documents may have been sent to may be helpful in developing further information about the case. MS KB article 102966 [24] provides some excellent information about the keys with the System hive (as well as within the user's hive) that pertain to printers known to the system.

## Firewall Policies

With Windows XP Service Pack 2, Microsoft introduced a firewall capability (which is now included with all versions of Windows [25]) with the operating system distribution. Previously, if you wanted some kind of firewall capability, you had to download and install one on your system, or you had to set up another system on your network to provide that capability. The Windows firewall is usually accessed and managed through a Control Panel applet or the *netsh* command locally, or through group policies in a domain environment; however, as one would assume, the configuration information for the Windows firewall is maintained in the Registry, in the following key path:

```
ControlSet00n\Services\SharedAccess\Parameters\
   FirewallPolicy\
```

There are two policies available in subkeys beneath the FirewallPolicy key: StandardProfile and DomainProfile. The StandardProfile key contains the firewall configuration for a standalone system (laptop, home system, and so on), while the DomainProfile maintains information about the firewall configuration while the system is connected to a Windows domain. These keys on a Windows XP system are illustrated in Figure 3.23.

Figure 3.23 is just a representative indication of the subkeys available beneath each profile key. Besides AuthorizedApplications, there may also be an ICMPSettings key, as well as GloballyOpenPorts key. The values beneath these keys (or beneath their respective List subkeys) essentially provide the firewall rules, if the firewall itself is enabled.

Why is this important? Well, there is a good bit of malware out there that, on infecting a system, will attempt to disable security

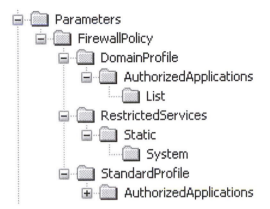

**Figure 3.23** Firewall Keys (Windows XP)

services, such as antivirus and even the firewall. Beneath the profile key are values such as EnableFirewall and DisableNotifications, and some malware (for example, fake security software [26]) will set these values such that the firewall and notifications (of such things like the firewall not being enabled) will be disabled. In these situations, it's a good idea to document the profile key's LastWrite time and see if it correlates to other malicious activity (i.e., malware installation, other files or Registry keys being created or modified on the system, and so on), as this may provide you with additional clues as to the extent of the infection or compromise. In other instances, malware has added entries to the list of applications authorized to communicate out through the firewall (for an example, see www.securelist.com/en/descriptions/old126765 [27]). The RegRipper fw_config.pl plug-in does a very good job of retrieving firewall settings information from Windows XP systems, and presenting it in an easy-to-understand format. For example, below is an AuthorizedApplications\List value I found during an examination of a Windows XP system thought to be infected with malware (wrapped for clarity):

```
C:\Documents and Settings\user\Local Settings\Temporary
  Internet Files\
  Content.IE5\DN3ZPPK2\EZWebUpdate [1].exe -> C:\Documents and
  Settings\
  user\Local Settings\Temporary Internet Files\Content.IE5\
  DN3ZPPK2\EZWebUpdate [1].exe:*:Enabled:EZWebUpdate
```

It's not often that you find an authorized application running from the user's temporary Internet files directory (or "Local Settings\Temp" directory, either, for that matter). This particular system also had entries allowing multiple peer-to-peer applications (Kazaa, Limewire, and so on), as well as other applications and games (WinVNC, Worlds of Warcraft, FarCry, WS_FTP, and so on), to communicate off of the system. Looking beneath this key, or beneath the GloballyOpenPorts\List key, will often provide indicators of possible issues on the system.

With Windows Vista came improvements in the network stack, along with some corresponding changes in how the firewall is configured and managed (see "Exploring the Windows Firewall" on Technet [28]). There were also changes to the Registry, as seen in Figure 3.24.

In Figure 3.24, we see the addition of a "PublicProfile," as well as key called "FirewallRules." According to MS KB article 947213 [29], the PublicProfile applies to a network interface when the system is not connected to a domain and the administrator has not specified that the network is private; this would apply to public Wifi connections, such as at coffee shops, libraries, and so on. Each of the profile keys contains values that indicate if the profile was enabled at the time that the image was acquired, as well as a Logging subkey that points to information such as the location of the firewall log file (C:\Windows\system32\LogFiles\Firewall\pfirewall.log, by default on Windows Vista and Windows 7), the size of the firewall log, and whether successful connections and dropped packets are logged.

A discussion of the FirewallRules key and the values/rules it contains is beyond the scope of this book; suffice to say that there is a good deal of information available at the Microsoft Web site (including MS KB article 947709 [30]) that provides information on interacting with the firewall through tools such as the *netsh* command. From an analyst's perspective, understanding how the firewall works may provide indicators or answers as to what may have occurred on the system.

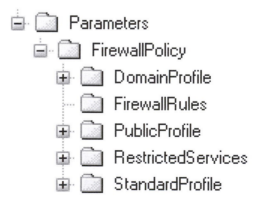

**Figure 3.24** Windows Vista Firewall Keys through RFV

As Windows 7 becomes more pervasive (and Windows XP fades into the mists of time), analysts are going to need to become familiar with analyzing firewall configurations and rules on these systems. The newer settings are a bit more complex, but will likely be used to allow access to and from the system, just as they were on Windows XP. The applications that protect a system will also likely be subverted in order to disable them, or to allow malicious functionality.

## Routes

One of the tricks that malware authors have used to "protect" their tools is to add entries to the hosts file so that critical assets (update sites for the operating system, applications, antivirus, and so on) cannot be reached. By forcing the query for a host or domain to resolve to a specific IP address, malware authors can inhibit the functionality. After all, you wouldn't want the installed antimalware product to update itself and then detect the presence of your malware, would you?

This is also something that can be used legitimately. According to the MS KB article on name resolution order [31], after checking to see if a name is its own, a Windows system will then check the hosts file. System administrators can add entries that redirect traffic to specific sites, and even some antimalware and antispyware applications will modify this file to force known-bad hosts or domains to resolve to the local host (i.e., 127.0.0.1). Parents can also do this with Facebook and MySpace!

Another technique that can be used is to modify persistent routes on the system. One command, which many incident responders run when collecting information is *route print*, which displays the current routing table for TCP/IP communications on the system. This facility also has the ability to add persistent routes that will remain in place between reboots, through the *route add* command [32]. If an added route is designated as "persistent" through the use of the "–p" switch, the command adds the routes to a Registry key within the System hive (which can be extracted using the routes.pl RegRipper plug-in). Interestingly enough, malware such as Backdoor.Rohimafo (a description of this malware is available at the Symantec Web site) appears to add persistent routes to the system in order to prevent the system from accessing sites that may result in updates that allow the malware to be detected.

As we discussed in Chapter 2, "Tools," Michael Hale Ligh requested me to review a chapter of an upcoming book entitled *Malware Analyst's Cookbook and CD: Tools and Techniques For*

*Fighting Malicious Code* (Wiley Publishing, no publication date available as of this writing), which he's coauthoring. In the chapter, the authors referred to the use of RegRipper and some plug-ins that they'd created for use in malware detection, and asked me to review the chapter to make sure that the information about RegRipper was technically correct (it was!). One of the plug-ins described in the chapter was, in fact, one that parses the persistent routes from the following key in the System hive:

```
ControlSet00n\Services\Tcpip\Parameters\PersistentRoutes
```

When I reviewed the chapter, I e-mailed Michael to let him know that I had recently written my own plug-in (routes.pl) to do the same thing. I'd been involved in examining a system where searches of the system for a specific IP address range had returned hits in the System hive, and a closer examination had revealed that the IP address was listed in the PersistentRoutes key.

## PendingFileRenameOperations

Another plug-in that the authors described in the chapter that Michael Hale Ligh asked me to review extracted the contents of the following key:

```
ControlSet00n\Control\Session  Manager\PendingFileRename-
Operations
```

Apparently, there are examples of malware that, in order to clean up behind itself, will attempt to delete files using the *MoveFileEx()* API function with the MOVEFILE_DELAY_UNTIL_REBOOT flag set; when this API function is used, the files to be deleted will be written to the PendingFileRenameOperations key. The next time that the system is booted, the Session Manager will parse the contents of the key for file name pairs; if the second entry is empty, the file is deleted.

There are two important factors to keep in mind about this information. The first is that in order to obtain and use the information in this key, you would need to detect and respond to an incident *before* the system is rebooted. The second is that if you are able to respond appropriately and collect the information, the LastWrite time of the key can give you an idea of when the system had been infected.

## Network Interfaces

Much like other devices, information about the network interfaces available on the system is maintained in the System hive. The main path for information about the network interfaces available on a system is the ControlSet00n\Services\Tcpip\Parameters\Interfaces key. Beneath this key, you'll find a number of subkeys whose names are globally unique identifiers (or GUIDs, pronounced *goo-idz*). Each of these subkeys refers to a specific interface, and the GUID names can be mapped to more easily readable names for the interfaces (see the "Network Cards" subsection later in this chapter).

The interface subkeys contain information about IP addresses assigned (static assignments or through DHCP), gateways, domains, as well as when DHCP leases were assigned, and when they terminate. This information can be extremely helpful during a wide variety of examinations, particularly when attempting to tie a particular system to entries found in router or Web or FTP server logs. An excerpt of what this information looks like in the Registry is shown in Figure 3.25.

| | | |
|---|---|---|
| DhcpDefaultGateway | REG_MULTI... | 192.168.1.1 |
| DhcpDomain | REG_SZ | chvlva.adelphia.net |
| DhcpIPAddress | REG_SZ | 192.168.1.10 |
| DhcpNameServer | REG_SZ | 192.168.0.1 |
| DhcpRetryStatus | REG_DWORD | 0x00000000 (0) |
| DhcpRetryTime | REG_DWORD | 0x0000a8bd (43197) |
| DhcpServer | REG_SZ | 192.168.1.1 |
| DhcpSubnetMask | REG_SZ | 255.255.255.0 |
| DhcpSubnetMaskOpt | REG_MULTI... | 255.255.255.0 |
| Domain | REG_SZ | |
| EnableDeadGWDetect | REG_DWORD | 0x00000001 (1) |
| EnableDHCP | REG_DWORD | 0x00000001 (1) |
| IPAddress | REG_MULTI... | 0.0.0.0 |
| IPAutoconfigurationAddress | REG_SZ | 0.0.0.0 |
| IPAutoconfigurationMask | REG_SZ | 255.255.0.0 |
| IPAutoconfigurationSeed | REG_DWORD | 0x00000000 (0) |
| IsServerNapAware | REG_DWORD | 0x00000000 (0) |
| Lease | REG_DWORD | 0x00015180 (86400) |
| LeaseObtainedTime | REG_DWORD | 0x4c739caa (1282645162) |
| LeaseTerminatesTime | REG_DWORD | 0x4c74ee2a (1282731562) |

**Figure 3.25** Excerpt of Network Interface Values (Windows XP)

The RegRipper plug-in nic2.pl does a really good job of extracting this information, and even goes so far as to translate some of the 32-bit time stamp values (LeaseObtainedTime, LeaseTerminatesTime, and so on) into something a bit more human-readable.

### File System Settings

The System hive also maintains information about the configuration of the file system, and there are several settings that may affect your analysis. For example, there is a value named "NtfsDisableLastAccessUpdate" [33], which, back in the early days of Windows XP and 2003, was intended as a setting that could be used to enhance the performance of the system. The intention was that on high-volume file servers, disabling the updating of last access times on files would improve overall performance; however, this was an optional setting at the time, as the value did not exist by default.

Interestingly enough, one of the surprises with the release of Windows Vista was that not only did this value exist, but also updating of last access times on files was disabled by default! Consider for a moment the effect that had on a lot of traditional computer forensic methodologies.

Beneath the same key is a value named "NtfsDisable-8dot3NameCreation"; if this value is set to 1 (and the file system is NTFS), then the creation of short file names will be disabled [34]. This may be an issue if you expect to see file names on the system similar to "PORTER~!.PPT" rather than "porter's latest widgets sales presentation.ppt." Enabling this functionality tells the file system to not create the shorter file names.

## Software Hive

The Software hive maintains a great deal of configuration information for the overall system as well as applications, and it can provide indications to a knowledgeable analyst of how the system and installed applications may have appeared, behaved, and

## Tip

Part of computer forensic analysis is not just recognizing what is out of place or unusual; it's also recognizing when some artifact should be present, but isn't.

responded when the system was running. Understanding the role that these keys and values play in configuration of applications and the operating system can provide the analyst with a great deal of insight into a variety of different types of examinations. Throughout this section, we will discuss various keys and values from the Software hive that play a significant role in the overall configuration of the system and applications. Keep in mind, though, that we cannot discuss every possible key and value because, quite simply, I need to finish this book at some point and send it to the printer! Also, there are constantly new applications being developed, as well as current applications (and the operating system) being updated to include new keys and values. What I hope to do is to provide you with insight into some of the keys and values that you can expect to find on a wide range of systems, including Windows XP all the way up through Windows 7.

There are a number of configuration settings that could affect your analysis, and ultimately, your case; in earlier books, I have referred to these as "time bombs," because at the time, they weren't something that I (or others) had seen on a regular basis. We've already mentioned some of these settings in the "System Hive" section of this chapter, and we'll be discussing some of the settings in the Software hive here in this section.

One example of a potential time bomb (or at the very least, something to be aware of) is the ClearPagefileAtShutdown value [35]. This value, when set to 1, tells the system to fill inactive pages in the page file with zeros when the system is shut down. This is described as a "security feature" that prevents information from being read by other processes; however, in some cases, this can also significantly hinder examinations.

An example of additional settings that may have a significant impact on examinations can be found within the Microsoft\Windows\CurrentVersion\Internet Settings key within the Software hive. The exact value names depend on the version of Internet Explorer installed on the system (per [36]), and for IE 7 and 8, the values are "BypassSSLNoCacheCheck" and "BypassHTTPNoCacheCheck," respectively These values, when enabled (i.e., set to 1) tell the system (through the appropriate API) to ignore the "Cache-control:no-store" and "Cache-control:no-cache" settings in HTML headers [37].

Now, these values do not exist by default, and need to be set ahead of time, but they can have a significant impact on examinations, in that malware authors have been seen using the WinInet API to allow their malware to communicate off of systems, notifying the author of infected systems, obtaining updates, uploading captured data, and so on. This, in itself, is nothing new, but it

## Warning

According to several sources, the "Cache-control:no-cache" (and "no-store") settings simply tell the browser to make its best attempt at not caching (or storing) the data; it does not guarantee that no artifacts of the transaction will be produced. These settings are usually used to force refreshing of data, as well as attempting to prevent sensitive information from being stored locally on systems.

can significantly impact your examination when the author uses the "Cache-control:no-cache" HTML header, telling the system to not cache data, meaning that indications of this communication activity will not appear in the index.dat or within the Internet cache (usually within the Temporary Internet Files folder).

Robert Hensing described in his blog [38] on 15 November, 2006 about how the user of specific API functions will cause the index.dat and Internet cache/Temporary Internet Files folder to be updated; in this case, he was referring to how using those APIs from a system-level account (as a result of a successful exploit, and rather than using a "normal" user account) will cause the Internet history of the "Default User" to be updated. So, in short, the use of the APIs results in this update, and in order to leave even fewer indications on the system, some malware authors have been seen using the "no-cache" setting. By "seen," in some cases, I mean that while no indications of the activity were discovered in the Internet history, there were indications found in the page file (had the ClearPagefileAtShutdown value been enabled, these indications may have been overwritten with zeros) or within captured network activity. Therefore, system administrators should consider setting the appropriate Internet Settings values described in MS KB article 323308 in order to tell the system to ignore the "no-cache" setting; however, as with any other settings, these should be thoroughly considered within the context of the overall system and network infrastructure.

There's another value of interest within the Software hive that may have an effect on your examination; the NukeOnDelete value beneath the Microsoft\Windows\CurrentVersion\Explorer\BitBucket key. What this does is allow someone to disable the Recycle Bin functionality; this is similar to the "Shift-Delete" functionality, only it applies across the board, for all actions. For example, if a user goes into Windows Explorer, selects a file, and hits the **Delete** key, under normal circumstances, the file goes to the Recycle Bin. However, if the NukeOnDelete value is present (it's not present by default) and set to 1, then you shouldn't expect to see any files in the Recycle Bin. Figure 3.26 shows the

# Tip

There are a number of Registry keys that exist in both the Software hive as well as within the user's NTUSER.DAT hive, and have identical paths. One example is the Run key [39]. The precedence of these entries will depend on the key itself and what is specified in vendor documentation. Just as with the key in the Software hive, the Run key in the user's NTUSER.DAT hive is also used as a persistence mechanism for malware. In some cases, the key paths are the same, but very different information is maintained within the keys. For example, with the Software hive, the key may maintain configuration information, while within the NTUSER.DAT hive, the key will contain settings, most recently used (MRU) lists, and so on. The Internet Settings values described in MS KB article 323308, for example, allow the system administrator to set the described functionality on a system-wide basis through the Software hive or on a per-user basis by applying those settings to the appropriate user profile.

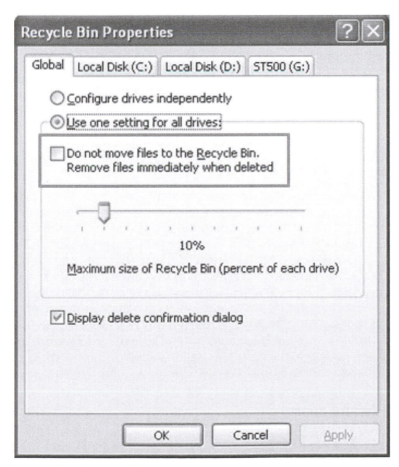

**Figure 3.26** Windows XP Recycle Bin Properties

Recycle Bin properties dialog from Windows XP, and where the NukeOnDelete value can be set. The properties dialog for Windows 7 is very similar, and in fact, uses the same verbiage for the setting.

One indicator that may be of interest is if the NukeOnDelete value is present, but set to 0. As this value does not exist by default on Windows XP or Windows 7, the presence of the value may indicate that the value had been set at one time. As part of your analysis, you may want to correlate the LastWrite time of the Explorer key to other artifacts from the system.

## Redirection

In order to handle some differences between 64-bit and 32-bit systems, Windows (XP, up through and including Windows 7) uses Registry redirection in order to maintain different logical "views" of the Registry, as different versions of software may use different Registry keys and values. In short, the major difference (from the perspective of Registry analysis) is that 32-bit applications run in WOW64 mode will access and write to keys and values beneath the Wow6432Node key [40] within the Software hive. As such, rather than the usual key path that appears as follows:

```
HKEY_LOCAL_MACHINE\Software\Microsoft\Windows\CurrentVersion
```

…you would then see the key path as appears below:

```
HKEY_LOCAL_MACHINE\Software\WOW6432Node\Microsoft\Windows\
    CurrentVersion
```

However, not all Registry keys are redirected on a 64-bit system; some are shared by both 32-bit and 64-bit versions of the operating system. Microsoft maintains a list of redirected and shared keys in the article "Registry Keys Affected by WOW64" [41]. What this means is that when analyzing the Registry from 64-bit systems, you'll need to be cognizant of the updated key path and how it applies when viewing hives through a Registry viewer, or be sure to modify your RegRipper plug-ins to take this into account.

Oddly enough, I have seen the Wow6432Node key play an important role on one engagement; several years ago, I was on an engagement where the customer had installed a 32-bit version of MS SQL Server on a 64-bit version of Windows 2003 Server.

## File Associations

In order to stay current in this profession, one of the activities I engage in is to be an active member of several lists and forums. This way, I get to not only ask questions of my own, but I can see questions posted and responded to by others, and this can be very educational. One of the questions I see time and again in a wide range of venues is "which application uses a file with this extension?" or something similar. In short, it appears that an analyst has found a file on a system with a particular extension, and wants to know which application uses or created that file. In most instances, if an application creates a file with a particular extension, it can then also be used to read that file, or process it in some manner.

The usual response to questions such as these is to refer the original poster to any one of a number of Web sites that maintain information such as this, but to me, this doesn't seem like a very good initial approach. The reason is that when an application is installed on a system, part of the installation process will be to associate particular file extensions with the application. For example, when I install ActiveState Perl on one of my Windows systems, files with the ".pl" extension are associated with the Perl executable. Information about file associations is maintained in the "Classes" key of the Software hive; simply navigate to the key and begin looking for subkeys whose names begin with a dot (i.e., "."). On my Windows XP system, I found the ".bat" extension, which usually refers to batch files. Within that key, the "(Default)" value contains simply "batfile." So, I locate the Classes\batfile key, and navigate through that key to the shell\ open\command key, where the "(Default)" value simply contains "'%1' %*," which indicates that this file type will be executed from the command line. If I were to locate a .bat file through the Windows Explorer shell and right-click on it, and choose **Open** from the drop-down menu, the commands within the batch file would be executed. However, if I navigate to the Classes\ batfile\shell\edit\command key, I see that batch file is associated with Notepad; therefore, if I were to choose "Edit" from the drop-down menu available from the shell, the contents of the file would be visible in Notepad. The RegRipper assoc.pl plug-in automates locating the file extension, and then looking up the shell\open\command value.

Another example of determining file associations involves a more manual approach, as I haven't seen a RegRipper plug-in for this methodology yet. When I open RegEdit on my system and navigate to the Classes key in the Software hive, I see a key named ".kar." The "(Default)" value within this key is empty, but there is a subkey named "OpenWithList" and beneath that key, another key named "QuickTimePlayer.exe." This indicates that file with the ".kar" extension may be opened with Quick-TimePlayer.exe. Other file extensions, such as ".jpe," have two subkeys beneath the "OpenWithList" key: "ois.exe" and "Picture-Viewer.exe."

Still other extensions have different information available through their "(Default)" values. For example, on my system, the ".js" extension has a "(Default)" value of "UltraEdit.js," indicating the files with this extension will be opened in the UltraEdit editor I have installed on my system.

I hope that this shows you that while the Internet can be a valuable resource for conducting searches and finding some interesting information, when attempting to determine a program or application association with a specific file extension, we should first consider the context of that system. I have yet to find a site or resource on the Internet that maintains a comprehensive list of all of the possible applications that could open, access, or create files with a unique extension. I'm not saying that you shouldn't turn to outside resources for assistance; rather, what I'm saying is that the question should first be considered in the context of the system being examined.

## Web Browser

With all this talk about the Internet, it's a good time to discuss some of the information available in the Software hive with respect to the Internet Explorer Web browser. Many times when beginning an analysis of a system, I've seen when analysts have said that they start by checking some of the Registry values specific to Internet Explorer (IE). This is fine … but why start there when there are a number of browsers available? Why focus on one browser from the beginning, when there are a number of possible targets?

There are a number of ways to determine which Web browsers had been used on a system. For example, on Windows XP, Vista, and Windows 7, you can check the available Prefetch files to see which browsers may have been executed. However, if you want to know the default browser in use on the system when a user double-clicks the appropriate file or link, there are a couple of Registry values you can check. One is the default (actually, "(Default)") value for the Clients\StartMenuInternet key. On my system, the value name is "IExplore.exe" (there are also two sub-keys: Firefox.exe and IExplore.exe), but when I log into the system, I double-click the Firefox icon on the desktop. It says this because when the "default browser" dialog appeared the first time I launched the Firefox Web browser, I told it no, I do not want to set Firefox to the default browser, and I disabled the dialog from appearing in the future.

Another place to check is the following key:

```
Classes\HTTP\shell\open\command
```

The "Default" value within this key tells you which Web browser the system will launch when a Web connection is attempted. However, as we discussed earlier in this chapter, there may be settings within a user's NTUSER.DAT Registry hive file that are different and supersede this setting. We will discuss in Chapter 4, "Case Studies: Tracking User Activity," how to determine specifics about a user's use of applications, including the Internet Explorer browser. For the system settings, the defbrowser.pl RegRipper plug-in will extract the necessary information from both of the keys that we've discussed.

If it does turn out that the Web browser in use on a system is Internet Explorer (IE), then another area that can be examined for indications of malware is the Browser Helper Objects (BHOs) listing, which is found in the following key in the Software hive:

```
Microsoft\Windows\CurrentVersion\Explorer\Browser Helper
  Objects
```

BHOs are DLLs that IE can load to provide additional functionality and allow for customization to the browser, much like plug-ins used for Firefox, or shell extensions for Windows Explorer (discussed in the "Shell Extensions" section later in this chapter). Examples of common BHOs include those for the Adobe Acrobat Reader, and the Google, Alexa, and Ask.com toolbars. Again, these are DLLs that are loaded by IE and not when the system is booted or a user logs into the system. If IE is not launched, the DLLs will not be loaded. However, if IE is used, then the DLLs will be loaded without any interaction with the user.

The use of BHOs to load malicious software is nothing new. In 2002, I was working in a full-time employment (as opposed to consulting) position at a company where someone had found something a bit unusual on her system. It turns out that the employee was in the marketing department, so what she found was indeed concerning. She was viewing the online content for our company Web site, and she noticed that in each instance where our company name was in the Web page, the name was now a hyperlink … which was not the behavior for which the Web page was designed. Out of curiosity, she clicked on the hyperlink (yeah, bad idea, I know…) and was taken to a competitor's Web page! It turned out that her system had been infected with a BHO that would look for specific words and names in Web pages, and modify the contents of the Web page to create hyperlinks to competitor's Web sites. I use the RegRipper bho.pl plug-in to extract information about BHOs installed on the system for every examination, particularly those that involve malware of some kind.

## Autostart Locations

Much like the System hive, the Software hive contains a number of locations from which applications and programs can be started with little to no interaction from the user beyond simply booting the system and logging in. Many of these locations are used by application authors for completely legitimate purposes; unfortunately, as we've mentioned with respect to BHOs, they're also used by malware authors.

Perhaps the most well-known of all of the autostart locations is the ubiquitous "Run" key (Microsoft\Windows\CurrentVersion\Run) described in MS KB article 199365 [42]. This key has long been used by both malware and legitimate applications as a refuge for persistence, and continues to be used, even today. Not only have I seen malware that creates a value beneath this key as recently as the summer of 2010, but I've seen systems infected by one variant of malware that were later infected by another variant of the same malware (as determined by reviewing the write-ups on the malware), so the Run key contained multiple values that pointed to the malware variants.

Another location of interest within the Software hive is the Microsoft\Windows NT\CurrentVersion\Winlogon\Notify key [43]. Entries beneath this key define packages (most often DLLs) that are to receive notifications from the WinLogon process. These notifications can include when the user logs in and the shell (i.e., Windows Explorer) loads, when the screensaver starts, when the workstation is locked or unlocked, when the user logs out, and so on. All of these actions cause an event to be generated, and packages can be designated to take some action when this occurs. The McAfee Web site includes a write-up of a generic downloader that uses the Winlogon\Notify key as a persistence mechanism [44]. Other examples of malware that makes use of this key include Virtumonde (a.k.a., Vundu) and Contravirus, and a backdoor identified at the ThreatExpert site as "Eterok.C" actually deletes entries from the Winlogon\Notify key.

When I say "location of interest," I know that sounds kind of hoity-toity, but one of the things I've found time and again over the years, especially with respect to autostart locations in the Registry, is that once you stop looking at the ones you know about, as well as for new ones, they start being used more often. Over the years, I've heard malware authors say that some autostart locations are no longer of use (the same has been said of

## Tip

Different malware families will use different persistence mechanisms using the Registry. For example, one of the hallmarks of a ZBot infection is the presence of a reference to the malware in the UserInit value in the Microsoft\Windows NT\ CurrentVersion\Winlogon key within the Software hive.

Other malware will leave various artifacts within the Registry; while not used to maintain persistence, these artifacts can be used as indicators to determine if (and possibly when) the system was infected. For example, some variants of Ilomo/Clampi have been found to create the Microsoft\9593275321 key within the Software hive. Virut is a file infector, but some variants have been found to add a value named "UpdateHost" to the Microsoft\Windows\CurrentVersion\ Explorer key in the Software hive, as well as adding an exception for themselves to the firewall policy (see the "Firewall Policies" section earlier in this chapter).

NTFS alternate data streams, but that's outside the scope of this book), but the fact of the matter is that there are a great deal of system administrators out there (as well as forensic analysts) who simply aren't aware of these locations and how they can be used. Add to that instances where antivirus applications do not detect the malware that's actually loaded (or the antivirus applications are disabled during the malware installation process) from these locations, and what ends up happening is that systems get and remain infected for a considerable period of time.

## Image File Execution Options

Yet another autostart location (I told you there were a lot of these!) can be found in the "Image File Execution Options" key. Now, Microsoft provides documentation on the use of this key, which is intended to provide debugging capability [45], and it can also be used to turn off the Windows Update feature in Windows XP [46]. Like many other tools and techniques that are useful to administrators, this technique can also be used for malicious purposes, and malware authors have been seen using this technique to maintain persistence of their applications. In fact, the Microsoft Threat Encyclopedia discusses the malware known as Win32/Bebloh.A, which uses this functionality to force Internet Explorer to be launched whenever any other browser (Opera, Safari, Firefox, and so on) is launched. And this is nothing new … Dana Epp wrote a blog post [47] on this issue in March, 2005. To get a lot of exposure to malware that uses this autostart functionality, Google for *inurl:nai.com "image file execution options"*.

## Note

In August, 2010, Microsoft released KB article 2264107 [48] in order to address issues related to the DLL Search Order vulnerability, specifically as it relates to remote resources (i.e., folders) accessible through SMB and WebDAV. Specific applications can be protected by adding the "CWDIllegalInDllSearch" value, with the appropriate data setting, to the Image File Execution Options key. The RegRipper imagefile.pl plug-in was updated to check for both the Debugger and CWDIllegalInDllSearch values.

In short, by adding a "Debugger" value to the application sub-keys beneath the Image File Execution Options key, you can force a debugger or another application to be loaded instead. You can demonstrate this easily by adding a key called "notepad.exe," and within that key, add a string value named "Debugger." Then, add the string "sol.exe" to the value. Now, use any method to launch Notepad. Pretty neat, huh? And this works with any application. If you were running a tool like Process Monitor while launching Notepad and monitoring for Registry accesses, you'd notice that the operating system accesses this key and attempts to locate a subkey for the application being loaded. So, this is functionality that, while included in Registry value, is implemented as a function of how the operating system … operates. Interestingly, I have seen this autostart location during engagements, and as such, wrote the imagefile.pl RegRipper plug-in to query the Image File Execution Options subkeys, looking for Debugger values.

## Shell Extensions

During an engagement, the team I was working with had collected data from a system using F-Response Enterprise Edition, and I had created a time line of system activity using several of the data sources that we had acquired. Fortunately, not only had we acquired the data within relatively close *temporal proximity* (a Star Trek-y term I first heard used by Aaron Walters, and try to use as often as possible…) to a user having logged into the system, but this system also had *Process Tracking* enabled through the Event Log. In short, we had a lot of really good data to work with, and we were trying to determine how one particular piece of malware was remaining persistent on the system. We had identified the malware itself through other techniques, but could not determine how it was remaining persistent and being activated on the system. The time line helped a great deal; in fact, the time line solved the problem for us, and what we were able to see was that the malware was remaining persistent by *using the Registry without using the Registry.*

If your reaction to this was, "huh?," then that's a good thing. What we determined was that this apparently novel approach to persistence was based on the use of approved shell extensions. There are a considerable number of articles available at the Microsoft Web site, as well as elsewhere on the Web, that address topics such as writing shell extensions and shell extension security. However, where shell extensions come into play as a persistence mechanism is that they are loaded when the Explorer.exe shell loads (when a user logs in, in part demonstrated by Event Log data in the time line) and provide some sort of functionality extension beyond the basic shell. Many of the approved shell extensions that are loaded by the shell have explicit paths that point directly to the DLL to be loaded, and in many cases, these are located in the Windows\system32 directory. However, some of the approved shell extensions (in the Software hive, as well as in the user's NTUSER.DAT hive) do not have explicit paths. Therefore, when Explorer.exe attempts to load the shell extension, it must first locate it, and in doing so, it begins searching in its own directory (C:\Windows) first. This DLL search order behavior is documented at the Microsoft Web site [49].

During the malware reverse-engineering panel at the "SANS What Works in Incident Response and Forensics" conference in July, 2010, Nick Harbour of Mandiant briefly described this persistence mechanism, as well, based on what his team had seen, and how they approached the issue (Nick is well known for his malware reverse-engineering skills). Nick's blog post addressed the DLL search order issue from a much wider scope, and appeared to refer to DLLs that are loaded based on their presence in an executable file's import table. To read more about how he described the issue, take a look at what Nick had to say about this persistence mechanism in an M-unition blog post [50]. Nick also mentions how to use the KnownDLLs (ControlSet00n\Control\Session Manager\KnownDLLs [51]) key to protect a system from this sort of attack.

From the perspective of the shell extensions, in short, by using the same name as a legitimate approved shell extension (albeit one that was located in the C:\Windows\system32 directory) and placing that DLL in the C:\Windows directory, the malware was able to ensure that it was loaded each time a user logged in; however, this persistence mechanism neither required modifications to any files on the system (outside of the creation of one new one), nor did it require any modifications to the Registry. From the Microsoft site, we can see that the

*SafeDllSearchMode* functionality is enabled by default (and can be disabled). However, close examination of the article reveals that regardless of whether the functionality is enabled or disabled, the DLL search order begins in "the directory from which the application loaded."

In order to assist in investigations where this functionality may have been used as a persistence mechanism, I wrote the shellext.pl plug-in for RegRipper. This plug-in parses through the values of the "Microsoft\Windows\CurrentVersion\Shell Extensions\Approved" key in the Software hive, and collects the names (GUIDs) and data (description of the shell extension) for each value, then navigates to the Classes\CLSID key to map the GUID to a DLL path. An excerpt of the output of this plug-in is provided as follows:

```
{6756A641-DE71-11d0-831B-00AA005B4383}  MRU AutoComplete List
 DLL: %SystemRoot%\system32\browseui.dll
 Timestamp: Mon Apr 4 17:43:08 2005 Z

{7BD29E00-76C1-11CF-9DD0-00A0C9034933} Temporary Internet Files
 DLL: %SystemRoot%\system32\shdocvw.dll
 Timestamp: Mon Apr 4 17:43:09 2005 Z

{f81e9010-6ea4-11ce-a7ff-00aa003ca9f6}  Shell extensions for sharing
 DLL: ntshrui.dll
 Timestamp: Mon Apr  4 18:37:13 2005 Z
```

As a result of the amount of data available, this plug-in can take several seconds to run; as such, I tend to run it through rip. exe, rather than as a RegRipper plug-in listed in a plug-ins file. However, from the output excerpt, you can see that two approved shell extensions (browseui.dll and shdocvw.dll) have explicit paths, whereas the third (ntshrui.dll) does not. In this case, in order to load the DLL, the Explorer.exe process must search for it in accordance with DLL search order: therefore, the search begins in C:\Windows, where Explorer.exe is located.

A very quick way to use this information during an examination is to collect all of the lines of the output that start with "DLL:" to a file, and then to parse the file looking at directory paths. For example, start with a command that appears as follows:

```
C:\tools>rip.exe -r D:\case\software -p shellext | find "DLL:" >
D:\case\file\shellext.txt
```

The result of the above command will be a file containing only the lines that start with "DLL:", and from there, you can strip out the entries that do not contain path information such as "%SystemRoot%\system32" or something else. Of the remaining

## Note

The use of approved shell extensions as a persistence mechanism is very insidious, due to its very simplicity. This mechanism requires only that a DLL file of a specific name be created in a specific directory, and does *not* require any modifications to the Registry. As long as the "subverted" shell extension does not remove regularly accessed functionality and the capability provided by the shell extension is not missed, the malware may be run without any complaints from the user.

To protect a system against the sort of attack that takes advantage of the DLL search order, there are two options available. One is to locate all of the shell extensions in the Registry that use implicit paths, and give each of them the appropriate explicit path. Another method is to add an entry for the DLL (ntshrui.dll) to the ControlSet00x\Control\Session Manager\KnownDLLs Registry key [52].

Overall, however, this is simply one example of a much larger issue that was originally identified as far back as the year 2000, but it became more evident in August and September, 2010 and was referred to as "DLL hijacking." In short, the use of shell extensions is but one example of a mechanism to get an executable to search for a DLL that it needs to load in order to perform some function. Readers interested in learning more about this issue should search for "DLL hijacking" through Google.

files, run a search for those files that appear in the C:\Windows directory. If they only appear in the C:\Windows directory, depending on the DLL in question, that may be expected; however, if files with that name appear in both the C:\Windows and the C:\Windows\system32 directory, you may have found something of value.

Using this technique, I mounted an acquired image as a read-only drive letter on my analysis system and ran the above command. I located a shell extension named "slayerXP.dll," and when running the search, I found instances of the DLL in a ServicePack directory, as well as in the C:\Windows\system32 directory. Both instances had the same size, as well as the same MD5 hash. Further examination of the DLL indicated that it was a legitimate Microsoft file.

## ProfileList

The Software hive maintains a list of the various profiles that are resident on the system, which includes both local and domain users. When a user logs into a Windows system, the system first checks to see if that user account has a profile on the system. This is located in the Software\Microsoft\Windows NT\CurrentVersion\ProfileList key, as shown in Figure 3.27.

# Tip

Information about the contents of user profiles and how they are created is available in the TechNet article, "User Profile Structure" [53].

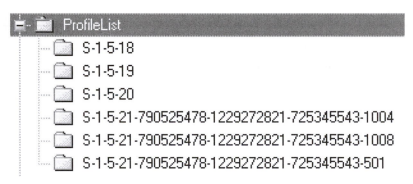

**Figure 3.27** ProfileList Key

| Value | Type | Data |
|---|---|---|
| ProfileImagePath | REG_EXPA... | %SystemDrive%\Documents and Settings\Paul |
| Sid | REG_BINARY | 01 05 00 00 00 00 00 05 15 00 00 00 26 76 1E |
| Flags | REG_DWORD | 0x00000000 |
| State | REG_DWORD | 0x00000100 |
| CentralProfile | REG_SZ | |
| ProfileLoadTimeLow | REG_DWORD | 0xFA2BF50E |
| ProfileLoadTimeHigh | REG_DWORD | 0x01C714E9 |
| RefCount | REG_DWORD | 0x00000001 |
| RunLogonScriptSync | REG_DWORD | 0x00000000 |
| OptimizedLogonStatus | REG_DWORD | 0x00000005 |
| NextLogonCacheable | REG_DWORD | 0x00000001 |

**Figure 3.28** Contents of a ProfileList Subkey

Each subkey beneath the ProfileList key is a security identifier, or SID, and you can find a list of well-known SIDs in MS KB article 243330 [54]. Each of the keys visible in the ProfileList key contains information about the user profile, as shown in Figure 3.28.

Some of the information visible in Figure 3.28 can be very useful for, well, some pretty obvious reasons. For example, the ProfileImagePath value tells us where the user profile and all of its associated files (NTUSER.DAT, for example) and subdirectories are located. On Windows 2000, XP, and 2003 systems, the default or usual path where we expect to find user profiles is in the path, "C:\Documents and Settings"; for Vista and later versions, it's "C:\Users." This value, in combination with the key name (i.e., the user's SID), provides a quick and easy means for associating the long SID to a username [55]. This also allows us to quickly find if the system was at one time part of a domain (refer back to the section in this chapter that discussed the Security hive) because if it was and domain users logged into the system, then some of the SID key names would be different (as opposed to just the last set of numbers ... the relative identifier or RID ... being different). Further, if the ProfileImagePath value points to some path other than what is expected, then that would tell us a couple of things, the first of which would be where to look for that user profile. The second thing it would tell us is that someone took steps to modify the default behavior of the operating system, possibly in an attempt to hide certain user activity.

The CentralProfile value is discussed in MS KB article 958736 [56]. Research conducted on the Internet (okay... "Googling") indicates that the State value may be a bit mask, whose value provides information regarding the state of the locally cached profile. However, MS KB article 150919 [57] indicates that this value has to do with the profile type, which can be changed through the System Control Panel applet, by going to the **Advanced** tab and clicking the **Settings** button in the User Profiles section, as shown in Figure 3.29.

## CHANGING USERNAMES

I've seen questions posted to forums where someone has asked how to determine when a user account name was changed. I've been fortunate in the past and examined systems where auditing for "User Account Management" was enabled, and found a record in the Event Log that indicated when the change was made. However, this isn't always the case. Another way to determine when this may have occurred would be to compare the LastWrite time for the user's key in the SAM (the one with the user RID in hexadecimal; for the Administrator, 000001F4 = 500) beneath the SAM\Domains\Account\Users key with the LastWrite time on the user's ProfileList key. Changing the user name will cause the appropriate value in the SAM hive to be modified, and the key's LastWrite time will be updated.

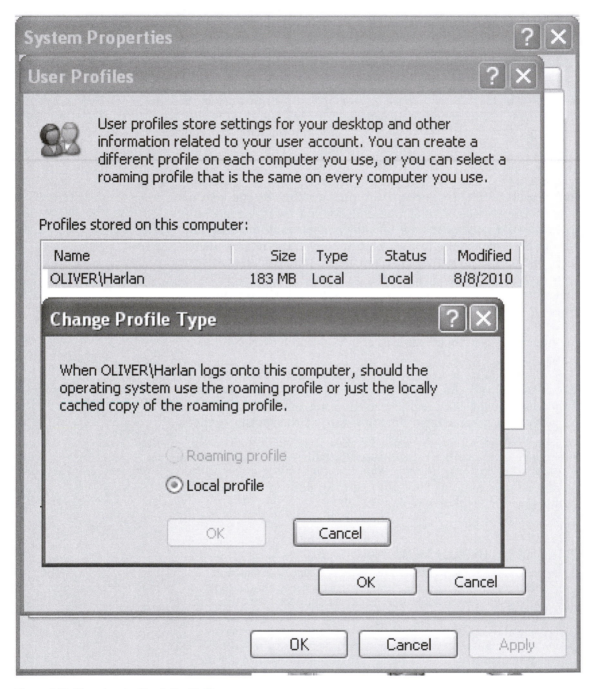

**Figure 3.29** Changing the User's Profile Type

## UAC

While we're on the subject of users and user profiles, Microsoft introduced something called *User Account Control* (or UAC) with Windows Vista. In short, this was something of a security measure, intended to prompt the user whenever something that might be considered untoward was going to happen; basically, there was a pop-up whenever something was going to make a change to the computer. This was intended to be a warning to the user, to alert them, but it quickly became something of an annoyance to most users and was disabled.

The behavior of UAC is controlled by several settings (value/ data combinations [58]) within the following key within the Software hive on Vista, Windows 2008, and Windows 7:

```
Microsoft\Windows\CurrentVersion\Policies\System
```

Of specific interest is the EnableLUA value; setting this value to 0 (or adding the DWORD value and then making the value 0) disables the prompt that appears each time a user attempts to do something that will make a change to the system.

Interestingly, there are several locations on the Internet that refer to this particular value as being related to malware or spyware, in particular Troj_Renos.SCMP, which (according to Trend Micro) disables Windows Defender, as well.

## Network Cards

Information about network adapters is also maintained in the Software hive. Beneath the "Microsoft\Windows NT\Current-Version\NetworkCards" key path, you may see several numbered subkeys, as illustrated in Figure 3.30.

Each of these subkeys refers to an interface, and the subkey generally contains two values, ServiceName and Description.

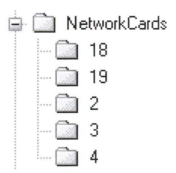

**Figure 3.30** Windows XP NetworkCards Key

The ServiceName value refers to the GUID for the interface, and the Description value contains a description of the interface, as illustrated in the output of the networcards.pl plug-in below:

```
Launching networkcards v.20080325
NetworkCards
Microsoft\Windows NT\CurrentVersion\NetworkCards

ADMtek AN983 10/100 PCI Adapter  [Mon Sep 30 21:01:28 2002]
Siemens SpeedStream Wireless USB  [Sat Apr 22 08:17:30 2006]
1394 Net Adapter  [Mon Sep 30 21:02:04 2002]
Instant Wireless USB Network Adapter ver.2.5  [Fri Jan 20
   07:30:12 2006]
```

The output of the plug-in provides an indication of the various interfaces on the system; in this case, we can see a PCI adapter, and two wireless adapters (one of which is USB). This information can provide an analyst with clues as to where to look for additional information, as the information from the Software hive supports that information about network interfaces available in the System hive (discussed earlier in this chapter).

## Wireless Connections

The Windows operating system maintains information about wireless access points to which the system has been connected. On Windows XP, this information is visible in the Preferred Networks box in the Wireless Network Connection Properties as illustrated in Figure 3.31.

How and where this information is maintained and visible depends on which process or application manages the wireless network connections. For example, some systems will use the Dell Wireless WLAN Card utility, and other systems may have their wireless connections and setting managed by an Intel application.

Information about wireless connections managed by Windows, such as those shown in Figure 3.31, can be found in the Microsoft\ WZCSVC\Parameters\Interfaces key. Beneath this key, you will find a subkey with the GUID for the wireless interface, and beneath that key you'll find several values that start with "Static#00xx," where "xx" is the number of the connection. Each of these values contains binary data that appears to be a structure that is very similar to the WZC_WLAN_CONFIG structure [59] (specific to Windows CE). The ssid.pl plug-in for RegRipper parses this structure and displays the SSID of the wireless access point (WAP), its Mac address, and the date that the system last connected to the WAP, as shown

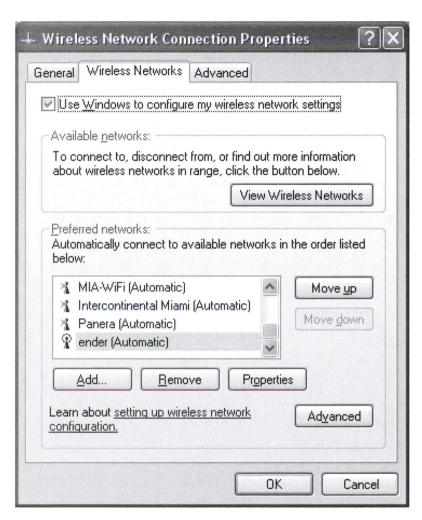

**Figure 3.31** Wireless Network Connection Properties (XP)

below (extracted from a Windows XP Software hive using the ssid.pl RegRipper plug-in):

```
NIC: 11a/b/g Wireless LAN Mini PCI Express Adapter
Key LastWrite: Thu Feb  7 10:38:43 2008 UTC

Wed Oct  3 16:44:25 2007 MAC: 00-19-07-5B-36-92  tmobile
Mon Oct  8 10:12:46 2007 MAC: 00-16-B6-2F-5B-16  ender
```

If you open the ssid.pl plug-in in an editor, you'll see that it also queries the Microsoft\EAPOL\Parameters\Interfaces key. In some cases, wireless SSIDs have also been found in this key. It's unclear to me as to how they end up there, which process is responsible for maintaining this information, or why some systems have the information while others don't, but now and again I've found information that has led me to look in other locations for additional artifacts. An example of the output of the plug-in from that key appears below:

```
NIC: 11a/b/g Wireless LAN Mini PCI Express Adapter
LastWrite time: Thu Sep 27 14:59:16 2007 UTC
1   ender
2   tmobile
```

Beginning with Windows Vista, this information was maintained in quite a different manner. This information is now maintained in GUID subkeys beneath the Microsoft\Windows NT\CurrentVersion\NetworkList\Profiles key in the Software hive, as shown in Figure 3.32.

The values and data within these keys provide a good deal more information than what is available on earlier systems. For example there is the profile name, the date that the profile was created (the first time that the system connected to the WAP), and the last time that the system was connected to the WAP. These values, and others, are shown in Figure 3.33.

You'll notice that the data within the DateCreated and DateLastConnected values are a bit bigger than we'd expect for Unix time (32-bit) or FILETIME (64-bit) objects. The data within these values is actually 128-bit SYSTEMTIME [60] objects. This is important as it's yet another time stamp format we have to be prepared to handle when analyzing Windows systems.

**Figure 3.32** Wireless Interface Profile Keys from a Vista System

| Value | Type | Data |
|---|---|---|
| ab ProfileName | REG_SZ | ender2 |
| ab Description | REG_SZ | ender2 |
| ab Managed | REG_DWORD | 0x00000000 |
| ab Category | REG_DWORD | 0x00000000 |
| DateCreated | REG_BINARY | D7 07 09 00 01 00 18 00 16 00 10 00 0A 00 52 00 |
| ab NameType | REG_DWORD | 0x00000047 |
| DateLastConnected | REG_BINARY | D8 07 08 00 06 00 10 00 0A 00 35 00 10 00 AD 03 |

**Figure 3.33** Wireless Interface Values from a Vista System

| Value | Type | Data |
|---|---|---|
| ab ProfileGuid | REG_SZ | {7A419400-FD53-4B2A-908E-B2DDF1ADD4D9} |
| ab Description | REG_SZ | ender2 |
| ab Source | REG_DWORD | 0x00000008 |
| ab DnsSuffix | REG_SZ | <none> |
| ab FirstNetwork | REG_SZ | ender2 |
| DefaultGatewayMac | REG_BINARY | 00 15 E9 EA 39 D2 00 00 |

**Figure 3.34** Values from Signature\Unmanaged Subkeys (Vista)

One piece of data that we don't see in these values is the WAP Mac address. If we go back to the Software hive and locate the Microsoft\Windows NT\CurrentVersion\NetworkList\Signatures key, we'll see Managed and Unmanaged subkeys. As the data for the Managed value shown in Figure 3.33 is 0, we go to the Unmanaged key, and we'll find a number of subkeys whose names are long strings. Within each of these keys, we find additional data that we can correlate to the data from the Profile key, using the ProfileGuid value, as shown in Figure 3.34.

I wrote the RegRipper networklist.pl plug-in to access a Vista or Windows 7 Software hive, and extract and correlate the above information, an excerpt of which (run against a Vista system Software hive) is shown below:

```
Launching networklist v.20090811
Microsoft\Windows NT\CurrentVersion\NetworkList\Profiles
linksys
```

```
Key LastWrite  : Mon Feb 18 16:02:48 2008 UTC
DateLastConnected: Mon Feb 18 11:02:48 2008
DateCreated    : Sat Feb 16 12:02:15 2008
DefaultGatewayMac: 00-0F-66-58-41-ED

ender
 Key LastWrite  : Mon Dec 22 04:09:17 2008 UTC
 DateLastConnected: Sun Dec 21 23:09:17 2008
 DateCreated    : Tue Sep 11 10:33:39 2007
 DefaultGatewayMac: 00-16-B6-2F-5B-14

ender2
 Key LastWrite  : Sat Aug 16 14:53:18 2008 UTC
 DateLastConnected: Sat Aug 16 10:53:16 2008
 DateCreated    : Mon Sep 24 22:16:10 2007
 DefaultGatewayMac: 00-15-E9-EA-39-D2

ender2  2
 Key LastWrite  : Mon Jan 12 12:42:49 2009 UTC
 DateLastConnected: Mon Jan 12 07:42:49 2009
 DateCreated    : Mon Aug 25 19:19:39 2008
 DefaultGatewayMac: 00-21-29-77-D0-2D
```

The above excerpt from the networklist.pl plug-in output provides an interesting view into activities on the system with respect to recording and managing the wireless connections. First, take a look at the "Key LastWrite" and "DateLastConnected" values for each profile listed; depending on the time of year, and the time zone settings (time zone, if daylight savings is enabled), these times are exactly either 4 or 5h off. Remember, Registry key LastWrite times are 64-bit FILETIME objects based on GMT/UTC, and the DateLastConnected values are 128-bit SYSTEMTIME objects. What this tells us is that when the dates and times are recorded for DateCreated and DateLastConnected values, the time zone and daylight savings settings are included in the computation. This is a very important piece of information for analysts, as assuming that these values are actually UTC will be incorrect and can make a mess of your analysis, a time line, and so on.

Second, in the above excerpt, we see two profiles that include the name "ender2," and the second one has an additional "2" as well as a different Mac address. In this case, I know what happened ... the original WAP with the SSID "ender2" had "died," and was replaced. Rather than replacing the original information, Windows (in this case, Vista) created a second profile, and left the original profile information intact. Understanding or just being aware of this can be very helpful to an analyst.

So, now we have this data, including a Mac address for the WAP that the system connected to (as well as a time frame for the connection) ... so what? Well, this information can be very useful ... for example, it can be used in WiFi geo-location; this means that we can use the WAP Mac address to perform a lookup, specifically through a company known as Skyhook. This company has information about WAPs in its database that was apparently collected by war-driving around major metropolitan areas. Submitting the WAP Mac address to an organization such as this may return latitude and longitude coordinates, if the information is available in the database. This lat–long pair can then be submitted to Google Maps to see where the WAP was actually mapped.

In order to demonstrate this capability, I wrote the maclookup.pl script, which is included on the CD that accompanies this book. This script is *not* part of RegRipper; instead, it is a stand-alone script that performs some lookups. Using the "tmobile" SSID and Mac address from the Windows XP example earlier in this chapter, we can provide the information to the script and get some information about the WAP:

```
C:\forensics\maclookup>maclookup.pl -w 00-19-07-5B-36-92 -s tmobile
OUI lookup for 00:19:07:5B:36:92...
 Cisco Systems
 80 West Tasman Dr.
 SJ-M/1
 San Jose CA 95134
 UNITED STATES
Google Map URL (paste into browser):
http://maps.google.com/maps?q=38.9454376,+77.4444653+%28tmobi
 le%2 9&iwloc=A&l=en
```

The first thing the script does is perform a lookup of the manufacturer of the WAP (based on the Mac address) using the Net::MAC::Vendor module. The script then submits the Mac address to skyhookwireless.com using a specified format (based on a similar script found here [61]). If the Mac address exists in the SkyHook database and the lat–long pair is returned, the script creates a URL that you can then copy-and-paste into a browser in order to see the Google Map with the location of the WAP represented by a pushpin, as shown in Figure 3.35.

As it turns out, the "tmobile" WAP was, indeed, a Starbucks store at the Dulles Airport. Again, keep in mind that not every WAP will have been mapped by a service such as SkyHook Wireless, so you're not guaranteed to get usable lat–long coordinates as a response to the query you submit. However, for major metropolitan areas (i.e., major cities such as Miami, Chicago, Los Angeles, and so on), it may be well worth a shot. I've heard from

**Figure 3.35** Google Map for tmobile WAP

analysts who have actually used the WAP information extracted from systems and been able to demonstrate that employees had visited competitor sites, and so forth.

## MRT

Windows systems that are regularly updated will often have the Microsoft Malicious Software Removal Tool (or "MRT" [62]), an antivirus micro-scanner, installed. When I say "micro-scanner," what I mean to say is that the MRT is not intended to protect a system from all malware threats, like a more comprehensive antivirus solution. Rather, the MRT is intended to protect the system against some very specific threats that Microsoft has identified as the most virulent.

MRT is updated monthly, and some months see only one update; for July, 2010, there was only an update for Win32/Bubnix; however, for August, 2010, there were nine updates, including Stuxnet and several Sality variants. Keep in mind that

**Tip**

When malware is suspected on a system, one of the steps of my examination process is to mount an acquired image as a read-only drive letter and scan it with antivirus scanners. Yes, I said "scanners" because I very often use more than one. However, one of the keys to this is to not use the same application as is already installed on the system. While I can't list all of the possible Registry keys used by antivirus scanning applications here (the list is just too long), a quick look at the file system and the Registry will tell me if the system had an antivirus application installed. Many times, by the time I receive the system or an acquired image, the local IT staff had already installed and run a (or more than one) scanner application on the system. Therefore, I include the check, which scanner(s) I opted to use and the results in my case notes. After all, I don't think the customer is going to be happy to receive a bill for doing what they already did and finding the same things.

the MRT is not an application that will protect a system from vulnerabilities, nor will it catch a wide range of malware and spyware. The MRT is intended to only protect a system from some very specific malware, and when used properly, the information provided about the MRT by the Registry can provide an analyst with considerable insight.

MS KB article 891716 [63] provides information about Registry keys where an analyst can find information to determine when MRT was last updated, as well as information regarding how to read the MRT log file. This can be very helpful in determining malware that may be on a system, or perhaps more appropriately, what malware may not be on a system (I've had several cases where I've been told, "we think it's this virus," and I have to set about proving or disproving that assumption, and documenting my findings). An analyst can use the mrt.pl RegRipper plug-in to extract the necessary information from the Software hive.

The MRT should not be confused with Windows Defender, which is a more comprehensive antispyware solution that comes installed by default on Windows Vista and Windows 7 systems. The Software hive (specifically in the "Microsoft\Windows Defender" key path) provides information about the last time a scan was run and what type of scan it was; this can be an additional resource when attempting to determine if a system was infected, and if so, when.

Again, the sections in this chapter are not meant to be all-inclusive and completely comprehensive lists of Registry keys and values that might be of interest during an investigation. Not every key and value can be discussed and presented; therefore, what I've attempted to do is present an overview of different keys and values that may be of interest during a variety of different types of investigations. Much of the information I've presented is based on my own experience, while some is based on events others have shared with me, and still others are based simply on research. By presenting a range of keys and values that might be useful, my hope is to convey the importance of the Registry as a valuable resource during incident response, as well as during computer forensic analysis.

## BCD Hive

On Vista and later systems, there is a BCD hive that contains boot configuration data, which is to say that it's a firmware independent means for managing boot options, replacing the boot.ini file that many analysts are used to seeing on Windows 2000 and XP systems. The BCD allows Windows to take advantage of the Extensible Firmware Interface (EFI) model found on newer computer systems.

A document at the Microsoft Developer Network (MSDN) site entitled *Boot Configuration Data in Windows Vista* provides a good deal of insight into the contents of the BCD hive file. The file uses the Registry hive structure, and MS refers to it as a "store" rather than a hive. However, because it uses the hive structure, we can open the file in Registry viewers, as shown in Figure 3.36.

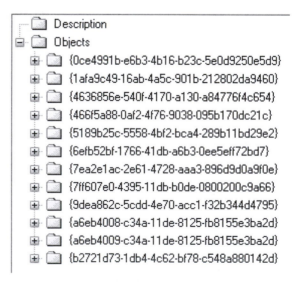

**Figure 3.36** BCD File Opened in MiTeC RFV

## Note

Microsoft reuses a lot of file structures; there are a number of applications on Windows 7, for example … such as Sticky Notes … that save their data files in the OLE or structured storage format. Most of us thought that this was a legacy format when MS Office file formats were changed and moved away from the use of OLE, but it's back!

As you can see in Figure 3.36, the various objects listed appear as GUIDs; many of these GUIDs (and their associated elements) are named and described in the MSDN document. As described in the document, the BCDEdit tool (bcdedit.exe) is used by support personnel and developers to manage and interact with the BCD store. The BCD is loaded into the Registry when the system is booted, as shown in Figure 3.37.

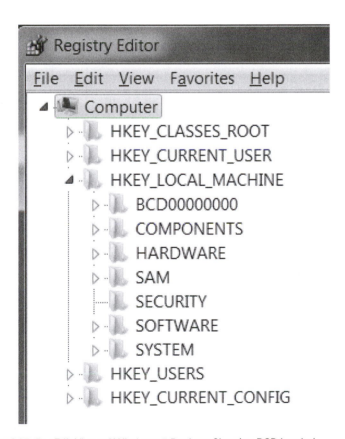

**Figure 3.37** RegEdit View of Windows 7 Registry Showing BCD Loaded

The BCD hive/store is visible in Figure 3.37, loaded as "BCD00000000." As of this writing, there isn't a great deal of information available as to the forensic usefulness or viability of information in the BCD store. As time goes on, I'm sure that additional information will be developed with regard to using information available in this hive.

## Summary

In this chapter, we've taken a good look at the Registry hives that pertain to the configuration and operation of the system as a whole, and we've seen how there is a good deal of information available that can be extremely valuable to an analyst during an examination. In many instances, we've also seen how the available information can be used as or developed into something more than just technical information, perhaps intelligence that can be used to support additional analysis and case work.

I've attempted to provide a quick snapshot of information available in the Security, SAM, System, and Software hives; no volume or tome will ever be able to encapsulate every possible key, value and setting that could possibly be included in each of these hives. Rather, I've tried to give you, the reader, an overview of what's available, including some of the most common entries. I've mentioned some of the Registry keys and values that I, and other analysts, look toward most often during examinations; however, that does not mean that these are all the keys and values that contain pertinent information. In fact, this will never be the case; there will always be a new application or new version, or some new malware or technique to compromise a Windows system that leaves a footprint in the Registry. What I hope I have done, and continue to do, is to provide you with an appreciation for how powerful a technique Registry analysis can be, particularly, when used in combination with other analysis techniques, such as time line analysis. The Windows Registry truly is a veritable treasure chest of data that can be used effectively by a knowledgeable analyst to add a great deal of context to an examination.

Other sources of information will be equally valuable as well, particularly after this book has been published. For example, an excellent source of information regarding autostart locations within the Registry is Microsoft's own AutoRuns tool. Another source of information, as Matt Churchill stated in a blog post to the SANS Forensic blog [64] on 16 August, 2010, is tools designed to be "evidence cleaners"; apparently, if some settings are important enough to be considered "evidence" and deleted, then they are very likely important to forensic analysts, as well!

# Frequently Asked Questions

**Q:** How can I find the location of the Task Scheduler log file through the Registry?

**A:** By default, the location of the Task Scheduler log file (i.e., SchedLgu.txt) is located in the Microsoft\SchedulingAgent key in the Software hive, and can be seen in the data for the LogPath value. On Windows XP, the file is usually located in the C:\Windows directory; on other versions of Windows, it's in the C:\Windows\Tasks directory (you can extract this information with the schedagent.pl RegRipper plug-in). Something else that may have an effect on your analysis, specifically concerning how much information may be available in the schedlgu.txt file, is the maximum size of the log file [65] (also extracted through the schedagent.pl plug-in).

**Q:** How can I determine, from the Registry, when the system was last shutdown?

**A:** The ControlSet00$n$\Control\Windows key within the System hive contains a value named "ShutdownTime," which is a 64-bit FILETIME object. This time should correspond to the LastWrite time of the key (which is also a 64-bit FILETIME object). You can use the shutdown.pl plug-in to extract this specific value and translate it into something readable.

**Q:** How can I determine, from the Registry, when the operating system was installed.

**A:** The installation date of the operating system is maintained in the Microsoft\Windows NT\CurrentVersion key within the Software hive. The value is named "InstallDate," and is a 32-bit DWORD value, meaning that rather than a FILETIME object, the data is a Unix time. This key also contains a good deal of other useful data, including the operating system version, Service Pack level, and so on. The winnt_cv.pl plug-in will extract this information for you.

**Q:** What are some other ways that malware can maintain persistence on a system?

**A:** The list is long … long, but finite. Some other ways to autostart malware (beyond what's already been discussed in this chapter) include modifying shell handlers (as described here [66]). Keep in mind that the HKEY_CLASSES_ROOT hive is actually a volatile hive, and consists of the Classes keys from the Software hive and the logged on user's hive on a live system. One example of malware that used this technique was SirCam [67]. Another method is to create a subkey beneath the "Microsoft\Windows NT\CurrentVersion\Image File Execution Options" key for a commonly used application and add a Debugger value that points to the malware (or replace an existing value). This technique has been used to disable antivirus applications (as described on the SANS Internet Storm Center blog [68]), as well as used to launch malware; I've seen this technique used during several engagements. Yet another tricky technique is to add an entry to the Microsoft\Command Processor\AutoRun value (in the Software hive; this also works for the Software\ Microsoft\Command Processor\AutoRun value in the user's hive). Give it a shot; navigate to the key and add "sol.exe" to the value, then run a command prompt. Now imagine what would happen if the value listed wasn't a nice, pretty GUI application, but instead some malware that run behind the scenes?

**Q:** Can the Registry be used to hide malware in other ways?

**A:** Without a doubt. I worked on an engagement with Don Weber while we were both part of the IBM ISS Emergency Response Services (ERS) team (as of this writing, Don is with InGuardians) in which we found that executable image files were being hidden in binary Registry values! We extracted the binary contents of the values and were able to perform static analysis of the files. As a result of this engagement, I wrote the findexes.pl plug-in, which can be run against any hive file (including not just the System and Software hives, but the NTUSER.DAT hive, as well), and attempts to locate binary values that include "MZ." We found that in some cases, the binary data started with bytes other than "MZ," and when we stripped those initial bytes from the data, we had what appeared to be complete executable files. I found this very interesting, as in an earlier consulting position I had created a proof-of-concept (PoC) tool that would reach out to the Internet and download an executable image file "disguised" as a GIF image, break that file up into blocks, and then write those blocks to various Registry values. This PoC tool did not use the WinInet APIs that are native to Windows systems, thereby minimizing the artifacts left behind by the use of this tool. There was an associated tool that would then reassemble the executable image file and launch it.

**Q:** How can I tell when the system was last booted using just the Registry?

**A:** While the Registry maintains a value called "ShutdownTime" (the value is found in the ControlSet00$n$\Control\Windows key in the System hive), there's no specific value within the Registry that says, "this is when the system was last booted." What I tend to do is go to the Services key in the System hive, and check the LastWrite time on keys for services that are configured to start at system boot. For example, kernel drives such as atapi.sys, cdrom.sys, and disk.sys will be pertinent to most systems, and are configured to start at system boot. Correlate this information with other information, such as event identifiers (IDs) 6005 and 6009 in the Windows 2000, XP, and 2003 System Event Logs.

# References

[1] Security Identifier. Wikipedia, http://en.wikipedia.org/wiki/Security_Identifier.
[2] How to determine audit policies from the Registry. Microsoft Support. http://support.microsoft.com/kb/246120 (accessed 01.11.06).
[3] Offline NT Password& Registry Editor. www.pogostick.net/~pnh/ntpasswd
[4] How to use the UserAccountControl flags to manipulate user account properties. Microsoft Support. http://support.microsoft.com/kb/305144 (accessed 03.12.07).
[5] Live View. http://liveview.sourceforge.net.
[6] How to use the SysKey utility to secure the Windows Security Accounts Manager database. Microsoft Support. http://support.microsoft.com/kb/310105 (accessed 30.10.06).
[7] Tarasco Security: Password Dumper – PWDump 7 for Windows. www.tarasco.org/security/pwdump_7.
[8] oxid.it – Cain & Abel. www.oxid.it/cain.html.
[9] LM Hash. Wikipedia, http://en.wikipedia.org/wiki/LM_hash.
[10] NTLM. Wikipedia, http://en.wikipedia.org/wiki/NTLM.
[11] How to prevent Windows from storing a LAN manager hash of your password in Active Directory and local SAM databases. Microsoft Support. http://support.microsoft.com/kb/299656 (accessed 03.12.07).
[12] Hacking Case. NIST. www.cfreds.nist.gov/Hacking_Case.html.
[13] How to turn on automatic logon in Windows XP. Microsoft Support. http://support.microsoft.com/kb/315231 (accessed 10.06.08).
[14] OphCrack. SourceForge. http://ophcrack.sourceforge.net
[15] SAMInside. InsidePro.com. www.insidepro.com/eng/saminside.shtml (accessed 25.08.10).
[16] L0phtCrack6. L0phtCrack.com. www.l0phtcrack.com.
[17] What are ControlSets? What is CurrentControlSet? Microsoft Support. http://support.microsoft.com/kb/100010 (accessed 1.11.06).
[18] CurrentControlSet\Services Subkey Entries. Microsoft Support. http://support.microsoft.com/kb/103000 (accessed 11.12.06).
[19] A description of SvcHost.exe in Windows XP Professional Edition. Microsoft Support. http://support.microsoft.com/kb/314056 (accessed 10.12.07).
[20] SANS Computer Forensic Investigation and Incident Response. http://blogs.sans.org/computer-forensics
[21] TrueCrypt. www.truecrypt.org.
[22] Windows 7, Windows 2008 R2, and Windows Vista setup log file locations. Microsoft Support. http://support.microsoft.com/kb/927521 (accessed 15.3.07).
[23] Microsoft Word bites Tony Blair in the butt. www.computerbytesman.com/privacy/blair.htm.
[24] Registry Entries for Printing. Microsoft Support. http://support.microsoft.com/kb/102966 (accessed 26.11.07).

[25] Windows Firewall. Microsoft TechNet. http://technet.microsoft.com/en-us/network/bb545423.aspx.

[26] FakeAlert-Winwebsecurity. McAfee. http://vil.nai.com/vil/content/v_153577.htm.

[27] Trojan-Proxy.Win32.Mitglieder.ee. SecureList. www.securelist.com/en/descriptions/old126765.

[28] Exploring the Windows Firewall. Microsoft TechNet. http://technet.microsoft.com/en-us/magazine/2007.06.vistafirewall.aspx.

[29] The "netsh firewall" command together with the "profile=all" parameter does not configure the public profile on a Windows Vista-based computer. Microsoft Support. http://support.microsoft.com/kb/947213 (accessed 1.02.08).

[30] How to use the "netsh advfirewall firewall" context instead of the "netsh firewall" context to control Windows Firewall behavior in Windows Server 2008 and in Windows Vista. Microsoft Support. http://support.microsoft.com/kb/947709 (accessed 5.12.08).

[31] Microsoft TCP/IP Host name resolution order. Microsoft Support. http://support.microsoft.com/kb/172218.

[32] 'P' Switch for route command added to Windows, Microsoft Support. http://support.microsoft.com/kb/141383 (accessed 20.02.07).

[33] NtfsDisableLastAccessUpdate. Microsoft Technet. http://technet.microsoft.com/en-us/library/cc758569%28WS.10%29.aspx.

[34] NtfsDisable8dot3NameCreation. Microsoft TechNet. http://technet.microsoft.com/en-us/library/cc959352.aspx.

[35] How to clear the Windows paging file at shutdown. Microsoft Support. http://support.microsoft.com/kb/314834 (accessed 20.07.10).

[36] Internet Explorer file downloads over SSL do not work with the cache control headers. Microsoft Support. http://support.microsoft.com/kb/323308 (accessed 15.11.07).

[37] HTTP/1.1 Header Field Definitions. W3.org. www.w3.org/Protocols/rfc2616/rfc2616-sec14.html.

[38] Robert Hensing's Blog. Microsoft TechNet Blogs. 15 November 2006, http://blogs.technet.com/b/robert_hensing.

[39] Definition of the RunOnce Keys in the Registry. Microsoft Support. http://support.microsoft.com/kb/137367 (accessed 19.01.07).

[40] Registry changes in x64-based versions of Windows Server 2003 and in Windows XP Professional x64 Edition. Microsoft Support. http://support.microsoft.com/kb/896459 (accessed 21.04.08).

[41] Registry keys affected by WOW64. Microsoft Developer Network. http://msdn.microsoft.com/en-us/library/aa384253%28VS.85%29.aspx.

[42] INFO: Run, RunOnce, RunServices, RunServicesOnce and Startup. Microsoft Support. http://support.microsoft.com/kb/179365 (accessed 21.11.06).

[43] Registry Entries. Microsoft Developer Network. http://msdn.microsoft.com/en-us/library/aa379402%28VS.85%29.aspx.

[44] Generic Downloader.z!1516DDBD. McAfee. http://vil.nai.com/vil/content/v_149604.htm.

[45] How to debug Windows Services. Microsoft Support. http://support.microsoft.com/kb/824344.

[46] How to turn off the Windows Update feature in Windows XP. Microsoft Support. 28 January 2005, http://support.microsoft.com/kb/892894 (accessed 28.01.05).

[47] Using image file execution options as an attack vector on Windows. http://silverstr.ufies.org/blog/archives/000809.html, 2005.

[48] A new CWDIllegalInDllSearch registry entry is available to control the DLL search path algorithm. Microsoft Support. http://support.microsoft.com/kb/2264107 (accessed 24.08.10).

[49] Dynamic-Link Library Search Order. Microsoft Developer Network. http://msdn.microsoft.com/en-us/library/ms682586

[50] Malware Persistence without the Windows Registry. Mandiant.com blog, 15 July 2010, http://blog.mandiant.com/archives/1207.

[51] REG: CurrentControlSet Entries PART 2: SessionManager. Microsoft Support. http://support.microsoft.com/kb/102985 (accessed 1.11.06).

[52] INFO: Windows NT/2000/XP Uses KnownDLLs registry entry to find DLLs. Microsoft Support. http://support.microsoft.com/kb/164501 (accessed 21.11.06).

[53] User Profile Structure. Microsoft TechNet. http://technet.microsoft.com/en-us/library/cc775560%28WS.10%29.aspx.

[54] Well-known security identifiers in Windows operating systems. Microsoft Support. http://support.microsoft.com/kb/243330 (accessed 12.01.10).

[55] How to Associate a Username with a Security Identifier (SID). Microsoft Support. http://support.microsoft.com/kb/154599 (accessed 27.02.07).

[56] The "Set roaming profile path for all users logging onto this computer" Group Policy setting also applies to local user accounts in Windows Server 2008. Microsoft Support. http://support.microsoft.com/kb/958736 (accessed 21.10.08).

[57] How to Prevent a User from Changing the User Profile Type. Microsoft Support. http://support.microsoft.com/kb/150919 (accessed 21.02.07).

[58] 2.2.11 User Account Control. Microsoft Developer Network. http://msdn.microsoft.com/en-us/library/cc232771%28v=PROT.10%29.aspx.

[59] WCZ_WLAN_CONFIG. Microsoft Developer Network. http://msdn.microsoft.com/en-us/library/aa448338.aspx.

[60] SYSTEMTIME. Microsoft Developer Network. http://msdn.microsoft.com/en-us/library/aa908737.aspx.

[61] Unnamed, Perl script by Joshua D. Abraham, http://spl0it.org/files/bssid-location.pl.

[62] The Microsoft Windows Malicious Software Removal Tool helps remove specific, prevalent malicious software from computers that are running Windows 7, Windows Vista, Windows Server 2003, Windows Server 2008, or Windows XP. Microsoft Support. http://support.microsoft.com/?kbid=890830.

[63] Deployment of the Microsoft Windows Malicious Software Removal Tool in an enterprise environment. Microsoft Support. http://support.microsoft.com/kb/891716.

[64] SANS Computer Forensic Investigation and Incident Response. SANS Forensic Blog. 16 August 2010, https://blogs.sans.org/computer-forensics.

[65] How to limit the maximum size of the Scheduled Tasks Log File. Microsoft Support. http://support.microsoft.com/kb/169443 (accessed 3.12.07).

[66] Changes to Shell Open Command. About.Com: AntiVirus Software. http://antivirus.about.com/od/windowsbasics/a/shellopen.htm

[67] You cannot start programs when your computer is infected with the SirCam virus. Microsoft Support. http://support.microsoft.com/kb/311446 (accessed 29.03.07).

[68] Abusing Image File Execution Options. SANS Internet Storm Center blog. 28 February 2008, http://isc.sans.edu/diary.html?storyid=4039.

# 4

# CASE STUDIES: TRACKING USER ACTIVITY

**INFORMATION IN THIS CHAPTER**

- Tracking User Activity

- Scenarios

## Introduction

When first I sat down to write this book, it occurred to me that this chapter ... one about tracking user activity ... might be the most useful and interesting chapter. Windows does a great job of providing a quality experience to the user and keeping track of documents they had opened, saved, or accessed, how they had set up and configured their favorite Solitaire game, which Web browser they used, which application is launched when the user double-clicks a file in the shell, and even the size and position of various application windows on the desktop. All of this information has to be tracked somehow, and for the most part, a great deal of it is tracked through the user's Registry hive files. The fact that this information is recorded in any manner at all is transparent to the user, but for a knowledgeable analyst, the Registry, and in particular the user's hives, can be veritable treasure trove of forensic data.

In Chapter 3, "Case Studies: The System," we discussed several of the Registry hives that pertain most directly to the system: the SAM, Security, System, and Software hives. In this chapter, we will be focusing primarily on two hives found within the User Profile directory: the NTUSER.dat hive and the lesser-known USRCLASS.dat hive. These two files, to varying degrees based on the version of Windows being examined, can provide a great deal of data regarding the user's activities on a system. In this chapter, we're going to take a look at the various ways this information can be used, and more importantly, how it can be used effectively to support a number of types of investigations.

As with the previous chapter, this chapter should not be considered a comprehensive and complete list of all possible Registry keys and values that might be considered important or valuable to an analyst. Although Windows XP systems are fairly well-understood, there is still a lot about Vista systems, and now Windows 7 systems, that require a great deal of research, particularly in the area of Registry analysis. Add to that the proliferation of applications on these systems, and there's an apparent never-ending supply of Registry locations that can be of value, including (but not limited to) used by malware to maintain persistence on the system. Rather than providing a long list of Registry keys and values of interest, it's more important to understand how some keys and values can be used, not only by an intruder or malware author but more so by a forensic analyst in order to paint a more complete picture of an examination. Understanding how the user hives can be used is far more important than maintaining a long list of keys and values that don't have any context or anything to indicate how they're important.

A final thought before we head into this chapter, as with previous chapters: the most important aspect of Registry analysis is to first understand your goals and what you are looking for or trying to demonstrate or prove. Many analysts kick off an examination by loading Registry hives into a viewer, without really understanding what it is they're looking for; this will often result in "no findings" and a great deal of time spent finding this out. If you understand what you're interested in and what you're looking for, you can not only find it very quickly but the absence of those artifacts is itself an artifact, and can often tell you much more about the user activity.

## REGRIPPER PLUG-INS

Throughout this chapter, as with Chapter 3, "Case Studies: The System," I'll be referring to a number of RegRipper plug-ins, particularly when discussing some Registry key or value of interest. Don't forget that we discussed in Chapter 2, "Tools," the use of rip.pl (or the .exe version), as well as the "Plug-in Browser" tool, to see the available plug-ins and what they're meant to do. I haven't discussed all of the plug-ins that are available on the CD that accompanies this book … as of this writing, there are 171 plug-ins. Some of the plug-ins are "twins," which means that they are based on other plug-ins and closely related, but slightly different in some small way (i.e., a small change in how the output is formatted, etc.). Feel free to browse through the plug-ins with either of the available tools, or open them in Notepad, and even use the ones that are available to write some plug-ins of your own!

# Tracking User Activity

The traditional approach to computer forensic analysis has relied heavily on file system time stamps and a few other artifacts (file contents) found on the system. However, systems are now often accessed via multiple user accounts, and the scope of many investigations has expanded beyond the boundaries and hard drive of just one system. Further, there are times when an analyst cannot trust file system time stamps, as either the updating of file last access times is disabled, or an intruder (or malware) modified those time stamps. As such, we need to look to other locations within the system to develop a better understanding of activity associated with a user account. The best place to start is within the Registry hive files within the User Profile; there is the well-known NTUSER.dat hive found in the root of the profile directory, and with more recent versions of Windows (Vista, Windows 7), the USRCLASS.dat hive is seeing greater usage. In this chapter, we'll focus on discussing and demonstrating how activity associated with a user account ("user activity") is recorded in the user's hives and how analysts can use that information to the benefit of their examinations.

## MRU Lists

The first thing I'd like to discuss is the concept of a "most recently used" list. A number of values (and keys) are maintained in the user's Registry hive as a "most recently used," or "MRU," list. What this means is that there is some sort of ordered numbering scheme that is used to track the entries, and in the case of some values, there may also be another value named *MRUList* or *MRUListEx* that will tell you the order of the MRU values. In some cases, the values are given numbers as names ("0000," "0001," and so on) as they are added to the key; the most recent value is named *0000*, and when the next value is added, it is named *0000* and the previous value is "pushed down" to "0001," and so on. This way, looking at the value names, you can get a very quick view of the order in which the values were added, and there is no need for an MRUList (or MRUListEx) value.

In other instances, the values are assigned numbers as names (which may begin with the letters "MRU," depending upon the key and the application that uses them), and there will be an additional value named *MRUList* or *MRUListEx* that maintains the order in which the values were "used" (again, this depends upon the application). For example, consider a Registry key for which the first value added is named simply "a." At this point, the MRUList value would indicate that the "a" value was the most recently used value. At some point, several other values (b, c, and so on) are added, and the MRUList value indicates the order accordingly (c, b, a). However, at some point, the user does something that reuses the first value (conducts a search for the same keyword, accesses the file, and so on); the MRUList value would now indicate that the MRU order is now "a," "c," "b." Even though all of the values keep their original names, the MRUList value indicates the order in which the values were "used."

Throughout the rest of this chapter, we'll encounter several Registry keys that maintain MRU lists. In each instance, we'll discuss how to interpret those specific values and how the values as a whole can be of use during an examination.

## Run

As discussed in Chapter 3, "Case Studies: The System," there are a number of Registry keys in the user hive that have the same name and path as keys in the Software hive. In some cases, as with applications, the keys in the user hive will maintain user-specific information, such as settings and MRU lists of accessed files, and so on, whereas the keys in the Software hive will maintain overall application configuration information. In other instances, the contents of the key within both hives are very similar and serve the same function, but those in one hive will supersede the values in the other hive.

The Run key is one of the latter. All of the available documentation at the Microsoft Web site indicates that when a user logs into a system, the contents of the Run key within the Software hive are run, and then the contents of the Run key within the user's hive are run; however, the entries within each key are run asynchronously, that is, in no particular order. The Run key within the user's hive is located in the following path:

```
Software\Microsoft\Windows\CurrentVersion\Run
```

One would think that after all this time, this particular key (and its counterpart in the Software hive) would no longer be quite as popular as they once were; however, nothing could be further from the truth. There are still a number of malware variants that rely on this key for persistence. In fact, on a recent engagement (during the summer of 2010), I examined a system that had been infected, not once but twice, by a bit of malware that used the user's Run key for persistence. I found two values in the user's Run key that pointed to different malware files that were later found to be different variants of the same malware family. Also, a friend of mine who primarily conducts forensic exams as a result of Payment Card Industry (PCI) data breaches has seen a good number of instances where the "Perfect Keylogger" is installed on systems; this tool maintains persistence by writing to the Run key in the Software hive. This indicates that for some, this key (regardless of the hive) is still a popular persistence mechanism.

## RunOnce

In addition to the Run key, there's also the RunOnce key … as the note indicates, entries in this key are run once. In fact, the data for each value is a command line, and by default, is deleted before the command is run; however, the deletion of the value can be deferred until after the command is run by prepending the value name with an exclamation point. You can also force the associated command within the RunOnce key to be run in Safe Mode (the contents of both the Run and RunOnce keys are ignored if the system is booted in Safe Mode) by prepending the name with a star (*). This is all documented in MS KB article 314866 [1].

Something else to consider is that this makes an excellent persistence mechanism. Imagine a piece of malware that included a mechanism, run either when the process is terminated or another designated time, to create an entry in the RunOnce key, rather than in, say, the Run key. When the system starts, the persistence mechanism would activate, but the system itself would delete the entry. However, the entry would be recreated at a designated time or based on a specific trigger, which would then allow the malware to be initiated again at the next system start. This possibility is an excellent example of why responders and analysts must be knowledgeable and take special care when acquiring and analyzing data. It's also an example of how analysts need to beware of becoming complacent during examinations; just because you haven't seen or heard of a particular persistence mechanism being used doesn't mean that it won't be used.

Programs can be configured via group policies to run when a user logins onto the system, as well. If an administrator goes to the **Group Policy** console and selects **Computer Configuration | Administrative Templates | System | Logon** (or the corresponding User settings), the programs added here will be added to the **Microsoft | Windows | CurrentVersion | Policies | Explorer | Run** key within the Software hive, or to the corresponding key within the user's hive, respectively (with the path the key in the user's hive prepended with "Software\," of course).

This can also be set up on a stand-alone system through the Local Security Policy, as illustrated in Figure 4.1.

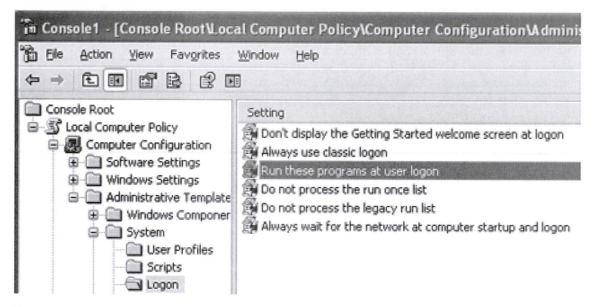

**Figure 4.1** Windows XP Local Security Policy

You should have noticed in Figure 4.1 that there's an additional setting called *Do not process the legacy run list*; there is also a corresponding setting within the User Configuration settings (**User Configuration | Administrative Templates | System | Logon**), and both of these refer to the respective **Windows | CurrentVersion | Run** keys. However, both Run keys (the "policy" and the "legacy" Run keys) are still used quite often by malware as persistence mechanisms. In fact, on August 19, 2010, the SpywareRemove Web site published a definition for malware named *Backdoor.Beastdoor.206* that uses the "policies" Run key for persistence (that is, installs as a value named *COM service*).

Now, these keys do not directly relate to user activity; rather, the contents of these keys can help you understand what other applications may have been running within the user context on the system. The purpose of identifying these keys and their contents, particularly during incident response or digital forensics analysis, would be to understand if the user purposely took specific actions that led to the issue (unusual or suspicious traffic observed on the network, and so on), or if the identified issue was due to some other processes at work, whether they are legitimate applications or malware. Understanding and examining malware persistence mechanisms (particularly those within the Registry) can also assist in addressing the "Trojan Defense," which we will discuss further later in this chapter.

## TEMPORAL PROXIMITY

The term *temporal proximity* is a Star Trek-y kind of term I first heard used in the fall of 2008 by Aaron Walters (of Volatility fame), and it refers to when response activities start in relation to the incident having occurred. I bring this up because keys such as the RunOnce key can really illustrate the importance of temporal proximity, as well as rapid incident detection and response. Something that differentiates the RunOnce key from the Run key is that items listed in the RunOnce key are run once. Any command line listed as a value beneath this key will be run the next time a user logs into the system and be deleted (before or after being run, per our previous explanation). The value of temporal proximity is also illustrated by issues such as deletions; when a Registry key is deleted, the space used by the key becomes part of the unallocated space of the hive file and may be reused (that is, overwritten) at some point (the same concept that applies to files in the file system). The sooner the response activities are initiated, the more likely you are to have access "fresh" data.

## USB Devices

In Chapter 3, "Case Studies: The System," we discussed tracking the use of USB devices (thumb drives, wallet drives, and larger drive enclosures connected via USB) on the system. It turns out that we can also track which user accessed those drives and when those drives were last accessed. According to research conducted by Rob Lee (of Mandiant and SANS fame) and published through the SANS Forensic blog, on Windows XP systems, the MountPoints2 key in the user hive will tell you which user accessed the devices, and the LastWrite time for that key will tell you when the device was last connected to the system. According to Rob's findings, this will work for thumb drives (but apparently not drive enclosures) on Vista and Windows 7 systems, as well. The full path to the key in question is

```
Software\Microsoft\Windows\CurrentVersion\Explorer\
  MountPoint2
```

Beneath this key are a number of long strings of numbers and letters that start and end with curly brackets; these are globally unique identifiers, or GUIDs (*goo-idz*). These are, in fact, the same GUIDs that are found in the MountedDevices key within the System hive. In Chapter 3, "Case Studies: The System," of this book, we discussed how the contents of this key can be used. The values within this key that start with "\??\Volume" and end in GUIDs refer to the volumes that were mounted on the system. For example, using the mountdev.pl RegRipper plugin, we are able to extract the following information from the System hive:

```
Device: \??\STORAGE#RemovableMedia#7&326659cd&0&RM#{53f5630d-
    b6bf-11d0-94f2-00a0c91efb8b}
    \??\Volume{567720f4-fff4-11db-ba6a-0016cf5d56b8}
    \DosDevices\E:
```

From this information, we see that the volume GUID refers to a removable storage device that was mounted as the E:\ drive on the system. Running the mp2.pl RegRipper plugin against the user's NTUSER.dat hive, we can extract the following information:

```
Thu Feb 7 13:37:11 2008 (UTC)
{567720f4-fff4-11db-ba6a-0016cf5d56b8}
```

Now, both of these pieces of information are just excerpts of the full output of the plug-ins used, but they serve to demonstrate how the information can be used to establish a time line of when the device was last connected to the system and by which user. Again, according to Rob Lee's research, this is specific to Windows XP systems.

## XPMode

With the release of Windows 7, Windows XP does not completely go away. Although some large organizations are looking at moving their users, a few at a time, to Windows 7, Windows XP is still very pervasive. On top of that, in order to insure that older applications can still be run on Windows 7, a special version of Windows XP called *XPMode* can be installed to provide a virtualized Windows XP environment for running those applications. In short, the user installs the application in XPMode and the icon for the application appears on the Windows 7 desktop. When the user double-clicks the icon, XPMode is automatically started. What this means for forensic analysts is that there may be sources of information or indicators in the XPMode environment that are not readily apparent in the Windows 7 environment, so keeping those analysis skills for Windows XP systems sharp will continue to be important for the foreseeable future.

## Searches

Users will often search for things (files by name, keywords within files, and so on) on their systems, as well as on other systems, and on the Internet. Sometimes, they even do this using the built-in search capability that comes with Windows XP, as is illustrated in Figure 4.2.

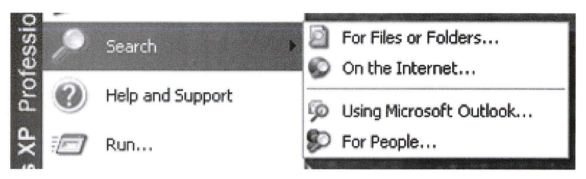

**Figure 4.2** Windows XP Search

When a user runs a search on Windows XP, the information about what is being searched for is maintained in the following Registry key:

`Software\Microsoft\Search Assistant\ACMru`

Beneath this key are several subkeys, each of which is named for a number, and each of these numbers corresponds to a particular portion of the Search Assistant, as indicated as follows:

- **5001** Contains list of terms entered via the "On the Internet …" search
- **5603** Contains list of terms entered via the Windows XP "For Files or Folders …" search
- **5604** Contains list of terms searched for using the "A word or phrase in the file" search
- **5647** Contains list of terms searched for using the "Computers or people" search

Figure 4.3 illustrates the portion of the Search Assistant in which entries populate the 5603 and 5604 keys, respectively.

I have found this information has proven to be very useful during a number of examinations. For example, the values beneath these keys are also numbered in an MRU fashion: 000, 001, 002, and so on. Therefore, the LastWrite time for the key itself lets us know when the search for the "000" value was conducted. Sometimes I find entries that are entirely normal for a particular user; in other cases, perhaps not so much. For example, I've seen where someone who had no business doing so was searching for terms such as *banking* and *passwords*. I've also seen where someone has perhaps had trouble spelling, searching for "bankign."

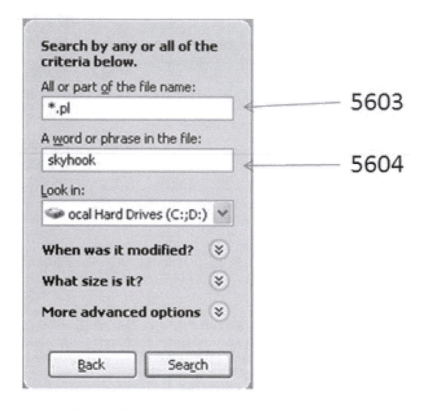

**Figure 4.3** Windows XP Search Assistant to ACMRu Subkey Mappings

On Vista systems, information about searches run by the user is maintained in a file, and not within a Registry key. With Windows 7, information about what the user searched for is again recorded in the Registry, this time in the WordWheelQuery key. The full path to this key appears as follows:

```
Software\Microsoft\Windows\CurrentVersion\Explorer\
    WordWheelQuery
```

Figure 4.4 illustrates how the contents of this key appear in Windows Explorer on Windows 7.

The values within the WordWheelQuery key are binary data types that are numbered ("0," "1," and so on), and there is also an MRUListEx value that is also a binary data type. As with many MRUListEx values, the MRU list is maintained as 4-byte DWORD values in sequence, with the value 0 × FFFF indicating the end of the list. As with the Windows XP ACMru key, the information in this key may shed some light as to the user's activity on the system.

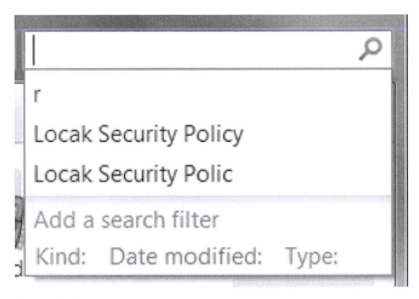

**Figure 4.4** Windows 7 Search History

## TIME STAMPS

Time stamps (key LastWrite times, time stamps in binary or string values) can be fairly important and revealing during analysis, particularly when the analyst creates a time line of activity from various data sources. I've seen instances where a user (specifically, an administrator) has had their credentials compromised, and the intruder accessed systems that the legitimate administrator had previously accessed. Many times, an intruder will access a lot of the same utilities and programs as an administrator, such as the Microsoft Management Console (MMC), or the Control Panel, and so on. So what will happen is that the analyst will see a good deal of activity that appears normal, but occurred after the date of compromise and was a result of the intruder's activities. So, when looking at values, particularly MRU lists, such as RunMRU, TypedUrls, or values regarding searches, it is important to note not only the entries and values but also the time stamps associated with those values.

## RecentDocs

Microsoft Windows does a very good job of tracking what documents a user has accessed, making them available in the Recent Documents menu, as illustrated in Figure 4.5.

This list of documents can be very revealing about a user's activities. In most cases, such as in a corporate environment, the documents listed here will be legitimate, business-oriented

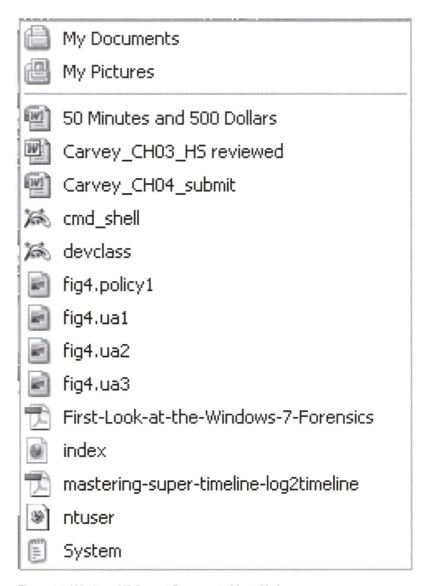

**Figure 4.5** Windows XP Recent Documents Menu Listing

documents. However, even in such environments, users may be found accessing documents that they shouldn't. Information about the documents that the user has accessed is maintained in the RecentDocs key, which is found in the following path:

```
Software\Microsoft\Windows\CurrentVersion\Explorer\RecentDocs
```

An example of RecentDocs key, as well as the subkeys and values, from a Windows XP system is illustrated in Figure 4.6.

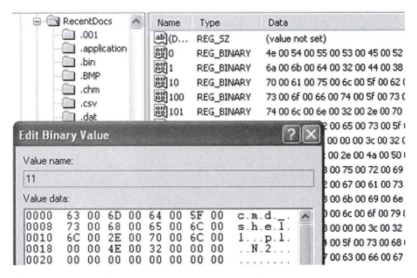

**Figure 4.6** View of RecentDocs Key/Values via RegEdit.exe

As you can see in Figure 4.6, the RecentDocs key itself contains numbered values (0, 1, and so on) that each contain binary data, as well as subkeys named for the various extensions of the files accessed. Each of these subkeys also contains numbered values with binary data, as well. All of these keys contain a value named *MRUListEx,* which is a sequence of DWORD values that list the order in which the documents or files were accessed. Vista and Windows 7 record this information in the same way, and the recentdocs.pl RegRipper plugin can be used to parse the necessary information from the binary value data on all versions of Windows. An example of information retrieved by the recentdocs.pl plugin from a Windows 7 system appears as follows:

```
Software\Microsoft\Windows\CurrentVersion\Explorer\
   RecentDocs\.jpeg
LastWrite Time Sat Mar 13 22:25:46 2010 (UTC)
MRUListEx = 2,1,0
 2 = anime_155.jpeg
 1 = 11.ca2.jpeg
 0 = roripara22_png.jpeg

Software\Microsoft\Windows\CurrentVersion\Explorer\
   RecentDocs\.jpg
LastWrite Time Tue Mar 16 15:43:58 2010 (UTC)
MRUListEx = 3,1,2,8,9,4,0,6,5,7
 3 = Picnik collage.jpg
```

```
1 = hether-446.jpg
2 = 09.jpg
8 = 1211720515959.jpg
9 = 016.jpg
4 = 25517_1260411908194_1166566081_30636671_8251529_n.jpg
0 = 25517_1260297105324_1166566081_30636173_6335083_n.jpg
6 = 25517_1260297145325_1166566081_30636174_7038891_n.jpg
5 = 25517_1260297185326_1166566081_30636175_5223984_n.jpg
7 = 25517_1260297225327_1166566081_30636176_4397882_n.jpg
```

This example illustrates the user's access to .jpeg and .jpg files; in short, images. One thing you'll notice is that the plug-in parses the MRUListEx value and then presents the files in the order in which they are listed in that value. Based on how the contents of these keys are maintained, we can that "anime_155.jpeg" was accessed on Saturday, March 13, 2010 at approximately 22:25:46 (UTC) and that "Picnik collage.jpg" was accessed on Tuesday, March 16, 2010 at approximately 15:43:58 (UTC).

## WHAT APPLICATION USES OR CREATED THAT FILE?

Many times while I'm perusing online forums, I'll see a question similar to, "what application is used to access/created this file?" Most of the time, the response is a reference to a Google search (or even a URL for lmgtfy.com) or to fileext.com. This may seem like the obvious answer, but it's not someplace I'd start. When I see a file extension listed on a file in an image, or in the RecentDocs key in the user's hive and I'm interested in determining the application that is associated with that file extension on the system, I'll run the assoc.pl RegRipper plugin against the Software hive (via rip.pl/.exe), redirect the output to a file, and then look to see what may be listed in the output file. This allows me to determine the file associations on that system; searching for this information via Google, while it may be useful, does not address the context of what applications are installed on the system being analyzed. The output of the assoc.pl plugin can also tell me about installed applications; for example, on a Windows 7 system, I found that all of the graphics files (.jpg, .img, .tif, and so on) were associated with the IrfanView application. So, not only did I now know that IrfanView was installed but I now had another application to check for an MRU list of opened or saved files. From this same system, I also found that OpenOffice was installed rather than Microsoft Office. Searching via Google may provide useful leads, but examining artifacts on the system being examined will many times provide much-needed context.

However, this information applies to the system itself; file association settings from the User Profile (found in the user's USRCLASS.dat hive) will supersede the system settings when the user logs in. This is covered in more detail in the "File Associations" section later in this chapter.

We can see from this that the values beneath the RecentDocs key and its subkeys will tell us what documents and files the user account was used to access (I say that, because that's all we know … we don't really know who was at the keyboard when the account was logged in …), as well as when the most recently access document was accessed (via the first item in the MRUListEx value and the key LastWrite time). A closer look at the binary data for the various values shows us the filename and a referenced Windows shortcut (.lnk) file, but not the full path to the file itself, so we don't know if the file was on the local hard drive, on a CD, on a thumb drive attached to the system or on a network share. In order to determine where the file originally existed, we can go to the application itself and see if it maintains an MRU list of its own. For example, while I was writing this chapter in MS Word 2007, I clicked on the Windows icon in the upper left hand corner of the application window and saw what was illustrated in Figure 4.7.

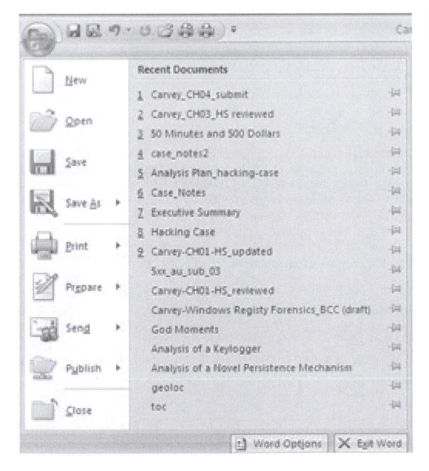

**Figure 4.7** MS Word 2007 Document MRU List

Many graphical user interface (GUI) applications on Windows systems maintain a similar list (you should note that Notepad does *not* maintain such a list) of recently accessed files. Another example of an application (in this case, MS Paint) MRU list is illustrated in Figure 4.8.

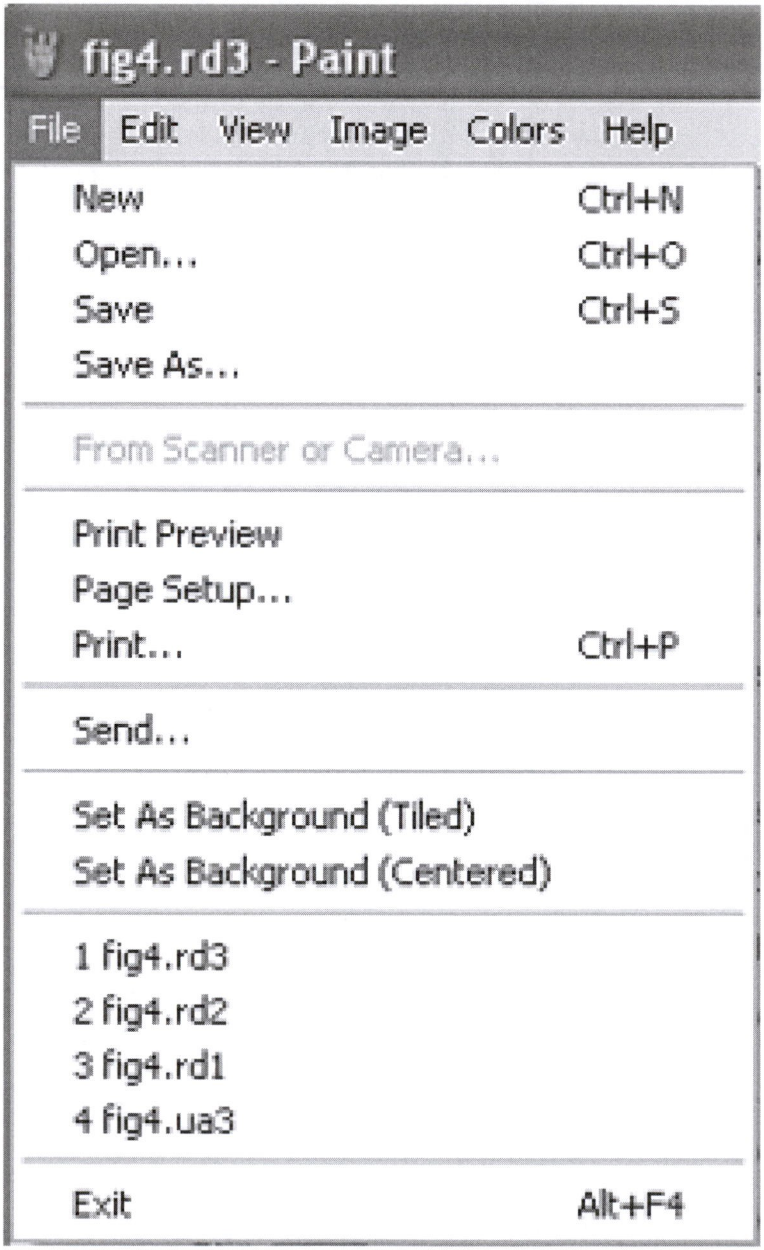

**Figure 4.8** MS Paint MRU List

As you can see in Figure 4.8, while I was writing this chapter (actually, this entire book), I would capture an image and use MS Paint to save the image in a TIFF format for inclusion in the book. Many other applications maintain similar lists, as illustrated in Figures 4.9 and 4.10.

Figure 4.9 illustrates the recently accessed files for Windows Media Player, while Figure 4.10 illustrates a similar file listing for Adobe Reader. As is often the case, these lists are maintained differently depending upon the application. For Windows Media Player, the list of files is maintained in the following key:

```
Software\Microsoft\MediaPlayer\Player\
    RecentFileList
```

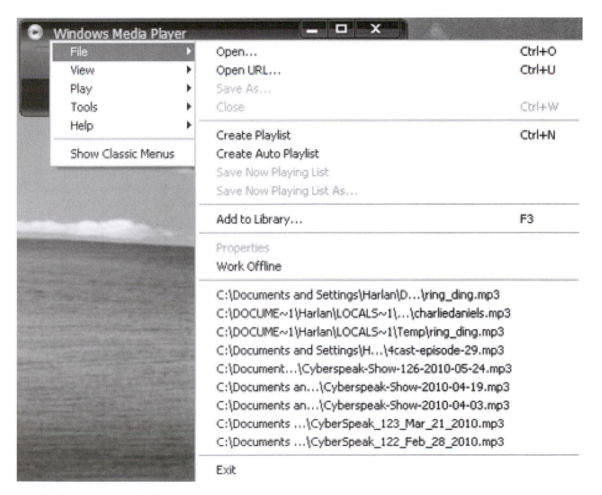

**Figure 4.9** Windows Media Player Recently Accessed Files

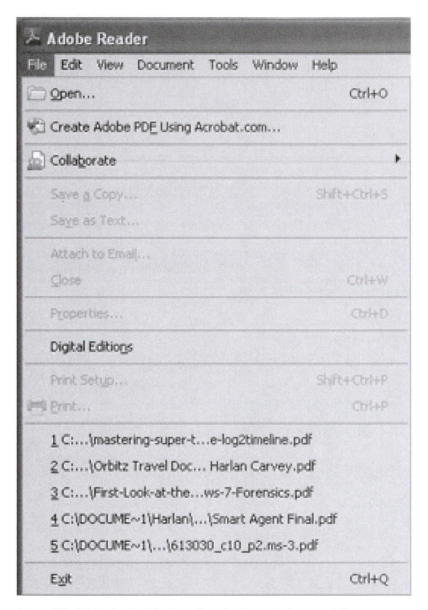

**Figure 4.10** Adobe Reader File Menu Showing Recently Accessed Files

The values beneath this key are named *File0, File1, File2,* and so on, with File0 being the most recently accessed file. The filenames are Registry string values and need no special parsing or interpretation, and as each new file is added to the list, it is written to the File0 value, and the other files are pushed down (that is, the original File0 becomes File1, and so on). The mpmru.pl RegRipper plugin will parse the RecentFileList key for the list of Windows Media Player recently accessed files.

## DisableMRU

Windows Media Player has a value named *DisableMRU* beneath the **Software | Microsoft | MediaPlayer | Preferences** key that, by default, is set to "0." If this value is set to "1," the list of recently accessed files will no longer be maintained. We discussed earlier in this book how a lack of artifacts can itself be an artifact; in this case, the lack of values beneath the RecentFileList key doesn't necessarily mean that no media files were accessed. Correlate the key LastWrite time with other data to see if there are indications that the values were deleted, but also check the DisableMRU value to see if an MRU list is being maintained.

For Adobe Reader (version 9.0, in this case), the list of accessed files is maintained below the following key:

```
Software\Adobe\Acrobat Reader\9.0\AVGeneral\cRecentFiles
```

Beneath this key are several subkeys whose names start with the letter "c" and are numbered (1 through 5, on my test system). If you like, open the Registry Editor (on a live system) or RFV to view an NTUSER.dat hive file from a system with the Adobe Reader installed and follow along. Within each of these keys are several values; the value named *sDI* is a binary value that contains the name of the accessed file, and the tDIText value contains the filename in ASCII text. Each time a new file is accessed and added to the list that new file replaces the information in the c1 subkey, and each subsequent file gets pushed down one ... the original c1 becomes c2, and so on. Therefore, under normal circumstances, all of the subkeys beneath the cRecentFiles key can be expected to have the same LastWrite time. The adoberdr.pl RegRipper plugin will attempt to determine the installed version of Adobe Reader and then obtain a list of recently accessed files from the cRecentFiles key, as shown below:

```
Launching adoberdr v.20100218
Adoberdr v.20100218
Adobe Acrobat Reader version 8.0 located.
Software\Adobe\Acrobat Reader\8.0\AVGeneral\cRecentFiles

Most recent PDF opened: Thu Feb 7 10:59:54 2008 (UTC)
  c1 /C/DOCUME~1/Harlan/LOCALS~1/Temp/CSD2007_Volatatile_Memory_
     Forensics.pdf
  c2 /C/DOCUME~1/Harlan/LOCALS~1/Temp/w_search_1098_print-1.pdf
  c3 /C/Documents and Settings/Harlan/Desktop/tbw1098.pdf
```

```
c4 /C/DOCUME~1/Harlan/LOCALS~1/Temp/w_search_1098_print.pdf
c5 /D/docs/WFA/complete/acmru.pdf
```

Again, although many GUI applications maintain a list of recently accessed files (commonly known as an "MRU" list) in the Registry, each of the lists may be maintained differently based on the application and/or the vendor (yes, even Microsoft maintains MRU lists for different applications differently). However, the filenames persist within the application MRU list even if the file is viewed and then deleted. For example, if someone views a movie file via Real Player (via the realplayer6.pl plugin) or Windows Media Player, and then deletes the movie file, the filename is not automatically deleted from the MRU list. Therefore, an analyst can see that the file was viewed, where the file was originally run from (that is, Temporary Internet Files, removable media, and so on), and when the most recent file was viewed. The presence of a filename within the application MRU list indicates that the user account and application were used to view the file in question.

## ComDlg32

The key "ComDlg32" refers to common dialogs available on Windows systems. Rather than requiring developers to recreate or code from scratch some of those dialogs that are used frequently, these are actually provided for use through the Windows application programming interface (API). The path to the key is **Software | Microsoft | Windows | CurrentVersion | Explorer | ComDlg32**, and the keys of interest beneath this key differ slightly between Windows XP, and Vista and Windows 7. Figures 4.11 and 4.12 illustrate the keys on Windows XP and Vista, respectively.

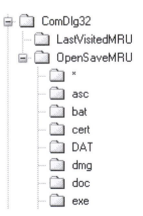

**Figure 4.11** Windows XP ComDlg32 Key, Viewed via RFV

ComDlg32
CIDSizeMRU
LastVisitedPidlMRU
OpenSavePidlMRU
*
3g2
bmp
BUP
doc
docx
exe
gif

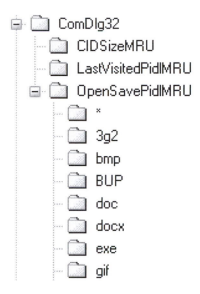

**Figure 4.12** Windows Vista ComDlg32 Key, Viewed via RFV

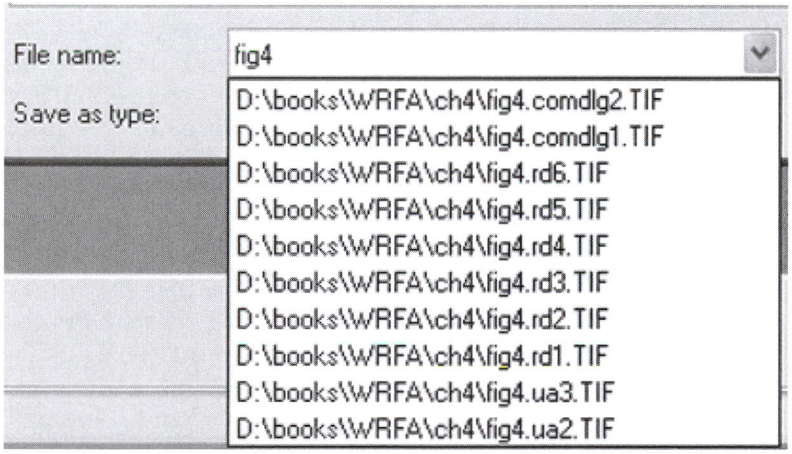

File name:
fig4
Save as type:
D:\books\WRFA\ch4\fig4.comdlg2.TIF
D:\books\WRFA\ch4\fig4.comdlg1.TIF
D:\books\WRFA\ch4\fig4.rd6.TIF
D:\books\WRFA\ch4\fig4.rd5.TIF
D:\books\WRFA\ch4\fig4.rd4.TIF
D:\books\WRFA\ch4\fig4.rd3.TIF
D:\books\WRFA\ch4\fig4.rd2.TIF
D:\books\WRFA\ch4\fig4.rd1.TIF
D:\books\WRFA\ch4\fig4.ua3.TIF
D:\books\WRFA\ch4\fig4.ua2.TIF

**Figure 4.13** MS Paint **Save As** ... Dialog Autocomplete Listing

The OpenSaveMRU (on Windows XP and 2003; OpenSave-PidMRU on Vista and Windows 7) tracks files that the user account is used to access via the **Open and Save As** ... common dialogs. You can see the use of these common dialogs when opening an application and clicking on the **File** menu item. From there, the drop-down menu will include **Open and Save As** ... options, and choosing these options will launch the common dialogs. This key and its subkeys also track previously opened or saved files as an autocomplete feature, as illustrated in Figure 4.13.

As you can see illustrated in figures 4.comdlg1 and 4.comdlg2, the OpenSaveMRU and OpenSavePidMRU keys contain subkeys that specify the extensions of the files opened or saved. In figure 4.comdlg1, we see a subkey named *asc*, which refers to files used by the Pretty Good Privacy (PGP) encryption application. Each of these keys contains values whose names letters and whose data points to the files in question. Each key also contains an MRUList value, which is a string that lists the MRU order in which the files were accessed. As such, the LastWrite time of the key would correspond to the time that the first file referenced in the MRUList value was accessed. The OpenSavePidMRU subkey values are different, in that the values are binary data types and need to parsed appropriately to retrieve the filename; also, the subkeys each contain a value named *MRUListEx* (as opposed to a value named *MRUList*), which is also a binary data type and needs to be parsed appropriately, as well.

One subkey beneath the OpenSaveMRU and OpenSavePidMRU keys that stands out is the key named "*." This refers to files of any extension, or no extension, and also maintains the list of most recently accessed files for each type. For example, beneath the OpenSaveMRU key in figure 4.comdlg1 is a subkey named *zip*, which contains six values. The most recently accessed file that ends with the ".zip" extension is not only listed in the MRUList value within that key but it is also listed as a value in the "*" subkey.

The LastVisitedMRU (LastVisitedPidMRU on Vista and Windows 7 systems) key serves a bit of a different function. This key tracks the application last used to access the files listed in the OpenSaveMRU key (and its subkeys), as well as the directory that was last accessed. The OpenSaveMRU values include the paths and filenames; also, remember that the common dialogs (in this case, **Open and Save As** ...) are not applications in and of themselves, but are instead accessed via other applications, such as MS Paint, Notepad, MS Word, the Web browser, and so on. Figure 4.14 illustrates a LastVisitedMRU value.

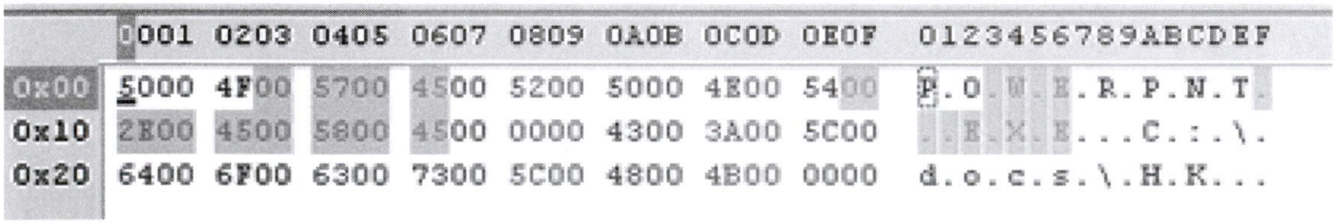

| | 0001 | 0203 | 0405 | 0607 | 0809 | 0A0B | 0C0D | 0E0F | 0123456789ABCDEF |
|------|------|------|------|------|------|------|------|------|------------------|
| 0x00 | 5000 | 4F00 | 5700 | 4500 | 5200 | 5000 | 4E00 | 5400 | P.O.W.E.R.P.N.T. |
| 0x10 | 2E00 | 4500 | 5800 | 4500 | 0000 | 4300 | 3A00 | 5C00 | .E.X.E...C.:.\. |
| 0x20 | 6400 | 6F00 | 6300 | 7300 | 5C00 | 4800 | 4B00 | 0000 | d.o.c.s.\.H.K... |

**Figure 4.14** Windows XP LastVisitedMRU Value Viewed via RFV

In Figure 4.14, we see the executable which was used to access the common dialog (Powerpnt.exe) and the directory that it was used to access (C:\docs\HK). Using this information, we can then correlate the values based on the LastVisitedMRU key's MRUList value to the values found beneath the OpenSaveMRU\* key, in order to obtain path information. For example, the first value referenced in the LastVisitedMRU MRUList value is "f," which points to Winword.exe, and includes the C:\docs\xcel directory in the binary data. We then go to the OpenSaveMRU\* key, and the first value listed in the MRUList value is also "f," which in this case points to C:\docs\xcel\xcel.doc. However, remember that these are MRU keys, so we shouldn't expect to find a great deal of historical data that would allow us to track file paths back several weeks or months.

### HISTORICAL DATA

Let's not forget that although some Registry keys (such as the ones that maintain MRU information) can show us not only the most recent documents that a user account had been used to access, but also documents accessed in the past; analysts can also find further historical data in Windows XP system Restore Points, or within Volume Shadow copies (as on Vista and Windows 7 systems).

Similar to the OpenSavePidMRU key values, the values listed within the LastVisitedPidMRU key (Vista, Windows 7) are binary data types and need to parsed appropriately. However, these values contain similar information as their counterparts on Windows XP and 2003 systems. The comdlg32.pl RegRipper plugin will extract the information from Windows XP and 2003 user hives, and the comdlg32a.pl plugin will also extract the information from Vista and Windows 7 user hives.

## Shellbags

One of the really useful aspects of the Windows operating systems is that when a user opens an application and modifies the location and size of the application window, those settings are saved so that the next time the user opens the application, the window is right back to where the user left it. This is addressed in part in MS KB article 813711 [2]. The window configuration and settings information is maintained beneath the following keys, found in the NTUSER.dat hive on Windows XP and 2003 systems:

```
Software\Microsoft\Windows\Shell\Bags
Software\Microsoft\Windows\ShellNoRoam\Bags
```

Again, this is where information about the windows settings is stored; information about the traversed path is maintained in the BagMRU key, which maintains an MRU list of the windows referred to in the Bags keys:

```
Software\Microsoft\Windows\Shell\BagMRU
Software\Microsoft\Windows\ShellNoRoam\BagMRU
```

This information can be very useful to an analyst, as it can provide a historic view of folders that the user has modified, including using Windows Explorer to access removable storage devices and remote network shares. The format of the BagMRU keys is cascading in nature, building on the path from the root outward. Within the keys, there are binary values that include information about the window (location, title); however, there is very little documented information about the information available in these binary values and how to parse that information. As such, a great deal of the information available is the result of testing and research. For example, the "Using shellbag information to reconstruct user activities" [3] provides some excellent information about the structure of these keys and values and describes an application (that is, "Tracehunter" [4]) that can be used to parse the value data. However, as of this writing, I have been unable to locate information regarding obtaining a copy of the application for use or testing. However, based on the description, the Tracehunter application does sound as if it would be a very useful tool for an analyst.

As of Windows Vista, the key paths still appear to remain in the NTUSER.dat file, but are sparsely populated within that hive. With Vista and Windows 7, the predominance of the values appears to have been moved to the USRCLASS.dat hive, in the following path:

```
Local Settings\Software\Microsoft\Windows\Shell\Bags
Local Settings\Software\Microsoft\Windows\Shell\BagMRU
```

## USRCLASS.dat

On Windows XP and 2003 systems, the USRCLASS.dat hive file is located in the following path:

```
%UserProfile%\Local Settings\Application Data\Microsoft\
   Windows
```

On Vista and Windows 7 systems, the hive file can be found in the following path:

```
%UserProfile%\AppData\Local\Microsoft\Windows
```

Again, these keys can provide information about the resources that have been accessed through the use of the user account. Even when removable storage devices have been removed or network shares disconnected, the information in the BagMRU values will persist. However, at the moment, detailed information about the creation and modification of the BagMRU values is extremely sparse and there needs to be more research and testing in this area.

## BagMRU PLUGINS

I've written two testing plug-ins (bagtest.pl and bagtest2.pl) that parse the BagMRU values from an NTUSER.dat hive file from a Windows XP system. At this point, those plug-ins simply traverse through the key paths to the values, providing the sequence of key names and the name of the resource or window accessed. For example, the output of the bagtest2.pl plugin appears as follows:

```
\0
\0\0                Entire Network ()
\0\0\0              Microsoft Windows Network (Microsoft
                        Network)
\0\0\0\0            Pitstop (Microsoft Network)
\0\0\0\0\0          \\192.168.1.103 (Microsoft Network)
\0\0\0\0\0\0        \\192.168.1.103\download (Microsoft
                        Network)
\0\0\0\0\1          \\Bob (Microsoft Network)
\0\0\0\0\1\0        \\Bob\SharedDocs (Microsoft Network)
\0\0\0\0\1\0\0      &My Music
\0\0\0\0\1\0\0\0    My Playlists
\0\0\0\0\1\0\1      My Videos
\0\0\0\0\1\0\2      My Pictures
\0\0\0\0\1\0\2\0    Sample Pictures
```

The next step for these testing plug-ins would be to align the entries so that the paths were consolidated, along with key LastWrite times. For example, in the excerpt from the output of the bagtest2.pl plugin provided above, rather than having a series of paths listed separately, provide consolidated paths, such as "\\192.168.1.103\download" and "\\Bob\SharedDocs\My Pictures\Sample Pictures." Ultimately, this format would be far more useful to analysts, particularly when correlated with relevant time stamps and incorporated into a time line of system and/or user activity.

## UserAssist

During a job interview about 11 years ago, the interviewer asked me what my favorite Registry key was; if I had to answer that question today, I'd have to say that it is the UserAssist key. Oddly enough, the key name is pretty descriptive … the contents of this key assist the user. Okay, I know it's a stretch but bear with me; beneath this key (we'll address exactly where shortly) are Registry values that track a user's interactions via the Windows Explorer shell, primarily when the user clicks or double-clicks certain items. This information is then used by the operating system to tailor the user experience; for example, I use a Windows XP SP3 laptop for work. Each morning when I log in to the corporate network, I click the **Start button**, go to **Programs**, then to "**Microsoft Office**," and in the final menu, I click **Microsoft Outlook**. After the first couple of times that I did this, when I got to that final menu, only the Microsoft Outlook choice was immediately visible; why would the operating system continue completely expand all of the menus in the path, when I'd demonstrated that I was primarily interested in only one or two items? It's a much better and preferable user experience to show those items I'm most interested in via customized menus based on my usage history. Given this and the data included in the relevant values, would lead you to believe that this key should really be called *forensics assist*!

So, to begin, the full path to the UserAssist key within the NTUSER.dat hive is as follows:

```
Software\Microsoft\Windows\ CurrentVersion\Explorer\
   UserAssist
```

Beneath this key (on all versions of Windows), you'll find two (I've seen three on a very few Windows XP systems) keys with names that appear to be GUIDs, as illustrated in Figures 4.15 and 4.16.

As you can see in Figures 4.15 and 4.16, each of these keys will have subkeys named *count*, and we're interested in the values located within the Count subkeys. Figure 4.17 illustrates what these values look like in a Registry viewer.

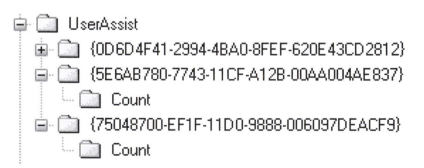

**Figure 4.15** Windows XP UserAssist Key

**Figure 4.16** Windows 7 UserAssist Key

| Value | Type | Data |
|---|---|---|
| HRZR_PGYFRFFVBA | REG_BINARY | A9 C2 38 0E DB 04 00 00 |
| HRZR_PGYPHNPbhag:pgbe | REG_BINARY | 01 00 00 00 02 00 00 00 00 00 00 00 00 00 0 |
| HRZR_HVFPHG | REG_BINARY | DB 04 00 00 AC 04 00 00 30 74 87 74 0A |
| HRZR_EHACNGU | REG_BINARY | DB 04 00 00 80 0F 00 00 00 10 F2 7A 0A |
| HRZR_EHACNGU:FO Nhqvtl ... | REG_BINARY | 01 00 00 00 07 00 00 00 80 83 67 E7 0C |
| HRZR_EHACNGU:P:\JVAQBJ... | REG_BINARY | DB 04 00 00 07 00 00 00 00 10 F2 7A 0A |
| HRZR_EHACNGU:Perngvir Cy... | REG_BINARY | 01 00 00 00 07 00 00 00 F0 EE 77 E2 0C |

**Figure 4.17** UserAssist\..\Count Key Values

The values illustrated in figure 4.ua3 don't look very useful, do they? Well, that's because the value names are "encrypted" via the ROT-13 substitution algorithm; that is, each letter is swapped with the one 13 positions further down in the alphabet. To undo (decrypt) the algorithm, we simply reverse the substitution. Fortunately, the userassist.pl (specifically for Windows XP systems) and userassist2.pl (will work for all Windows systems) RegRipper plugins will handle this translation easily using the following code:

```
$value_name =~ tr/N-ZA-Mn-za-m/A-Za-z/;
```

Before we proceed, it's important at this point to mention that Didier Stevens [5] has conducted a considerable amount of research into the values beneath the UserAssist key, particularly with respect to Windows 7. In fact, Didier has not only published his findings in [IN]SECURE magazine [6] but he also created a tool (called *UserAssist*) to decrypt the value names and parse the data for pertinent information. Without question, Didier deserves a great deal of credit for the current understanding of, and interest in, the contents of the UserAssist key within the computer forensics community.

## VIGENERE ENCRYPTION

During his research into the UserAssist key, Didier discovered that in the beta version of Windows 7, rather than ROT-13 "encryption," the value names were encrypted using Vigenere encryption, a polyalphabetic substitution cipher originally described by Giovan Battista Bellaso in 1553. The final release of Windows 7 switched back to the use of ROT-13 encryption. According to a Microsoft employee I spoke with, the use of the encryption or obfuscation technique isn't to protect any sensitive information; rather, it's intended as a deterrent to prevent the user from modifying any information in the value name or data.

Okay, so how is all of this important? Well, remember that the operating system uses some method for keeping track of a user's actions (which items they click, which shortcuts and applications they access, and so on), and then uses that information to provide an improved (beyond the default installation) experience to the user. Both testing and analysis indicate that the information embedded within the binary data associated with many of the values beneath the UserAssist key includes a 64-bit time stamp (that is, our familiar FILETIME structure), as well as a counter (referred to as a "run count") that appears to indicate how many times the user has interacted with the shell in the manner in which these values would be created or modified.

## RUN COUNT

When the counter value embedded within the UserAssist value binary data was first examined, it appeared that the count actually started at 5, rather than 0. There seemed to be no apparent reason for this (the internals of any algorithms that may use this information are not known), Ovie Carroll and Bret Padres (of the CyberSpeak podcast fame) came up with a very funny mnemonic device; the name "Gates" (as in "Bill Gates") contains five letters. Regardless of the reason apparently starting the count at 5, testing indicated that this was, in fact, the case; performing an action and then parsing the information on live system would result in a count value of 6 (the first time that the action was recorded, plus 5).

In short, the binary data can be parsed (by RegRipper plugins) to determine how many times the user had taken this action (that is, navigated through the Programs menu to launch MS Word, double-clicked a desktop icon, and so on) via the shell and when they last did so. An important aspect of this is that in order to create/modify these values, the user needs to interact with the Explorer shell; that is, if the user clicks **Start** and then types "cmd" into the **Run** box on Windows XP, you don't get the same artifacts as if the user clicks **Start | Programs | Accessories** and chooses "**Command Prompt**," and you won't be able to "see" what the user did in the command prompt.

Let's take a look at example; this example is an excerpt from the output of the RegRipper userassist2.pl plugin, run against an NTUSER.dat hive extracted from a Windows XP system:

```
{75048700-EF1F-11D0-9888-006097DEACF9}
Thu Feb 7 13:37:26 2008 Z
 UEME_RUNPATH:E:\FTK Imager.exe (1)
Thu Feb 7 12:41:42 2008 Z
 UEME_RUNPATH:C:\Program Files\Microsoft Office\OFFICE11\
   WINWORD.EXE (120)
Thu Feb 7 11:27:41 2008 Z
 UEME_RUNPATH:C:\WINDOWS\regedit.exe (5)
Thu Feb 7 10:39:55 2008 Z
 UEME_RUNPATH:Lotus Notes 7.lnk (142)
 UEME_RUNPATH:C:\Program Files\Lotus\notes\notes.exe (142)
Thu Feb 7 10:38:38 2008 Z
 UEME_RUNPATH:C:\Program Files\AT&T Network Client\
  NetClient.exe (147)
 UEME_RUNPATH:{5D5A8163-501D-4F38-8B17-23488A324D64} (146)
 UEME_RUNPATH:{AC76BA86-1033-0000-BA7E-100000000002} (112)
```

As you can see from the above excerpt, the userassist2.pl plugin decrypts the value names beneath the UserAssist subkeys and then, where applicable, parses the associated binary data for the run count and the last time the action was taken. First, we see the GUID that we mentioned which is one of the UserAssist subkeys; opening the Software hive from the system from which the NTUSER.dat hive was extracted in the MiTeC Registry File Viewer (RFV) and searching for that GUID, we find that it refers to a class identifier (CLSID) beneath the Classes key that points to "Active Desktop."

Next, we see an indication that on February 7, 2008, at approximately 13:37:26 Z (see the "Time References" sidebar) FTK Imager was launched from the E:\ drive. Well, that's where I placed a CD in the system and ran FTK Imager in order to collect specific files from the system, including the Registry hives. That reference begins with "UEME_RUNPATH," which indicates an executable file was accessed; in this case, by double-clicking the program icon as it appeared in Windows Explorer (opened to the CD, of course). According to the run count (that is, the number in parentheses after the application path), at this point, FTK Imager was only run once.

# TIME REFERENCES

Most of the RegRipper plugins report time with "Z" or "UTC" at the end. The "Z" refers to Zulu, or Greenwich Mean Time (GMT). This is analogous to Universal Coordinated Time, or UTC. When performing analysis across multiple systems, or across multiple time zones, normalizing the time stamps to a common format and reference point can make that analysis much easier. I've had several cases where an intruder accessed systems within an organizations infrastructure that were dispersed across multiple time zones and normalizing all time stamps on all of the affected systems to UTC made it much easier to follow his trail, and more importantly, illustrate it to the customer.

Next, we see that regedit.exe was launched and that Lotus Notes (our e-mail application at the time) was run for the 142nd time by double-clicking the Windows shortcut (on the desktop). Beneath that, at 10:38:38 Z, we see that the AT&T Network Client (VPN solution) was accessed and that there are two GUIDs, as well. Once again, opening the Software hive from this system in RFV and searching for "{5D5A8163-501D-4F38-8B17-23488A324D64}," we find that this also appears as a subkey name beneath the Microsoft\Windows\CurrentVersion\Uninstall key and that subkey contains a value named *DisplayName* set to "AT&T Network Client." The other GUID (AC76BA86-1033-0000-BA7E-100000000002) appears in 24 locations (keys and values) throughout the Software hive and appears to refer to the Adobe Acrobat Reader version 7.0 installer.

Other entries may appear with different prefixes in the output of the userassist2.pl plugin (and other tools). For example, rather than being preceded by "UEME_RUNPATH," some decoded values may begin with "UEME_RUNPIDL" (a "PIDL" is a pointer to an ItemIdList structure, which is used to identify objects in the Shell namespace [7]), referring to a folder or shortcut, and others may begin with "UEME_RUNCPL," which refers to Control Panel applets being clicked.

I should point out that the RegRipper userassist.pl plugin was written specifically for the NTUSER.dat hives from Windows XP systems, whereas the userassist2.pl plugin was written for all current versions of Windows (Windows XP through Windows 7), in that it does not look for specifically named subkeys beneath the UserAssist key.

Personally, I've used the information within the UserAssist keys to great effect during a number of examinations. I've seen where users and intruders have installed and then run Cain.exe, in order to collect passwords from a variety of applications (see Chapter 3, "Case Studies: The System," for an example of how analysts can make use of tools like Cain); even after deleting the application, the entries in the UserAssist key persist. I've seen where programs were run from an external resource, such as a CD or thumb drive, because the user double-clicked the icon via the Windows Explorer shell. I've also seen where system administrators who stated that once a system had been confiscated and "secured," they "didn't do anything" had actually installed, run, and then uninstalled two consecutive antivirus scanning applications, one after another. I guess they were just trying to be thorough … but their actions were "recorded" and accounted from some of the artifacts that I was seeing, as well as some I wasn't seeing. I've seen where intruders have installed malware on systems that we weren't immediately aware of, and this information helped us a great deal in our examination.

I've also examined systems where there were apparent disparities with time stamps recorded on the system and, in parsing the UserAssist key information, found "UEME_RUNCPL" entries referencing "timedate.cpl," the Date and Time Control Panel applet that allows the user to modify the system time. The user can change the system time in this manner by either double-clicking the **Control Panel** applet, or by right-clicking the clock on the far right of the TaskBar and choosing **Adjust Date/Time** from the context menu that appears.

As we saw in Figures 4.15 and 4.16, Windows 7 uses a different set of GUIDs for the UserAssist subkeys and that's not all that's different. Those values that contain time stamp data are also formatted differently and possibly contain a bit more information. Again, Didier Stevens has some testing and analysis in this area, in an attempt to identify the various pieces of information (that is, such as how long the application had focus, and so on) and reviewing some of what he's published, it's easy to see how an analyst can use them to support his/her findings during an examination. This is an area that will require significantly more research and testing.

## XPMode AND UserAssist

Windows 7 allows the user to install legacy applications into what is called "XPMode," allowing those applications to run in a specific Windows XP virtual machine. So, the user installs the application and the icon appears on their Windows 7 desktop, but when they double-click the **Programs** icon, "under the hood," the Windows XP virtual machine (a .vhd file) is launched, and the application is loaded and run.

For fun, I installed Skype on a Windows 7 laptop, but installed the application in XPMode, and ran it several times. Afterward, I extracted the pertinent Registry hive files from both the Windows 7 platform and the Windows XP .vhd file and, parsing the UserAssist entries from both, found that double-clicking the icon on the Windows 7 desktop leaves artifacts in the Windows 7 UserAssist key, as expected. In addition, I found the following key and value in the Windows 7 USRCLASS.dat hive:

```
Key: 198afac9.Windows.XP.Mode\shell\open\command
Value: (Default)
Data: "C:\Windows\System32\VMSAL.exe" "Windows XP Mode"
 "||198afac9" "Skype" "%1"
```

This illustrates the mechanism by which applications installed in the Windows 7 XPMode are launched and provides clues to other possible artifacts.

One final note with respect to the UserAssist key: there have been two additional Registry values identified that may significantly affect the information maintained beneath the UserAssist subkeys. Both of these would be values added (they do not exist by default on any system I've seen) to a Settings key (beneath the UserAssist key). The first value NoEncrypt, is discussed in MS KB article 239062 [8] and when set to a DWORD value of "1," can apparently be used to disable the ROT-13 encryption. The other value NoLog, when set to a DWORD value of "1," can apparently be used to disable logging all together. Remember, though … if the logging or recording of user interaction data is disabled, the user experience will be significantly altered, as data used to enable customized menus based on usage history is no longer available. Now, I haven't seen either of these values during an engagement, but they are important for an analyst to be aware of, as the absence of entries beneath the UserAssist subkeys could be the result of deletion (manually, or via an "evidence eraser" program or script), or through the addition of the NoLog value.

## NOINSTRUMENTATION

Another Registry value mentioned in MS KB article 292504 [9] is "NoInstrumentation." This is a value that can be set via Group Policies and would be added to the user's CurrentVersion\Policies\Explorer key. When set to a DWORD value of "1," this value will "prevent the system from remembering the programs run, paths followed, and documents used"; apparently, this value may have more wide-ranging effects than simply disabling recording of information beneath the UserAssist key.

## MuiCache

The MuiCache key is one of those Registry keys that seems as if it might be very useful, but for which there is very little documentation available. On Windows XP and 2003 systems, the path to the MuiCache key within the user's NTUSER.dat hive is

```
Software\Microsoft\Windows\ShellNoRoam\MUICache
```

On Vista systems and above, the key path is located in the user's USRCLASS.dat hive, in the following key path:

```
Local Settings\Software\Microsoft\Windows\Shell\MuiCache
```

So, how is this key useful? Several years ago, I was doing some research on specific malware samples and looking to see what some of the antivirus (AV) vendors had already documented with respect to the variants they'd seen. In some instances, I began to see references to malware creating a value (according to the AV vendor write-up) within the MuiCache key when run, and not being familiar with this key, I wanted to see if I could determine the reason for this value being created. As it later turned out, the malware wasn't creating the value … the value was being created by the operating system, as a result of how the malware was being launched within the testing environment. This proved to be very interesting and very useful.

We've already seen how we can track the user's activity on a system when they interact with the shell, whether they're conducting searches, or launching applications. However, in some instances, we'll see that a command prompt was launched (as indicated by the UserAssist key or RunMRU entries) and then nothing afterward. In some instances, we may be able to get an idea of what the user may have done (or more correctly, what the user account may have been used to do …) by examining the contents of the MuiCache key. By default, when an account is first created (or shortly after it is first used), the MuiCache key may contain value names and data similar to what is illustrated in Figure 4.18.

As you can see in figure 4.mui1, the value names start with "@" and appear to refer to shell-based functionality available as part of a default installation, through various DLLs. As the user begins to use and interact with the system, other values begin to appear, as illustrated in Figure 4.19.

As you can see in Figure 4.19, many of the new value names that begin to appear beneath the key once the user account begins to be used do not begin with "@" and instead point to executable application files (rather than DLLs). Also, the data for the values appears to be populated from one of a number of locations, including perhaps the window title (from when the application is launched) as well as perhaps the file version information embedded within the portable executable (PE) file. None

| Value | Type | Data |
| --- | --- | --- |
| LangID | REG_BINARY | 09 04 00 00 |
| @sstpsvc.dll,-35001 | REG_SZ | Secure Socket Tunneling Protocol |
| @netlogon.dll,-1010 | REG_SZ | Netlogon Service |
| @snmptrap.exe,-3 | REG_SZ | SNMP Trap |
| @PlaSrv.exe,-10005 | REG_SZ | Performance Logs and Alerts |
| @C:\Windows\explorer.exe,-7024 | REG_SZ | Internet |
| @C:\Program Files\Internet Explorer\iexplore.e... | REG_SZ | Internet Explorer |
| @C:\Windows\explorer.exe,-7025 | REG_SZ | E-mail |
| @C:\Program Files\Windows Mail\msoeres.dll,... | REG_SZ | Windows Mail |
| @C:\Windows\system32\brcpl.dll,-1 | REG_SZ | Backup and Restore Center |
| @C:\Windows\system32\unregmp2.exe,-4 | REG_SZ | Windows Media Player |
| @C:\Windows\System32\ie4uinit.exe,-733 | REG_SZ | Launch Internet Explorer Browser |

**Figure 4.18** MuiCache Key Contents from a Windows Vista System

| Value ▲ | Type | Data |
| --- | --- | --- |
| C:\Program Files\Adobe\Photoshop Album Sta... | REG_SZ | Adobe Photoshop Album Starter Edition 3.2 (Viewer) |
| C:\Program Files\Adobe\Photoshop Album Sta... | REG_SZ | Adobe Photoshop Album Starter Edition 3.2 |
| C:\Program Files\AIM6\aim6.exe | REG_SZ | AIM |
| C:\Program Files\AIM6\anotify.exe | REG_SZ | AOL |
| C:\Program Files\Apple Software Update\Soft... | REG_SZ | Apple Software Update |
| C:\Program Files\Dell\QuickSet\quickset.exe | REG_SZ | QuickSet |
| C:\Program Files\Google\Picasa3\Picasa3.exe | REG_SZ | Picasa |
| C:\Program Files\Google\Picasa3\PicasaPhot... | REG_SZ | Picasa Photo Viewer |
| C:\Program Files\HP\Digital Imaging\bin\hpqdi... | REG_SZ | hpqdirec.exe |
| C:\Program Files\Internet Explorer\iexplore.exe | REG_SZ | Internet Explorer |
| C:\Program Files\iTunes\iTunes.exe | REG_SZ | iTunes |

**Figure 4.19** Additional MuiCache Key Contents (Windows Vista)

of the applications (with the exception of the Dell QuickSet application) that appear in Figure 4.19 were installed by default on the system; rather they were installed and run by the user after the user account was created. This key can provide us with an indication of the various applications and tools that had been run within the context of the user account.

This key also provides a sort of historic, persistent record of the applications that the user account has been used to run, albeit without any sort of time stamp specific to each application. During an engagement, I was parsing the NTUSER.dat file from a compromised Windows 2003 system (using RegRipper's mui-cache.pl plugin), and I noticed that there were several unusual value names that referenced non-native executable files in the C:\Windows\Tasks directory. It appeared that the intruder was placing his/her toolset in this directory, as by default, when viewing the Tasks directory via the Windows Explorer shell on a live system (which is how most system administrators tend to do so), the .exe files do not appear in the viewing pane. This means that the intruder's tools are effectively hidden from view from most of the likely first responders, should any unusual activity be detected on the compromised system. It turned out that we were able to locate several of the tools in the Tasks directory, but several others had apparently been deleted. This provided an interesting indication of the intruder's other activities on the system (that is, they'd apparently added, used/run, and then deleted other command-line tools) that remained persistent after the intruder had apparently deleted several of the tools used.

## MuiCache KEY HISTORICAL DATA

Although the only time stamp associated with the MuiCache key is the LastWrite time of the key itself, we may be able to get some sense of when the applications were run by attempting to correlate the value names we find here with other data sources, such as data found within the UserAssist key, as described previously in this chapter. Another source might be Registry hives included in System Restore Points and/or Volume Shadow Copies.

Several years ago, I used to present pretty regularly at local High Tech Crime Investigation Association (HTCIA) conferences (our local chapter became known as the Regional Computer Forensics Group, or RCFG) and spoke to a number of law enforcement officers about the issue of steganography, or hiding programs or files inside other files. Although steganography was mentioned in the media, as well as within a number of training courses, I was curious as to how prevalent it was seen within the law enforcement community. Interestingly enough, not one of the law enforcement officers I spoke to could recount ever having seen or suspected the use of steganography in any of their examinations. Although there are a number of freely available tools for embedding or hiding files (executable files, images, text, videos, and so on) within other file, many of them do not get installed on a system in the usual sense; instead, the application files are simply added to a directory by the user. The contents of the MuiCache key may indicate the use of steganography applications, particularly those that may have been copied to a system or run from external media, such as a CD or thumb drive.

Virtualization may also present issues during an examination. Many analysts are familiar with virtualized environments such as Microsoft's Virtual PC (VPC, the basis for Windows 7s XPMode) as well as VMWare. However, there are a number of virtualized environments that allow a user to connect a thumb drive to a system and launch the virtual environment, perhaps running a Linux-based operating system … all without shutting down the Windows system. This can allow a user with physical access to a system to perform a number of malicious activities, all while leaving almost no footprints at all on the Windows system. Diane Barrett, an associate professor at the University of Advanced Technology, has published several presentations that describe artifacts left behind as a result of the use of a number of portable virtual environments, including MojoPak [10] and Moka5 [11]. Apparently, Professor Barrett identified very few artifacts indicating the use of these environments, one of which was an entry in the MuiCache key.

Overall, the point of this is that, under most normal circumstances, values beneath the MuiCache key generally appear as a result of interaction of some kind with the shell. When an executable file path is found as a value name beneath this key, it appears to indicate that the user account in question was used to run the application. Follow-on analysis steps might be to attempt to locate the file within the file system (or unallocated space), a Prefetch file, or perhaps an MFT entry (particularly if the file path indicates that the file was on a local hard drive). This key can provide some very interesting indications of activities that occurred within the context of the user account.

## File Associations

We discussed in Chapter 3, "Case Studies: The System," how file association information from within the Software hive can be used to answer questions regarding the relationship between file extensions and applications on a system. However, information about file associations is also maintained on a per-user basis, as well. If you open the Registry Editor on a live system to the HKEY_CURRENT_USER hive and expand the tree beneath the Software key, you'll see a Classes subkey with information similar to that which appears in the Software hive. This information is mapped into the HKEY_CURRENT_USER hive from the user's USRCLASS.dat hive file and supersedes information available in the Software hive.

As an example of this, we can start with the discussion of the default Web browser from the "Web Browser" section of Chapter 3, "Case Studies: The System." In that particular case, the information

## Note

As we've seen, there are a number of instances where Registry artifacts that indicate the installation or use of applications persist after the application is removed or deleted. This applies to many applications that simply have a GUI, but do not require an installation routine (that is, the application files are simply copied to a directory). However, many applications that utilize an installation routine and set file associations in the Registry will also "undo" those settings when the application is uninstalled. This is yet another example of how Registry hives from System Restore Points (Windows XP) or Volume Shadow Copies, as well as deleted keys extracted from unallocated space within Registry hive files (via regslack.exe), can provide significant historical data from a system.

from the Software hive indicates that Internet Explorer is the default Web browser for the system. However, the "Default" value from the following key (from the live system, accessed via regedit. exe) points to the Firefox Web browser:

```
HKEY_CURRENT_USER\Software\Classes\http\shell\open\command
```

This maps to the following key found in the USRCLASS.dat hive within my User Profile:

```
http\shell\open\command
```

What this shows is that when I log into the system with my account, the system settings for file associations (and in this particular case, the default Web browser) are superseded by settings found in my USRCLASS.dat hive.

## Scenarios

Talking to folks after some of my previous books had been published, one of the consistent things we'd discussed was that while I'd mention this Registry key or that file in the Windows\system32 directory, there was really nothing in the book that tied the mentioned or described artifacts together, which wove them into an overall investigative tapestry that allowed the analyst to tell the story of what happened. This is something many folks said that they wanted to see; that is, they wanted to see examples of how to go from artifact A to artifact B, and so on, until a story has been written. Personally, like many others, I find long lists of Registry keys and values with no real investigative context tying them together to be, well, kind of boring … not only to read but also to write, as well. As such, I wanted to provide some scenarios that describe steps I and others have taken to correlate multiple sources (specific to the Registry) and build as complete a picture as possible.

## Tying It Together

I worked an engagement several years ago where the intruder had gained access to the infrastructure via Remote Desktop; it later turned out that local law enforcement had worked with the employee whose home system had been compromised and found a key stroke logger. The organization was on the verge of implementing RSA SecurID for remote access, but simply had not been far enough along when the incident occurred. The intruder accessed the infrastructure with the pilfered credentials and then switched to using a dormant domain administrator account; though it was available, this account had not been disabled and simply had never been used in the infrastructure. This made the intruder relatively easy to track across the various systems that he accessed, as each system had a newly created profile for the account he was using, with the associated NTUSER.dat hive. Examining this file, we were able to see what the intruder had done; we saw indications in the ACMru key of searches that he'd run, as well as files accessed in the RecentDocs key. We were also able to see other systems that the intruder had accessed via a Remote Desktop Connection; these systems were recorded in the following Registry key:

```
Software\Microsoft\Terminal Server Client\Default
```

Beneath this key are values that start with "MRU," followed by a number, indicating the order in which these systems had been accessed [12]. The associated data provided use with names and IP addresses of other systems that the intruder had accessed. When we showed up, the customer had pointed us to about a dozen systems they knew to be compromised; using the contents of this key, we were able to locate another dozen or so systems that had been accessed, and using time stamps, we were able to literally map the intruder's progression through the infrastructure.

Most importantly, however, we were able assist the customer with a much more important question: was sensitive data possibly exposed? Had the intruder accessed files known to contain sensitive data? Using all of the data available to us, including the contents of the RecentDocs keys from the intruder's User Profile created on each system, as well as the MRU keys for applications used to open files, we were able to put together a convincing argument that there were no indications that the intruder had accessed the files in question (the customer had already identified specific files that were known to contain sensitive information). In fact, from what we saw, the intruder did not appear to be aware of type of organization he/she compromised, and the contents of the ACMru keys from several of the systems indicated that he/she was looking for passwords. Correlating this information with other data derived from other areas of the infrastructure, we were able to provide strong indications that the intruder had not accessed the files to regulatory bodies, which was very beneficial to our customer.

## The "Trojan Defense"

The *Trojan defense* is a term that has become more popular since it hit the scene in 2003 when it was used in court. Aaron Caffrey had been accused of attacking military computer systems and his defense was that, in fact, he hadn't done so. Rather, he claimed that his system had been infected with malware, which was responsible for the attacks. Law enforcement sees this defense raised often, and as such, has become concerned about having to address it. After all, how do go about proving that a virus or Trojan wasn't responsible for the actions (downloading illegal images and movies, attacking other systems, and so on) when we see security experts deriding antivirus scanning applications as being insufficient?

Well, how about if you take the argument from a different direction? Rather than (or, in addition to) attempting to disprove the existence of the malware, how useful would it be to show that the user account had been used to view the files? That would certainly obviate the "the malware put it there and I had no idea" defense, wouldn't it? One place to start would be the MUICache and UserAssist keys, to see which applications for viewing files or movies had been launched. From there, check the RecentDocs keys, as well as the contents of the OpenSaveMRU (or OpenSavePidMRU, as appropriate) keys for names of files that may be inappropriate. Remember, if a user launches an application to view a file, and the filename is recorded in the RecentDocs (or OpenSaveMRU) key, and then the file is deleted, the value within the key will remain. For additional information and correlation, you may also want to extract the MRU or recently accessed file lists from other applications, such as Windows Media Player or Real Player. Remember, however, that only filenames are listed here, and although we often tend to believe that names of files may indicate their contents, this really isn't the case. Therefore, be sure to correlate all appropriate information. What these Registry locations indicate is that whomever was accessing the user account was aware that the files were on the system and was using specific applications (that is, image viewers, Web browser, movie viewers, and so on) to view them.

Another area to look into, that is often not considered, is one avenue through which file can get on systems. Yes, many times files are downloaded from the Internet through the Web browser, or as an attachment to e-mail. Sometimes, however, files of all types arrive on systems in a compressed archive. In fact, when writing this book (and my previous books), I would submit my draft chapters to the publisher in a zipped archive, and once a chapter is ready for final submission, the archive will often contain the chapter submission as an MS Word document, as well as image files, scripts, and so on. The 7Zip application, for example, maintains a list of archives accessed in values beneath the following key within the user's hive:

```
Software\7-Zip\Compression\ArcHistory
```

The 7Zip application also maintains a list of archive extraction paths beneath the following key within the user's hive:

```
Software\7-Zip\Extraction\PathHistory
```

In both cases, the value names and data beneath the two above listed keys are easy-to-read strings. The WinZip application maintains similar listings of accessed archives and extraction directories beneath the "Software\Nico Mak Computing\WinZip\filemenu" and "Software\Nico Mak Computing\WinZip\extract" keys, respectively (the winzip.pl RegRipper plugin will extract and display the value names and data from beneath each key, as well as each key's LastWrite time). The WinRAR application maintains similar listings of accessed archives and extraction directories beneath the "Software\WinRAR\ArcHistory" and "Software\WinRAR\DialogEditHistory\ExtrPath" keys, respectively. In most instances, the value data contains the full path to the file being accessed, which can lead an analyst to external devices. Further, although these keys contain filenames and not content, they can still provide an analyst with indicators that may help determine whether or not the "Trojan" or malware was the culprit, or if it was the user.

## Connecting to Other Systems

Many times, as a responder or analyst, I'm asked to determine if the system was associated with any "suspicious or unusual activity." Most times, that's far too general of a goal to really address, as I could end up spending hours or even days developing a list of indicators that I thought could be "suspicious or unusual," only to find out that those were actually part of the user's job description.

One activity that may be "suspicious," or even a violation of acceptable use policies, is accessing other systems. By this, I don't mean such as accessing Web sites; instead, I mean accessing other employee's systems. In my experience as a security administrator, this is something that should be and is usually limited to a very few specific individuals, as various issues could be raised. However, suffice to say that in most instances, an employee accessing another employee's system is something could be "suspicious or unusual activity." The artifacts that we would look for and hope to find depend largely on the method used to access other systems. For example, earlier in this chapter, we saw where to find artifacts of connected to systems via a Remote Desktop Connection (the user clicks **Start | Programs | Accessories | Remote Desktop Connection**). If the user maps a share (we saw in Chapter 3, "Case Studies: The System," how to determine the shares that were available on a system, via the RegRipper shares.pl plugin) via the Map Network Drive Wizard (on Windows XP, right-click the **My Network Places** icon and choose **Map Network Drive** from the drop-down menu), the shares that the user account was used to connect to will appear in the following Registry key:

```
Software\Microsoft\Windows\CurrentVersion\Explorer\Map
    Network Drive MRU
```

As you can see, this key is an MRU key; on Windows XP systems, the values listed beneath this key are named for lowercase letters (a, b, c, and so on) and there is an MRUList value that provides the MRU listing. Users can also access shares via universal naming convention (UNC) paths entered into the **Run** box; these entries will appear in the following Registry key:

```
Software\Microsoft\Windows\CurrentVersion\Explorer\RunMRU
```

On Windows XP, this key maintains its values in a manner similar to the "Map Network Drive MRU" key (values named for lowercase letters, MRUList value, and so on). Systems connected to via these means, as well as via the command line, will lead to an entry for the remote system being added to the ComputerDescriptions key:

```
Software\Microsoft\Windows\CurrentVersion\Explorer\
    ComputerDescriptions
```

The contents of the ComputerDescriptions key will provide an indication of remote systems to which the user account had been used to connect, albeit without a date or other associated context. However, it can be useful in providing an indication that the user may have been performing "suspicious or unusual activities."

Windows 7 systems have a TypedPaths key that seems to be something of a cross between Windows XP's RunMRU key and the TypedURLs key used by Internet Explorer. The full path to the TypedPaths key appears as follows:

```
Software\Microsoft\Windows\CurrentVersion\Explorer\TypedPaths
```

The values beneath this key are named *url1* and *url2*, and the data is a string that can include the UNC path to remote systems. These values appear in the Windows Explorer Address Bar on Windows 7 systems.

## PRESERVING PRIVACY

Tools to protect a user's privacy have been around almost as long as Windows has been around. The marketed purpose of these tools, be they open-source, free, or commercial, is to protect a user's privacy by removing all traces of their activity. As you might assume, many of these tools not only delete files or alter file contents but also delete Registry keys and values. In some cases, analysts can determine Registry keys and values that might be valuable sources of information by tracking these tools. For example, downloading and running some of these tools, or searching user forums for these tools, will provide some interesting Registry locations for a variety of potentially useful artifacts.

Keep in mind that there are other ways to connect to systems remotely, as well. One example is the use of the Virtual Network Computing (VNC) application, originally from the Olivetti & Oracle Research Laboratory (ORL) in the United Kingdom. This application provides access to a remote system similar to the Remote Desktop Connection, and in addition to a client application (usually vncviewer.exe) requires an appropriate server component to be installed on the remote system. Similar to other remote access applications, VNC maintains a list of systems connected to beneath a Registry key, and the path to that key depends on the version of VNC used. For example, for VNC version 3 from ORL, the key path is

```
Software\ORL\VNCViewer\MRU
```

A variant of the original, RealVNC version 4 maintains its MRU list in the following key path:

```
Software\RealVNC\VNCViewer4\MRU
```

There may be other applications or techniques that can be used to access systems remotely, and those applications may maintain their own MRU lists of systems that the user had accessed. Some that come to mind include GUI-based FTP/file transfer utilities, for example. As such, you should take steps to determine if such tools have been installed and used on a system and if it maintains such an MRU list. Information in an MRU list may provide indications of other affected systems, and this can be extremely important when dealing with a prolific intruder (as in the "Tying It Together" scenario described earlier in this chapter) or with a particularly stealthy and persistent intruder.

## Summary

As you can see, there is a great deal of information in the user's hives (NTUSER.dat, and on Vista and above systems, USRCLASS. dat) that will provide indications of not only what the user did but also when they did it. This can help demonstrate that a system was in use during a specific period; for example, the creation date and last modification time of the NTUSER.dat file will provide indications of when the user account was first used to log into the system and when it last logged out, respectively, but information from many of the keys (including key LastWrite times and data derived from binary and string values) will provide indications of actions the user took and when they took them. An analyst can use all of this information to develop an understanding of and add context to other activity found on the system. As with the other hive files, analysis of the user's hives can also assist in determining if the system was infected with malware, or if the user (or an intruder) was responsible for the observed activity.

By now, I hope that I've done a good job of illustrating to you, the reader, the immense value that can be derived through Registry analysis. Over the years, I've tracked user and intruder activity, provided information to obviate the "Trojan Defense," and even exonerated falsely accused employees, all by including Registry analysis in my overall examination.

Keywords: Registry, NTUSER.dat, USRCLASS.dat, UserAssist, MuiCache, virtualization, RecentDocs, WordWheelQuery, user

## References

[1]  A definition of the Run keys in the Windows XP Registry. Microsoft Support. 1 December 2007, http://support.microsoft.com/kb/314866.

[2]  My view settings or customizations for a folder are lost or incorrect. Microsoft Support. 15 July 2009, http://support.microsoft.com/kb/813711 (accessed 15.07.09).

[3] Y. Zhu, P. Gladyshev, J. James, Using shellbag information to reconstruct user activities, Digit. Invest. 6 (Supp. 1) (2009). http://cci.ucd.ie/content/using-shellbag-information-reconstruct-user-activities.

[4] TraceHunter. The UCD Centre for Cybercrime Investigation. http://cci.ucd.ie/tracehunter.

[5] Didier Stevens. http://blog.didierstevens.com/programs/userassist/.

[6] INSECURE-Mag-10.pdf. [IN]SECURE Mag. (10) (2007). http://www.net-security.org/dl/insecure/INSECURE-Mag-10.pdf (issue 10, pp. 72–77, last accessed 3.11.2010).

[7] ITEMIDLIST structure. Microsoft Developer Network. http://msdn.microsoft.com/en-us/library/bb773321%28VS.85%29.aspx (accessed 19.10.2010).

[8] WD2000: general information about Word 2000 instrumented version. Microsoft Support. http://support.microsoft.com/kb/239062 (accessed 23.10.02).

[9] Policy settings for the Start menu in Windows XP. Microsoft Support. http://support.microsoft.com/kb/292504 (accessed 02.07.10).

[10] MojoPac. Wikipedia, http://en.wikipedia.org/wiki/MojoPac.

[11] MokaFive. Wikipedia, http://en.wikipedia.org/wiki/MokaFive.

[12] How to remove entries from the remote desktop connection computer box. Microsoft Support. http://support.microsoft.com/kb/312169 (accessed 01.11.06).

# INDEX

Page numbers followed by *f* indicates a figure and *t* indicates a table.